A gift has been made by:

Fred Darragh Foundation

In honor of

CALS

A MASSACRE IN MEMPHIS

A MASSACRE IN MEMPHIS

THE RACE RIOT THAT SHOOK THE NATION ONE YEAR AFTER THE CIVIL WAR

STEPHEN V. ASH

Hill and Wang
A division of Farrar, Straus and Giroux
New York

Hill and Wang
A division of Farrar, Straus and Giroux
18 West 18th Street, New York 10011

Library of Congress Cataloging-in-Publication Data

Ash, Stephen V.
   A massacre in Memphis : the race riot that shook the nation one year after the Civil War / Stephen V. Ash.
     pages   cm
   Includes bibliographical references and index.
   ISBN 978-0-8090-6797-8 (hardback)
   1. Memphis Race Riot, Memphis, Tenn., 1866.   2. African Americans—Violence against—Tennessee—Memphis—History—19th century.   3. Memphis (Tenn.)—Race relations—History—19th century.   I. Title.

F444.M557 A75 2013
305.896′07307681909034—dc23

                                         2013015255

Designed by Abby Kagan

Hill and Wang books may be purchased for educational, business, or promotional use. For information on bulk purchases, please contact the Macmillan Corporate and Premium Sales Department at 1-800-221-7945, extension 5442, or write to specialmarkets@macmillan.com.

www.fsgbooks.com
www.twitter.com/fsgbooks • www.facebook.com/fsgbooks

1 3 5 7 9 10 8 6 4 2

CONTENTS

PART III: THE AFTERMATH

Maps of 1866 Memphis

THE MEMPHIS RIOT

NAVY YARD

STONEMAN'S HEADQUARTERS

CITY HALL

DOWNTOWN MEMPHIS

WASHINGTON STREET

POLICE STATION

ADAMS STREET

JEFFERSON STREET

COURT SQUARE

FRONT ROW

MAIN STREET

SECOND STREET

THIRD STREET

UNION STREET

GAYOSO STREET

GAYOSO HOUSE

FREEDMEN'S BUREAU HEADQUARTERS

FRONT ROW

MAIN STREET

SECOND STREET

THIRD STREET

Mississippi River

Area of detail

Mississippi River

MEMPHIS

0   1/4
MILES

© 2013 Jeffrey L. Ward

May 1–3, 1866

MEMPHIS

Mississippi River

Area of detail

River

Mississippi

Mississippi

COURT SQUARE

FRONT ROW

MAIN STREET

SECOND STREET

THIRD STREET

UNION STREET

GAYOSO STREET

GAYOSO HOUSE

FREEDMEN'S BUREAU HEADQUARTERS

CITY MARKET

BEALE STREET

HOLLYWOOD'S GROCERY

PONTOTOC STREET

VANCE STREET

SAINT MARTIN STREET

CAUSEY STREET

HERNANDO STREET

SHELBY STREET

MAIN STREET

SOUTH MEMPHIS

DESOTO STREET

DILTSES' HOUSE

MORRIS CEMETERY

RANKIN'S SCHOOLHOUSE

PENDERGRAST'S GROCERY

SOUTH STREET (AKA CALHOUN STREET)

BAYOU BRIDGE

RAYBURN AVENUE

M&T RAILROAD DEPOT

FORT PICKERING, NORTHERN PARAPET

0   1/4

MILES

© 2013 Jeffrey L. Ward

AUTHOR'S NOTE

That no book-length study of the Memphis riot of 1866 has been written before this one is surprising, considering that the riot influenced the course of our nation's history at a critical juncture, shaping in important ways how Americans thought about the pressing questions of the post–Civil War period. But what is even more surprising about the dearth of books on the riot is the enormous amount of evidence available to the historian. The riot is, in fact, one of the best-documented episodes of the American nineteenth century.

In its immediate aftermath, the Freedmen's Bureau, the U.S. Army, and a specially formed congressional committee interviewed hundreds of witnesses: men, women, and children, black and white, from all walks of life. Their recorded testimony is a voluminous trove of information not only about the riot but also about the living and working conditions, family and gender relations, racial and ethnic conflicts, and communal institutions, politics, and ideology of the people in Memphis in the spring of 1866. Most who testified were ordinary folks, many of them poor and illiterate, the sort of people whose voices are absent or only faintly heard in the vast majority of sources we have from that era.

One of my intentions in this book is to revive, as it were, the individuals who gave Memphis its vitality and character, and who may have died in the riot—to restore to them the personhood that death and history have taken. This seems especially important in the case of the freed people, some of whom were emancipated only a year or so before the riot, and probably forty-six of whom were murdered in the rioting. They were newly visible in their own time and almost uniformly illiterate, and so unable to bequeath their actions, thoughts, and hopes to posterity. It is a historical and moral imperative to re-member as many as we can as individuals, not as a mass of people whose characteristics can be summed up in a paragraph, and certainly not as the dull-witted, unimprovable flotsam many Rebels (and many Yankees) saw them as.

Another of my intentions is to illustrate the nature of the violence that has resulted from race hate in America; here, too, the rich sources make possible an unusually vivid portrait. The events in Memphis in the spring of 1866 were so appalling that it is perhaps hard for many of us to fit them into our understanding of our nation's past. We may struggle to recognize any common ground with the bloodthirsty rioters or the federal authorities who sat idly by—it is easier to dismiss them all as products of a uniquely pathological time and place. But when we move from a close examination of the riot to a longer view, the event begins to resonate across centuries. The riot can be seen both as a continuation of older forms of racial brutality and as a harbinger of a new kind of violence: the organized terror Southern whites would carry out against blacks well into the twentieth century. In this sense, the 1866 Memphis riot not only sheds light on a turning point in American history and allows us to write ordinary people back into that history, but also is crucial to understanding one of our original and most intractable matters, the role of race in American life.

A MASSACRE IN MEMPHIS

Prologue

Memphis, Tennessee, May 22–24, 1866

The last 140 miles of Congressman Elihu Washburne's railroad journey from Washington to Memphis spanned the flat countryside of west Tennessee. Cotton plantations dominated the landscape: from the train window Washburne would have seen broad stretches of fenced and tilled land alternating with patches of woods, with here and there a planter's manor and a scattering of laborers' cabins. Black people were at work in the fields with hoes and plows. The fields were green, not white, for the full ripening of the crop was still months away.

It was Tuesday, May 22, three weeks to the day since the outbreak of the horrific race riot in Memphis that had riveted the nation. Washburne, a long-serving Republican member of the House of Representatives from Illinois, had been charged with overseeing Congress's investigation of the riot. This was an important assignment: the bloody, three-day upheaval, the most sensational event outside Washington since the death of the Confederacy, would no doubt play a key role in the crucial decisions now facing the nation.

Washburne already knew a good deal about the riot and its causes. In the months leading up to the riot he had received letters from acquaintances in Memphis concerning the situation there, particularly the city's racial and political tensions. Newspapers had provided considerable information on the riot itself. Moreover, both the local military commandant and the Freedmen's Bureau had already investigated the riot, although not as extensively as Washburne planned to, and he had been informed about their findings.[1]

From these various sources he had learned that there was a bitter, long-standing antipathy between Memphis's blacks and lower-class whites. The Union army had taken the city early in the war, in 1862, paving the way for emancipated slaves from the countryside. This had the effect of greatly aggravating the old bitterness, because the newly arrived blacks began to compete with the lower-class whites for jobs. The city police—who were all white, nearly all Irish immigrants, and notoriously unprofessional—especially detested the freed people and regularly abused them. The thuggishness of the police went unchecked by the leading civil officials of the city, who were themselves mostly Irish and contemptuous of the blacks. The soldiers of the black U.S. Army regiment that had garrisoned the city until they were mustered out just before the riot were a special target of white resentment; this resentment was not altogether unjustified, however, for the unit was poorly disciplined and some of its men stirred up trouble or committed crimes when off duty. The native-born Southern whites of Memphis had been, with few exceptions, devout secessionists during the war—many hundreds had served in the Confederate army—and they remained unrepentant now, resentful of Union victory and federal authority, furious about their political disenfranchisement, hostile to equal rights for the freed people, and contemptuous of the Yankee newcomers in their city. Almost all the local newspapers were controlled by such Rebels, and in the months leading up to the riot they ran lurid editorials that further inflamed the prejudice against blacks and Northerners.

The riot, which was triggered by clashes between black men and police officers on April 30 and May 1, was an explosion of rage and violence directed against the freed people and perpetrated by the white underclass. Policemen and firemen were among the rioters, as were certain higher-ranking officers of the city government. By the time the rioting ended on May 3, at least forty blacks had been murdered, dozens more wounded, several raped, and many others robbed. Many black churches, schools, and residences had been torched.

Many of these shocking details made it into the reports of newspapers around the country, which rightly saw the riot as a major development in the increasingly rancorous debate over the future of the South, and indeed the whole nation. The Civil War had resolved two momentous, long-standing issues: the attempt of eleven Southern states to gain independence was crushed, and slavery was abolished. But new questions soon arose: How were the seceded states to be restored to the Union? How was the devastated Southern economy to be rebuilt? How were the defeated Rebels to be dealt with? And what about black Southerners, whose freedom was assured but whose status was otherwise undefined? Implicit in these questions were others even more profound and far-reaching: Did this task of postwar reconstruction, as Abraham Lincoln had hinted at Gettysburg, offer the opportunity to forge an essentially new and greater American nation? If so, how could that be achieved?

Congressman Washburne's judgments on the great postwar questions placed him squarely in his party's mainstream. Republicans insisted that the Rebels who had fought so hard to fracture the Union and preserve slavery must truly accept defeat and emancipation, must confess and atone for the sins of secession and rebellion, and must demonstrate by word and deed that they were now loyal U.S. citizens. Until they did, their states must be denied congressional and electoral representation and their own political activity must be circumscribed. Republicans also insisted that the freed slaves must have sufficient legal—and, if necessary, military—protection to give substance to their freedom and to prevent their abuse and exploitation at the hands of the Rebels. Restoring the South to the Union and fully reenfranchising its white citizenry without reforming its flawed society and institutions and ideology would, as the Republicans saw it, invite continued sectional disputes of the kind that had brought on the war, render meaningless the terrible sacrifices the North had made in putting down the Southern rebellion, and prevent the realization of Lincoln's vision for the nation's future.[2]

In the first postwar Congress, which was dominated by Republicans, Washburne was named to the newly created Joint Committee on Reconstruction. In early 1866 the committee held hearings on conditions in the South and generated evidence that put the Republicans more and more at odds with President Andrew Johnson. Johnson, a Southern Unionist and Democrat, wanted the former Confederate states to be speedily restored to the Union with no fundamental changes besides the abolition of slavery. He also wanted the Rebels to be reenfranchised with minimal qualifications, and he was content to let them deal with the freed people pretty much as they saw fit. In the immediate postwar months he liberally granted amnesty and pardons to former Confederates and allowed them to take part in elections and constitutional conventions that set up new state governments. (Those in Tennessee, however, were subject to somewhat different terms and remained disenfranchised.) Democrats in Congress and across the nation cheered Johnson's policy. The president's vetoes, in February and March 1866, of two bills intended to protect the emancipated slaves outraged the Republicans, who then began formulating a constitutional amendment that would make their demands into law.[3]

The unthinkable carnage of the Memphis riot thus occurred at a particularly charged moment. It threw the debates in Washington into stark relief—it made what was at stake in them unavoidably clear and, because many policemen had not just condoned but had taken part in the massacre, called into question the very foundation on which every classically liberal government rests its legitimacy: its guarantee to protect its citizens from being murdered. Something had to be done; to some congressmen, it may have seemed that the nation's future, which had supposedly been decided by the war, was again hanging in the balance. Eleven days after the riot finally ended, the House of Representatives passed a resolution creating the Select Committee on the Memphis Riots.

Washburne, its chairman, arrived in the city with his fellow committee members on the twenty-second, at the Memphis and Ohio Railroad depot on the city's north side. From there it was a one-mile hack ride south along Main Street to the Gayoso House, the city's finest hotel, where a room had been reserved for the committee's hearings. Little or no evidence of the riot's violence and destruction was visible along this route, so Washburne and his colleagues did not immediately see the charred, collapsed remains of houses, shanties, schools, and churches and, in some of the cemeteries, the dozens of freshly filled graves.[4]

At this time of year, if the weather was sunny and dry as it was on this day, one of the first things a visitor such as Washburne could not have helped noticing was the dust. It rose in clouds from the streets and billowed outward, stirred up by the ceaseless traffic of buggies, hacks, carts, drays, and wagons, some driven at breakneck speed, in violation of the law. For years the city authorities had considered paving the major thoroughfares but so far had done nothing more than talk about it. Business owners on a few of the primary commercial streets, including Main, pooled money to hire a man to ply their streets in a cart equipped with a barrel of water and a sprinkler. This helped, but dust in lesser quantities wafted in from unsprinkled streets nearby. Everywhere in the city, dust settled on clothing, drifted down onto porches and sidewalks, and crept indoors through open windows. Housewives, maids, and shopkeepers battled it with brooms and feather dusters as they prayed for rain. But when rain came it turned the streets into a muddy quagmire, six inches deep or more, and the people prayed for clear skies.[5]

Another thing that immediately struck the visitor to Memphis was the crowding. The city proper stretched for more than two miles along the east bank of the Mississippi River and more than a mile inland, but even with the adjacent unincorporated neighborhoods commonly regarded as part of the city, there was scant room for the thirty-five or forty thousand people who now lived there—or were thought to, for the number of inhabitants was uncertain. All anybody knew for sure was that the population had swelled since the census takers of 1860 had counted twenty-three thousand Memphians. Newcomers, whites in addition to newly freed blacks, had inundated the city after its capture by Union forces in June 1862, and the end of the war and of military rule in 1865 had not stemmed the tide. The streets teemed with people and the horses, mules, and oxen that served them; in many residences two families crammed into a space meant for one.[6]

On the day of his arrival, Washburne assembled the committee and opened the proceedings in parlor 398 of the Gayoso House, formally confirming the committee's credentials for the record. The real work began at ten o'clock the next morning. The first witness was a prominent U.S. Army officer, Major General George Stoneman, commander of the Department of the Tennessee, with headquarters in Memphis. During his lengthy testimony, Stoneman answered questions about his dealings with municipal officials during and after the riot, the threats made during the riot against the city's Northern-born population, the makeup of the riotous mobs, and the sentiments of the Memphis newspapers. He contradicted reports in the Rebel papers that blacks had actually perpetrated the violence. It "was no negro riot," he said firmly. "The negroes had nothing to do with the riot, except to be killed and abused."[7]

The next day, the committee questioned several Memphis residents who had witnessed the rioting. One was Ellen Dilts, a homemaker and Yankee immigrant. She told of hearing a policeman exclaim to a crowd of whites, "Kill every nigger, no matter who, men or women." Also questioned was a shoemaker and former slave named Albert Harris, who was not just an eyewitness to the riot but one of its victims. On the night of May 2 a gang of white men, some of them policemen, had forced their way into his house, held a pistol to his head in front of his frantic, sobbing wife, robbed him, and threatened to burn his place down.[8]

That day, the twenty-fourth, Washburne wrote a letter to one of his Republican colleagues on the Joint Committee. The Select Committee had begun work, he reported, "and it is plain to see we have a long job before us." There were many more witnesses he intended to call and, although he had already reached some general conclusions, there was much more he wanted to know about the origin and course of the riot, about its perpetrators and victims, and about this dusty, crowded, deeply divided city. Fueling this quest was Washburne's fervent engagement with the great postwar questions, and his intuition that the riot held the answers to many of them. "I intend to remain here," he vowed, "till we get to the bottom of this business."[9]

PART I

A CITY DIVIDED

1

Yankee Memphis

I have always counselled [the freed people] that liberty meant
the right to work for themselves, to get their own living, and live
honestly as white people do; . . . I have told them . . . that they
must be obedient to their employers, and peaceable.
                    —Testimony of Benjamin P. Runkle, superintendent of
                                Memphis Freedmen's Bureau office

[The Rebels] call me a pimp. I have served the United States
government in the army five years, and I am called a pimp in
the public press. . . . I came here ready to take these people by
the hand, but they have met me with insults, because I wear the
uniform of the government.
                                —Testimony of Benjamin P. Runkle[1]

One day in the latter part of April a Northern-born man in Memphis named William Wilder sat down and wrote a short, bitter
letter to Congressman Thaddeus Stevens of Pennsylvania, a leader of
the Republican Party's Radical wing. Wilder was a Union army veteran whose regiment, the 6th Illinois Cavalry, had endured much hard
campaigning in Tennessee, Mississippi, and other parts of the South.
He had left the service in 1864, settled in Memphis, and started a
business. His political sentiments were Radical. Now he had decided
he must leave the city, and he thought Stevens might be interested in
knowing why. "Enclosed please find an editorial clipped from the
Avalanch[e] of this City," Wilder wrote. "This article shows the state of
feeling now existing in this city against all northern men. I came here

to engage in business about two years since, but from the fact that I have served two years [in] the Federal Army . . . I shall be obliged to seek another home."[2]

Congressman Stevens saved the letter in his files, but not the clipping. The editorial that so troubled Wilder probably appeared in the *Avalanche*'s April 3 issue. In it, the editor took note of the Yankee businessmen in Memphis who espoused Radicalism, men "who are, with [Massachusetts senator Charles] SUMNER and STEVENS, for confiscation, disenfranchisement, and everything calculated to degrade, ruin and embarrass the people to whom they propose to sell their wares." The editor then suggested a way to deal with these miscreants: if his readers would identify them he would publish their names, so "that the Southern people may shun them as they would a leprosy [*sic*]. The Radicals are for war—let them have it. We have enlisted as a volunteer."[3]

How many Yankees were living in Memphis in the spring of 1866 was uncertain. (The term applied to Northerners who had recently moved to the city, not to those who had lived in the city or elsewhere in the South for many years and regarded themselves as Southerners.) Certainly there were many hundreds, perhaps a couple of thousand or more. Some had been called to Memphis by duty, some by conscience, some by ambition; some were the wives or children of those called. Most were middle-class and educated. Many intended to make Memphis their permanent home, while others were anxious to leave. All had come to the city after its capture by federal forces on June 6, 1862; the Yankees living there when the war began had abandoned the city and fled north.[4]

The U.S. Army had maintained a presence in Memphis ever since that day in 1862—a substantial one during the war that dwindled thereafter. And when the 3rd Colored Heavy Artillery mustered out at the end of April 1866, there remained only the headquarters of the Department of the Tennessee, a detachment of the 16th U.S. Infantry Regiment (a white unit), and a few quartermaster troops and other support personnel. Most of the officers and men of the 3rd remained in the city and in uniform, waiting for their back pay, but they were no longer members of the military.[5]

From June 1862 to June 1865, Memphis was under military rule, although for the first two years the municipal government was allowed to operate. In June 1865, with the war over and a Unionist-controlled state government in place in Tennessee, the army ended military rule in Memphis and returned power to the city government. But because politicians in Washington had not yet settled the pressing questions of how the former Confederate states would be restored to the Union, how the defeated Rebels would be dealt with, and what the status of the freed slaves would be, the army forces posted in Memphis and other Southern cities continued to wield considerable influence in local affairs.[6]

From the war's end through early 1866, the ranking army officer in Memphis was Major General John E. Smith, commander of the District of West Tennessee. Although he embraced Republican Party principles, Smith dutifully followed President Johnson's policy of magnanimity and reconciliation with regard to the defeated Confederates. He was skeptical, however, about the Rebels' willingness to reconcile and especially about their acceptance of black freedom. "The white people of the South," he wrote in June 1865, were still influenced by "the wicked leaven of slavery" and were "blind to the lessons of this war. . . . The former master would still induce the black to think that he is as much a slave as ever." At the same time, he doubted the freed people's capacity to exercise freedom wisely. While sympathetic to their plight, he believed that the degradations of slavery had rendered them incapable of meaningful citizenship, at least for the time being. On their own they were "an incubus upon society, a helpless, useless, unproductive class," desiring nothing more than "a life of idleness" and potentially "vicious and unsafe to communities." From these facts, as he saw them, he drew a firm conclusion: "Both races yet need to be controlled by the strong arm of Federal authority."[7]

Smith thus insisted on the need for federal troops in Memphis, but not black ones. While those in the city were generally well behaved in his opinion, he recognized that their mere presence infuriated whites. "The prejudices of the southern people against the negro troops," he told his friend Elihu Washburne in a private letter in December, "seem to be insurmountable." Public peace was in danger as long as they were posted in the city, Smith thought, and he had no doubt that a lot of white Memphians would welcome a racial clash. The best insurance against that, he told Washburne—and, repeatedly, his own superior officer—would be to replace the black troops with white ones. That recommendation was not acted on during his tenure in Memphis.[8]

Although military rule in the city had formally ended, Smith unhesitatingly asserted his power whenever he thought it necessary to do so. The most notable instance occurred in December 1865, when a freedman named Billy Clarke was shot to death by Mike Maloney, a policeman. An investigation revealed that, in the act of arresting Clarke with no substantial cause, Maloney had fired a fatal pistol bullet into him and then, as he lay in the street dead or dying, had shot him twice more. Smith, well aware of the bad reputation of the police and certain that no white who murdered a black would ever be found guilty in the district criminal court, had Maloney arrested by the provost marshal, confined in the military jail in irons, and tried by a military commission. The civil authorities howled in protest and the criminal court judge issued a writ of habeas corpus, which Maloney's attorneys presented to Smith—who dismissed it out of hand, telling the lawyers that "any act of encroachment upon the rights of the negro . . . is in violation of military law" and that, given "the notoriously loose administration of criminal law in this city," justice demanded that the case remain under army jurisdiction. The military commission sentenced Maloney to five years in prison, and he was dispatched to the state penitentiary in Nashville.[9]

Not long before Maloney's sentencing in late January, Smith was succeeded as ranking army officer in Memphis by Major General George Stoneman. Born in upstate New York in 1822, Stoneman was a West Pointer and a veteran of service in the Mexican War and on the frontier. During the Civil War he had been a prominent cavalry commander in both the eastern and western theaters. Given command of the Department of the Tennessee (embracing all U.S. Army forces in Tennessee) following the war, he was Smith's immediate superior. He maintained his headquarters in Nashville until January 1866, when he relocated to Memphis and moved into the combined office and residence that Smith had occupied, a building on Promenade Street opposite the old federal navy yard in the First Ward—comfortable accommodations, but a long way from Fort Pickering, where the troops were quartered. Smith moved to another building, but not long afterward his command was abolished and he left the city. From that point on, the garrison force in Memphis reported directly to Stoneman.[10]

In contrast to Smith's, Stoneman's political sentiments were Democratic. Although he was determined to protect the freedmen from gross abuse, he was at least as skeptical as Smith about their capacity for productive citizenship and far more critical of the black troops. He had not been long in Memphis before he started cracking down on the misconduct of the men of the 3rd Colored Heavy Artillery. He was, furthermore, less hostile to the Rebels than Smith and more willing to accede to their political demands. Their anger and agitation would subside, Stoneman believed, if they were reenfranchised, and he did not worry that, once restored to power, they would persecute their political enemies or reenslave the freed people. The Rebel newspapers in Memphis were rabid and vituperative, he admitted, but no more so than some Northern Radical papers he was familiar with. And, too, he was more inclined than Smith to trust the city's civil authorities and leave law enforcement wholly in their hands. He was, in fact, somewhat disengaged from this assignment in Memphis; compared to his wartime adventures at the head of cavalry brigades, it seemed petty and dull.[11]

Even had he been as ready as Smith to intervene in municipal affairs, Stoneman did not have the same manpower at his disposal. With the mustering out of the 3rd Heavy Artillery, the military force remaining in Memphis was quite small. It consisted of four understrength companies of the 16th U.S. Infantry—180 men and five officers, all told, a contingent barely larger than the Memphis police force.[12]

Commanding this detachment was a young captain named Arthur W. Allyn. He had five years of military service to his credit, having enlisted just days after the war began as a private in a volunteer regiment in his home state of Connecticut. A few months later he accepted a commission as first lieutenant in the 16th, a newly created regular-army regiment assigned to the western theater, and he went on to fight in many of the greatest campaigns and battles of the war: Shiloh, Corinth, Perryville, Stones River, Chickamauga, Chattanooga, Atlanta. Well educated, well-read, and attentive to duty, he was breveted captain in late 1861, assumed company command, and in 1864 was granted that rank in full.[13]

Like the other young Yankees among that first wave of enlistees in the spring of 1861, Allyn was aglow with nationalistic ardor—in one of his frequent letters to his family he described himself as a "patriot defender of our country's honor." His fervor did not wane over the years of hard soldiering, and with the surrender of Robert E. Lee's army in April 1865 he exulted in "the very glorious successes of our arms" and the Confederacy's imminent demise. But then came the shock of President Lincoln's murder by a Rebel sympathizer, and with it not only grief but rage: "Vengeance upon the traitor hearts that conceived so cowardly a deed," Allyn declared, and he prayed to "the great and wise God who rules the destinies of our race [to] preserve the nation now and guide Abraham Lincoln's successor in a path that will give us a quick and lasting peace though it be purchased at the price of the blood of every traitor who has borne arms against our good country."[14]

In August 1865, Allyn's company and several others of the 16th were assigned to garrison duty in Nashville. When the order came down for the 3rd to muster out, he was instructed to take command of a detachment consisting of companies A, C, G, and H of the 16th and move it to Memphis. This force arrived by train on the evening of April 12 and moved into empty barracks in Fort Pickering, a large, fortified army camp that stretched along the Mississippi River and straddled the city's southern boundary. Stoneman informed Allyn that his main task would be to guard the considerable stockpile of army stores and equipment in the city. At that point, Allyn was simply the commanding officer of his detachment, but when the colonel of the 3rd was mustered out with his regiment on April 30, Allyn formally assumed command of the Post of Memphis.[15]

Four days after arriving in the city, Allyn issued an order that set the daily routine for his troops: reveille at daybreak, followed by breakfast; sick call at six thirty; drill from seven to eight; dinner at noon; retreat and inspection at six, followed by supper; tattoo at eight; taps at eight thirty; fatigue and guard duty as required. No off-duty enlisted man would be permitted to leave Fort Pickering without permission from his first sergeant and a written pass from his company commander. "Men upon pass," Allyn added, "are particularly reminded that they are in a peaceful city, and ordered to deport themselves . . . with the dignity of the uniform they wear[,] remembering they are the representatives of a greate [sic] and dignified Republic. . . . [They] will refrain from intoxication and all disorders which inflict disgrace upon a soldier of the United States Army." Because the land on which Fort Pickering stood would soon be returned to its owners (it had been appropriated by the army during the war), Allyn assigned a detail of men with carpentry experience to fix up some of the buildings in the navy yard to serve as barracks after the move. With these soldiers trooping off to the First Ward each morning and others dispatched to do guard duty or work in the post hospital as nurses or cooks, and still others sick or confined in the military jail for various infractions, there were times when Allyn had as few as fourteen men on duty in the fort.[16]

In the wake of the Union military force that captured Memphis in 1862 had come another band of Yankee invaders, a far gentler cohort with a very different mission, armed not with muskets and cannons but with schoolbooks and Bibles. These were civilian women and men dedicated to aiding the freed people, the women mostly teachers, the men mostly ministers. They were inspired by evangelical Protestantism and by the reform movements that had stirred much of the Northern middle class in the antebellum years, especially the abolitionist crusade. During the war, as Union armies conquered Rebel territory and slaves flocked to the occupied towns, Northern benevolent societies—the American Missionary Association, the United Presbyterian Association, the American Baptist Home Mission Society, the Western Freedmen's Aid Commission, and others—sponsored representatives willing to go south and labor on behalf of the liberated blacks. In Memphis these agents founded schools, churches, and an orphanage. Their efforts were aided and coordinated by the army until the summer of 1865, when the newly established Freedmen's Bureau office in the city took charge.[17]

In the early months of 1866 there were approximately thirty such men and women in Memphis, nineteen of them teachers (white men and women, that is; at least four Northern-born blacks also did benevolent work in the city). The women were almost all young and unmarried, the men mostly so. They ran a dozen schools, several churches, and the Colored Orphan Asylum. Their financial compensation was modest (those sponsored by the United Presbyterian Association, for example, were paid forty-five dollars a month). Most of them lived together in a boardinghouse known as the Teachers' Home, run by the

Western Freedmen's Aid Commission, or in a similar establishment run by the American Baptist Home Mission Society.[18]

One of the more prominent Yankee missionaries in Memphis—although untypical in some ways, for he was in his late thirties and married and did not board with the others—was the Reverend Ewing O. Tade. He had come to the city in March 1865 as an agent of the Christian Commission, which provided Union soldiers and sailors with religious literature and other comforts. With the war's end and subsequent military demobilization, the Christian Commission closed up shop in Memphis and Tade went to work for the American Missionary Association. In correspondence with AMA officials prior to his hiring, he described the type of person ideally suited to work with the freed people, and in doing so described himself: "He must be *enthusiastic* in this great & glorious work. Education, apt ability to teach, good preaching abilities, patience & great love for perishing souls, these are all very necessary but to these *must be added a genuine abolition enthusiasm,* to lift up these poor degraded & still despised people."[19]

As soon as he was hired, Tade got to work establishing a church for the freedmen, the nondenominational Lincoln Chapel. He was assisted by his wife, Amanda, and his brother, James, and by donations of money and labor from various sources, including black Memphis. The church building, constructed mostly by Ewing and James's own hands, was dedicated in a grand ceremony on January 1, 1866, the third anniversary of the Emancipation Proclamation. Thereafter Lincoln Chapel offered not only Sunday services, led by Ewing, but also a Sunday school and a day school run by James, Amanda, and two other Northern women.[20]

Ewing Tade held strong political views—of the Radical sort—but he mostly kept them to himself. His message to the freed people, reiterated in every sermon he gave and in his frequent visits to parishioners' homes, was one of salvation and social uplift. His sympathy for the former slaves and his heartfelt concern for their future touched his listeners, but he invariably expressed these sentiments in the language of racial paternalism and class chauvinism. (In this he differed not at all from most other Yankee missionaries.) Southern blacks, he was convinced, had been not just physically exploited by slavery, but morally debased. Even the most ostensibly pious freedmen were egregiously dissipated: "Their ministers . . . are filthy tobacco worms," he reported to the AMA, "the 'Leaders,' many of them, use whiskey, the young people dance." To be fully worthy of God's grace and American citizenship, blacks must redeem themselves from the odious legacy of slavery. They must, Tade thought, take middle-class Yankeedom as their model and Northern reformers as their guides, and so embrace the virtues of self-control, temperance, chastity, and punctuality. The chief purpose for which he and other benevolent workers labored, Tade declared, was to "control & mold the intellect & the religion of the colored people," not just to get them into heaven but also to "fit them to take care of themselves" on earth.[21]

While Lincoln Chapel's day and Sunday schools thrived, Tade struggled to attract a steady congregation. But his optimism and enthusiasm remained undiminished. "My heart is greatly encouraged," he wrote. "I feel that I never had so great & so good a field in which to labor for my blessed Savior." He was certain that "this humble chapel in Union Street, Memphis Tenn., [is] the starting point of good influences which shall grow brighter & brighter, long after the sun has become cold & dark." The last days of April found him feeling "encouraged hopeful & strong."[22]

Along with the army and the benevolent association agents, a third cohort of Yankee invaders came to Memphis during and after the war, and in far greater numbers. These were men on the make ("carpetbaggers," as they would eventually be branded by the Rebels) who saw the postslavery South as a new frontier of business opportunity. Among them were merchants, bankers, lawyers, insurance agents, restaurateurs, and physicians. The majority had served in the Union army or navy, mostly as officers, and a good number had been posted in Memphis at some point. Those who had spent time there had been struck by its potential.[23]

Before the war, the trade in cotton and slaves had made Memphis the most important city on the Mississippi between Saint Louis and New Orleans. The war years had been hard on the city's economy, but in early 1866 commerce was surging—minus the trade in human beings, of course—as evidenced by the frequent arrivals and departures of heavily laden steamboats on the riverfront, the bustling scenes at the city's three railroad depots, and the press of customers in the well-stocked stores lining Main, Front, and other streets. Memphis was a dazzlingly attractive place to many ambitious men of Northern birth. The Yankee presence in the commercial and professional life of the city in the postwar months was substantial, perhaps predominant; as one Memphian remarked in the spring of 1866, "I think one half of the business [here] is transacted by Northerners."[24]

The person who wrote those words was himself a Yankee entrepreneur, a young man named Peter Eltinge. He had grown up in New Paltz, New York, but had lived in New York City before and during the war, working as a clerk. In August 1862, at age twenty, he had joined the 156th New York Volunteer Infantry Regiment as a second lieutenant and eventually rose to the rank of captain. He served for over three years, seeing far more of the South than did the typical Yankee soldier. His regiment was transferred repeatedly from one theater to another: first to Louisiana, then to Virginia, Georgia, North Carolina, and finally (in the postwar months) back to Georgia.[25]

Eltinge had been caught up in the antebellum North's reformist and political enthusiasms, but he was no zealot. In New Paltz he had joined a young people's temperance society and in New York City he had taught in a Sunday school for poor children. In 1860 he supported Abraham Lincoln, but he did not consider himself a Republican or, for that matter, a Democrat; and he had a special dislike for the extremism of the abolitionists. He thought of himself simply as a "conservative Union man." What really inspired him was a dream of success in business. After he mustered out of the army in the fall of 1865, he formed a partnership with his sister's husband, George Lord, who had been an officer in the Union navy's Mississippi River squadron. Since Eltinge had never been anywhere near Memphis, it was no doubt Lord who suggested that city as the place to seek their fortune. Pooling their savings and agreeing to give the retail trade a try, the two aspiring businessmen arrived in Memphis (by themselves, for Eltinge was a bachelor and Lord's wife remained in the North for the time being) on the afternoon of March 13, 1866, with $2,200 in capital.[26]

It was an inauspicious day. "[We] found the place in a horrible condition," Eltinge reported in a letter to his father. "There is about six inches of mud in the streets and it is terrible getting about." But he and his partner went to work enthusiastically, staying at the Gayoso

House while they searched for a rental building for their business and to live in. Before long they found one (for seventy-five dollars a month), secured their city and state business licenses (twenty dollars apiece), and began stocking the store, mostly with groceries and general merchandise for the local market but also with plantation supplies that they hoped to sell to the planters of west Tennessee, north Mississippi, and east Arkansas who trekked to the city periodically to buy provisions. With no place to cook for themselves, the two young men found a boardinghouse where, for seven dollars a week each, they could eat.[27]

They worked hard, keeping the store open from six in the morning until nine at night, six days a week, and doing everything themselves—clerking, stocking, bookkeeping, dusting, and sweeping—until the end of April, when they hired a black person to do the cleaning. The enterprise was profitable from the start, but just barely. Fire insurance was another problem: "We cant get our stock of goods insured," Eltinge told his father. "The building is frame and the whole block is frame. This makes the insurance companies unwilling to take it." But he and Lord remained optimistic, calculating that their sales would increase as they learned more about the retail trade and cultivated more business contacts. They even began thinking about expanding into cotton speculation. "We hope," Eltinge wrote his sister on April 20, "for better times soon."[28]

Yet another Yankee cohort in the city—a relatively recent arrival—was the staff of the Memphis subdistrict of the Freedmen's Bureau. Officially the Bureau of Refugees, Freedmen, and Abandoned Lands, the Freedmen's Bureau had been created by Congress near the end of the war primarily to aid black Southerners in their transition from slavery to freedom. It was a War Department agency, and the men who staffed its hierarchy, from the headquarters in Washington down to the local level, were mostly army officers. The Memphis subdistrict, which comprised the city and a large expanse of rural west Tennessee, was established in the summer of 1865. Like every other local Freedmen's Bureau office across the South, it had a broad range of duties. These included overseeing the signing of labor contracts between planters and black field hands, providing for indigent freed people and caring for the helpless sick, regulating the apprenticing of black orphans, assisting the educational work of Yankee missionaries, and adjudicating legal matters involving blacks.[29]

The original superintendent (chief officer) of the Memphis subdistrict was Brigadier General Davis Tillson. He did not stay long in that post, nor did any of the three men who held it between Tillson's departure and late February 1866. These four superintendents differed in some ways in their approach to the job, but they shared three things: a determination to protect the freed people against legal inequity, physical abuse, and reenslavement; an assumption (similar to that of Smith, Stoneman, and Tade) that slavery had degraded blacks and rendered them incapable of responsible citizenship; and a conviction that Memphis was teeming with indolent freedmen who must be forced into productive labor.[30]

One of the first things Tillson did after arriving in July 1865 was meet with the city's mayor to find out whether black testimony was accepted in the local courts. Learning that state law forbade it, Tillson immediately set up a Bureau judiciary to take charge of all legal cases involving blacks. This court, which was presided over by a Freedmen's Bureau agent and could call on troops in the city to enforce its decrees, handled both civil and criminal cases: disagreements between white employers and black laborers, marital disputes among the freed people, brawls between white and black hack drivers, charges of public drunkenness or theft brought by the city police against blacks, and every other legal matter involving the freedmen. And it did so impartially, thus winning praise from many blacks and scorn from many whites.[31]

But this does not describe the response to every one of the Bureau's actions. Tillson and his successors firmly believed, just as the departed Smith had, that the freedmen needed to be protected from white hostility. "I am determined," Tillson wrote the month he arrived, "that . . . no person shall escape punishment in my sub dist[rict], who is guilty of wrong or injustice to the Freed people." But he also believed that blacks had to be protected from their own foolishness and base passions. His Bureau would steer them to productive pursuits. "Their ignorance," said Tillson, "for which they can not be justly blamed, makes them insensible to their best interests." In the very same sentence in which he vowed to punish their abusers he declared himself "equally determined that the Freed people shall not become a worthless, lazy set of vagrants living in vice and idleness." Two months later his successor echoed those words, claiming that Memphis was overrun by "lazy, worthless vagrants who will never be induced to leave the life they are now leading, except by the use of force." This was no empty threat. The superintendents regularly dispatched armed soldiers to arrest every freedman who merely appeared to be unemployed. Those arrested were deposited in jail, where they sat until they agreed to take work on a plantation. The roundups infuriated the city's blacks.[32]

The Memphis Bureau agents fought a running battle with the municipal authorities, who protested the fact that the Bureau court kept the fines it levied on black offenders but made the city use its jail to hold those offenders before trial, and to continue to hold those who were convicted and unable to pay their fines. (The military jail was too small for that purpose.) This cost the city a lot of money, and the mayor threatened to deny the Bureau the use of the jail unless it paid the city for the privilege, although he never made good on that threat. Meanwhile, the Bureau officers chastised the civil authorities for refusing to take responsibility for black paupers as they did for white paupers: not a penny of city or county revenues went to the missionaries' orphanage, the Bureau-operated Freedmen's Hospital, or any other sort of relief for needy blacks, forcing the Bureau to devote a portion of its meager funds to those purposes. The city and county fathers replied that Congress, in creating the Freedmen's Bureau, had relieved the South's civil officials of all responsibility for black indigents. But the Memphis Bureau agents saw this intransigence not as a matter of legal principle but of racism and schadenfreude: as one of them put it, Southern whites, "having always prophesied that the emancipation of these people would [lead to] their extermination," relished the suffering of the freed people. Whatever the truth, the matter remained unresolved. On more than one occasion, the body of a homeless black person who had died in the street lay unburied for days while the Bureau and the city argued over who would provide a coffin and see to the interment.[33]

At the end of February 1866 a new superintendent took charge of the Memphis subdistrict, the fifth in eight months. Benjamin P. Runkle was a thirty-year-old Ohioan, a college-educated lawyer, and a U.S. Army officer. His military service had begun just ten days after the attack on Fort Sumter in April 1861, when he accepted a commission as captain in a volunteer regiment. A year later, at Shiloh, he suffered a ghastly wound to his jaw, but eventually recovered and resumed active service. He rose quickly in rank, survived two more battle wounds, and won much praise from his superiors. Partially disabled by his injuries, he was mustered out in July 1864 as a brevet brigadier general; but a month later he accepted a commission as lieutenant colonel in the army's Veteran Reserve Corps (also known as the Invalid Corps), which assigned soldiers who could no longer take the field to desk jobs or other light duty.[34]

Runkle and his wife moved into a house a mile and a quarter beyond the city limits. He was surprised at the state of the Bureau. The previous superintendent had been lax; the office records were a mess and important business had gone untended. Reviewing an inspection report on the Freedmen's Hospital and learning that it was "in a most deplorable condition," Runkle immediately ordered the surgeon in charge to get it into proper shape. Meanwhile, he concluded that the office was understaffed, so he asked his superior officer in Nashville for at least one more agent. He also decided that the Bureau's accommodations were unsatisfactory. The office was in a building in the Fourth Ward near the heart of downtown. Runkle made plans to find something closer to the southern part of the city where most of the freedmen lived.[35]

Runkle was less skeptical than his predecessors about the former slaves' capacity for productive citizenship. "The condition of the Freedmen," he wrote in his first monthly report to Nashville, "is all that could be expected under the circumstances: that a race kept in total ignorance for more than a century should conduct themselves as well as they do, should be so earnest in their desires, and so eager and persevering in their efforts to acquire education is a matter of astonishment." Yes, they crowded into the city in far greater numbers than was good for them; but most did so, he thought, not to avoid work but to take advantage of the missionaries' schools or because they had been mistreated on the plantations. As for the accusation, leveled by many whites, that Memphis was awash in black crime, Runkle doubted that black crime was a greater problem than white crime. Still, he acknowledged that there were many black idlers and criminals in the city, and he tolerated them no more than had the previous superintendents.

The periodic roundup of vagrants continued under his administration, but he was at least more diligent than his predecessors in ensuring that no one was packed off to a plantation who did not deserve to be.[36]

Scrupulously fair, Runkle achieved a first for a Bureau superintendent: he won the full trust of the city's blacks. His predecessors had recognized that black cooperation was essential for both the handling of able-bodied freedmen who refused to live productive lives and for the general welfare of the black populace. They had called on Memphis's black leaders for assistance but had been, unsurprisingly, rebuffed. But in a series of meetings with Runkle, these leaders agreed to rally their community in support of the Bureau. This new spirit was manifest in April, when blacks joined in a sanitation campaign, launched by Runkle, to clean up their homes and neighborhoods in anticipation of the onset of cholera season.[37]

As he oversaw the Bureau's dealings with black Memphis, Runkle kept an eye on white Memphis. It was as obvious to him as to his predecessors that the Bureau, and the military force that backed it, were necessary to protect the freed people. Without this federal presence, he noted in his report for March, blacks "would be in a worse condition than when in a state of Slavery." He found little that was encouraging in the attitudes of white Memphians, Yankees excepted. The fecklessness of the city government and the brutish unprofessionalism of the police disgusted him, but he reserved his outrage for the vengeful, troublemaking Rebel newspapers.[38]

Runkle soon secured new accommodations for the Bureau in a more comfortable and attractive building. It was on the west side of Second Street between Gayoso and Beale, in the Fifth Ward—closer, in other words, to the people its purpose was to help. Runkle and his staff moved into it on the last day of April.[39]

A great many of the Yankees in Memphis, Runkle among them, were politically engaged, and of those a sizeable majority were Republicans (or "Union men," as they also called themselves). While these Memphis Republicans disagreed among themselves on certain issues, all sided with the Republican-dominated Congress in its increasingly bitter confrontations with Democratic president Johnson. Only a minority aligned with the Radical wing of their party; but all were routinely labeled Radicals by their opponents, the Democrats of Memphis (who generally referred to themselves as Conservatives).[40]

Fed up with Conservative newspaper agitation and Irish municipal misgovernance, Memphis Republicans decided in late 1865 to organize, with the dual aim of presenting a united front against Democratic propaganda and winning control of the city and county governments. By April 1866 they had founded the Union Republican Party of Memphis, appointed an executive committee, and passed resolutions declaring their general principles—among them "that all men are created equal" and that the federal government had a duty to protect citizens' rights. They then began formulating plans to run candidates in Memphis elections.[41]

One of the executive committee members was thirty-seven-year-old John Eaton, Jr., a brevet brigadier general in the Union army during the war and now chief editor of the *Memphis Post*, one of the city's two Republican papers. Before the war, no one who knew him would have predicted that Eaton would one day rise to prominence in the military and in politics, for he had originally devoted himself to different pursuits: first to teaching and public-school administration, eventually to the ministry. When he went to war in 1861 it was not as a combatant but as the chaplain of the 27th Ohio Infantry. Although he had always rejected abolitionism as extreme, he sympathized with slaves and, after coming to the attention of General Ulysses S. Grant, was appointed in November 1862 to oversee the care of the thousands of runaway slaves who had made it to the lines of Grant's army in west Tennessee and north Mississippi.[42]

Eaton remained in charge of the "contrabands" in that theater for the rest of the war, after which he joined the Freedmen's Bureau in Washington, D.C. But before long he felt another calling: to return to west Tennessee and establish a newspaper. The paper's mission would be to uphold the cause of the Union, to defend and uplift the freed people, to enlighten the benighted South, and to serve as a rallying point for Republicans in the region. Calling on like-minded friends, Eaton secured investors for the enterprise. He then resigned from the army and the Bureau and in late 1865 moved to Memphis with his wife, Alice.[43]

The first issue of the *Post* appeared on January 15. In it Eaton forthrightly proclaimed his purpose and his convictions. The newspaper would "be the exponent of staunch, unconditional loyalty to the Union." Emancipation was a great boon, not just to blacks but to the South as a whole: "Slavery tarnishes the honor of labor and makes industry a disgrace. Slavery poisons the air, and gives barrenness to the soil. Liberty clears the one, and enriches the other." But black freedom was under continuing attack, Eaton warned, and disloyalty still festered in the South. "The Post will give special attention to the correction of these evils."[44]

Eaton threw himself into the paper. He put out daily and weekly editions, and scrambled to secure enough advertising to keep the paper afloat. Alice worried about him, sensing that the long hours and stress were aging him prematurely. She herself hated Memphis and missed Washington, but was comforted by the thought that her husband was doing righteous work.[45]

The *Post*'s editorial columns quickly established the newspaper as the voice of moderate Republicanism in Memphis. It had much to say on the great question of national reunification: to Eaton's mind, the rebellious South did not yet deserve readmission to the Union. His editorials also addressed the matter of the freed people, for whom he had not only great sympathy but great hope. He pointed out that white Southerners' predictions about the consequences of emancipation had been thoroughly falsified by events. They had claimed that blacks "would murder their former masters," but in fact "the murders . . . [have been] chiefly committed by the whites. Then it was cried from pulpit and rostrum, and repeated by the press, that the negro, as free, would not work. The season closed, the crops were less than usual, but the fact stood confessed that the negroes, though only partially paid and allowed little of true liberty, were the chief cultivators of the soil."[46]

Eaton applauded the passage (over Johnson's veto) of the Civil Rights Act in early April. The act granted the former slaves citizenship and legal equality but not the franchise, which Eaton thought they were as yet unready to exercise responsibly. The same month, the *Post* addressed the freed people directly in a series of homilies written in the tone of a parent instructing a child. On the thirteenth the subject was education, which presumably the freedmen had to be convinced was good for them: "While you remain in a state of ignorance you must be content to perform the very lowest class of labor and receive the lowest rates of wages. . . . Now [with the end of slavery] you should have an ambition to be something else besides mere 'hewers of wood and drawers of water.' . . . You will never be able to command the respect and esteem of those with whom you associate . . . till you are in the possession of an education." Five days later there was a lesson on the necessity of "*keeping your contracts*, or, in other words, [we] say to you that *you must do as you agree*. One of the greatest obstacles in the way of your improvement is to be found in your failure to keep your promises, or in your want of reliability." This applied not just to work but to marriage: "You must learn that this obligation can not be thrown off whenever fancy or dislike shall dictate. You can not have a new husband or wife every few months or years." On April 29 came a lecture on black "habits": "Habits are of two kinds, good and bad. You have both. The good we wish to encourage you in; the bad we wish you to abandon." One of the bad ones was "*spending your hard-earned money foolishly*," especially on liquor. "The world has never seen an instance yet where any man or woman was made the better for the use of liquor; but from the days of Noah down to the present time its effects have been only evil."[47]

Eaton also called for the economic restructuring of the South. This was a matter on the minds of Republicans throughout the nation. Long held back by slavery and the power of the planter class, the South's economy was badly in need of a transformation: Southerners should emulate the North's economy, Eaton and others argued. The plantation system exploited laborers and exhausted the soil; planters ought to divide their estates into family farms, and blacks as well as poor whites should be encouraged to purchase them. The Southern economy was too dependent on agriculture and commerce; industries must be established to create new wealth. The South must invite immigrants of the right sort—in other words, Yankees and Germans (no more Irish, please), whose hard work, thriftiness, progressive ideas, and bountiful investment capital would invigorate the listless region.[48]

The Republicans of Memphis were almost all from the North, but their ranks included a handful of native Southerners ("scalawags," as the Rebels would soon begin to call them). These men had been Unionists during the war, and had suffered for it until the Yankee army arrived. Some now held political appointment, thanks to Governor William G. Brownlow (himself a Unionist, from east Tennessee, who had been persecuted by Rebels during the war). Among these office-holders was thirty-seven-year-old William Wallace, the district attorney general and a stockholder in the *Post*.[49]

Another Southern Unionist, B.F.C. Brooks, was the chief spokes-man of the Memphis Republicans' Radical minority. A physician and Alabama native, he had lived in Memphis since 1854. He boasted of the fact that, in the statewide referendum of June 1861, he was one of only five men in the city who voted against secession. The secession-ists had consequently turned their wrath on him; fearing for his life, he fled the city. After the Yankees captured Memphis he returned to serve as a surgeon in a military hospital. Nurturing a permanent grudge against the Rebels, he became active in Republican politics after the war and established a weekly newspaper, the *Memphis Republican*, to make his views known. It had a small circulation compared to the *Post's*, for it breathed a fire too hot for most of the city's Republicans. While Eaton criticized President Johnson and the Memphis Conser-vatives in temperate terms and urged no severer penalty than dis-enfranchisement for any Rebel, Brooks denounced his opponents, lauded Thaddeus Stevens (who advocated enfranchising the freedmen and confiscating the property of rich Rebels), and called for punish-ment of the Rebels commensurate with their guilt: for the rank and file, disenfranchisement; for the lower stratum of Confederate leaders, banishment; for those at the top, the gallows.[50]

The vast majority of native whites in Memphis, along with the Irish, were Conservatives. By the spring of 1866 their hostility to the city's Republicans, moderate and Radical alike (they made no distinc-tion), had reached an intensity disturbing, even frightening, to many Yankees. Urged on by the Conservative newspapers, especially the *Avalanche*, the Rebels and Irish seemed determined to make life so miserable for any whites who favored Rebel disenfranchisement or black rights that they would pack up and leave. Overt threats of vio-lence were rare; Conservatives made their position known through ominous hints, insults on the street, social ostracism, and talk of boy-cotting businesses. But some Yankees suspected that the U.S. military presence in the city was the only thing keeping Conservatives from launching an all-out assault on them.[51]

Few bowed to this pressure. The Freedmen's Bureau agents and army personnel, of course, did not have the option to leave. The missionaries, called to the city by God, were determined not to forsake their duty. A number of other Yankees were apolitical or even sympathetic to the Conservatives, and thus encountered no threat sufficient to drive them away, for the Conservatives insisted that they opposed only Northerners whose politics were hostile to the white South. A few Yankee entrepreneurs, such as William Wilder, closed up shop and left town under threat of boycotting; but the rest stuck it out, hoping that Rebel and Irish rage would eventually dissipate.[52]

2

Rebel Memphis

There is not a bit more love for the laws and the Constitution of the United States and the Union [among the former Confederates in Memphis] than there was in the hottest days of the rebellion.
—Testimony of Ira Stanbrough, businessman and Southern Unionist

I was a slaveholder myself. . . . I know there is no feeling on the part of our people of enmity or dislike to the colored population; but, on the contrary, so far as the older citizens are concerned, I may say that their feelings toward the colored population are almost universally kind. The colored people that belonged to me I believe regarded me as their best friend.
—Testimony of Treadwell S. Ayers, lawyer and Memphis resident for twenty-two years[1]

The Rebels of Memphis were wary of talking to the Yankees in their city. Much of what the Yankees knew about the opinions of Southern-born whites (aside from the newspaper editors) they picked up by eavesdropping on conversations on the sidewalks, in hotel lobbies, and on public transportation. For instance, one morning in late December 1865, as he rode a train through the west Tennessee countryside toward the city, J. T. Trowbridge, a Northern journalist, listened closely but unobtrusively as white men and women in the seats around him commented on the small groups of ragged black people they occasionally passed who were warming themselves around open fires and who they assumed were homeless. Trowbridge recorded what he

heard: "That's freedom! that's what the Yankees have done for 'em";
"Niggers can't take care of themselves"; "The Southern people were
always their best friends. How I pity them! don't you?" "Oh, yes, of
course I pity them! How much better off they were when they were
slaves!"; "They'll all be dead before spring."[2]

Two months later Benjamin Runkle had a similar experience while
traveling to Memphis by rail. He was going there to begin his new job
as the head of the local Freedmen's Bureau, but he was in civilian
clothes and thus did not arouse the suspicion of a group of Southern
men seated nearby. From what Runkle could pick up, half of them
were Memphians, the rest were from the surrounding region, and all
had just attended a big Conservative political meeting in Nashville.
They addressed each other as "judge" or "colonel" or "general." One
seemed despondent: "I have got no country; I have nothing to live
for; I don't care a damn." But the others seemed determined and
had many plans for the future. They returned time and again to the
problem of blacks and Yankees in Memphis. "We will never stop,"
one of the group vowed, "until the last one of them goes out or goes
under."[3]

"Rebels" was not what the Southern-born whites of Memphis called
themselves. They preferred "old citizens" to distinguish themselves
from the city's freed people, foreign immigrants, and Yankees. Of
course, the term would appear to apply to Southern Unionists as well,
but there were so few of them that it hardly mattered. "Old citizens" was
virtually synonymous with native-born Southern whites who had supported the Confederacy.[4]

Although most old citizens had opposed secession throughout the
winter and early spring of 1860–61, the period when the Deep South
states left the Union and formed the Confederate States of America,
their sentiments had changed abruptly in the wake of the Confederate
attack on Fort Sumter on April 12 and President Lincoln's subsequent
call for troops from the loyal states to put down the Southern rebellion. Faced with the choice of making war on their fellow Southerners
or joining with them to repel the Yankee invaders, all but a handful
took their stand with the Confederacy, as did the vast majority of
whites throughout west and middle Tennessee (east Tennessee remained a Unionist stronghold). Well before the state formally seceded
on June 8, 1861, native-born white Memphians had been mobilizing

for war. Many hundreds of Memphis men volunteered for the Confederate army; at least fifty infantry companies, cavalry companies, and artillery batteries were recruited in whole or in part in the city. Many would lose their lives in the war.[5]

Memphis's Confederate period ended on June 6, 1862, when a Union naval squadron, followed by army units, took control of the city. During the three years of Union military rule, many of the city's Rebel citizens fled to parts of the South still under Confederate control. Those who stayed chafed under the hated Yankees and prayed to be rescued by the Rebel army. But their prayers went unanswered, and the war ended in the spring of 1865 with the city still in Yankee hands.[6]

That spring and summer the refugees and the surviving Confederate soldiers returned home. They found a city very different from the one they had left, both physically—three years of occupation by thousands of enemy troops had generated much destruction and construction—and socially. The city teemed with newly arrived black people, Yankee civilians were back in force, and the population of foreign immigrants had swelled. Before the war, Southern-born whites had comprised nearly half the city's population; by 1866, perhaps one-fourth or less. There were dramatic political changes, too: the old citizens were now disenfranchised and the Irish dominated the city government.[7]

Rebels of the elite class were particularly traumatized by these revolutionary developments. Educated, cultured, and—at least before the war—affluent, they had owned the majority of the slaves and largely controlled antebellum Memphis's professions, wealth, commerce, and government. When the war broke out, the elite men had, with a few exceptions, devoted themselves to Confederate service, some assuming high positions in the army or government.

After the war, they found themselves not only slaveless and disenfranchised but also threatened in a way that the Rebel common folk were not. Late in the spring of 1865, President Johnson began issuing a series of proclamations. He did so unopposed, at first; Congress had adjourned in March and would not reconvene until December. One proclamation set forth a policy of amnesty and pardon: amnesty for the Rebel masses, *potential* pardon for Rebel leaders. On signing a simple oath to recognize the abolition of slavery and be loyal to the

United States, most who had supported the Southern rebellion would receive presidential amnesty. But this general amnesty would not apply to certain Rebels—fourteen classes of people in all, including those who had held certain federal civil or military positions before the war; those who had held a civil office (however minor) in the Confederate government; Rebel army officers above the rank of colonel and navy officers above the rank of lieutenant; and those whose property was worth $20,000 or more. Nearly all the elite men of Memphis and across the South were in one or more of these fourteen classes. To obtain absolution, the president declared, these people must not only take the oath but also apply to him for an individual pardon. If they were not pardoned, they could be prosecuted for treason—which could mean confiscation of their property, imprisonment, banishment, even hanging.[8]

Rebels throughout the South quickly took the oath. Those denied amnesty then began preparing their pardon applications, but with no assurance of success. Johnson was an east Tennessean and stalwart Unionist who, while serving as Tennessee's military governor (by appointment of President Lincoln) from early 1862 to early 1865, had earned a reputation as a harsh, uncompromising, even vindictive enemy of the Rebels, especially the leaders. Petitioning him for pardon was humiliating to these proud men. Many felt compelled to swallow their pride, deny that they were ever enthusiastic secessionists, and minimize their service to the Confederacy. Some of those in Memphis had known Johnson before the war and mentioned this in their petitions; some who could reasonably do so attempted to establish a bond with the president, who came from a very humble background and detested aristocratic pretension. "Allow me to say that I have long been known to your Excellency," wrote William T. Avery, a former U.S. congressman, wealthy slaveholder, lieutenant colonel in the Confederate army, and Confederate government official. "For more than thirty years [Memphis] has been my home, beginning here my life, a boy without money [and] without friends, and with but little education. I have ever endeavored to act upon principle. Upon principle it is now my firm purpose henceforth and in good faith to maintain inviolate my allegiance to the government of the United States of America."[9]

To the astonishment of many Americans north and south, Johnson quickly approved the vast majority of petitions, denying or postponing only those of the very highest-ranking Confederate leaders and certain other notorious Rebels. (Avery, his petition dated June 5, was pardoned on July 10.) Not only that, but the president also put into place in most of the former Confederate states (Tennessee being an exception) a reconstruction program that enfranchised all amnestied and pardoned Rebels, allowed them to participate in elections and constitutional conventions to restore their state governments, and encouraged the swift reincorporation of all the seceded states into the Union (on which Congress would have the final say), while denying the freed people any role in the process.[10]

Johnson's motives were mysterious. Some speculated that he hoped to build a coalition of white Southerners, Northern Democrats, and moderate Republicans that would carry him to victory over the Radical Republicans in the 1868 presidential election. (Johnson himself was a lifelong Democrat. He had run in 1864 as the vice-presidential candidate of the National Union Party, which is what the Republican Party called itself in that campaign to attract loyal Democrats.) Whatever his motives, a growing number of Northerners subsequently turned against him, while Rebels hailed him as their champion.[11]

Johnson's bold and controversial reconstruction policies inspired a dramatic shift in mood among many of the defeated Confederates, from one of humble acquiescence to one of feisty confidence in the possibility of reconstructing the South on their own terms. Those in Tennessee were perhaps less confident than most other Rebels, for their state government (restored before the war ended under a program devised by President Lincoln) was controlled by native Unionists who denied them the franchise. But still, the news from Washington through the summer and fall of 1865 was encouraging; and even the convening of the heavily Republican-dominated Congress in December and its opposition to the president's plan—notably its refusal to seat the congressmen elected in the former Confederate states and its passage of the Civil Rights Act in April over Johnson's veto—failed to extinguish hope among Tennessee Rebels that things would work out well in the end.[12]

The old citizens of Memphis, although shorn of the franchise, were not wholly impotent. The elites, in particular, continued to wield a great deal of influence. They had lost their slaves and seen their Confederate bonds rendered worthless, but their other property was still generally intact. (In some cases their real estate had been seized during the war for military use or nonpayment of taxes, but virtually all of it was eventually returned.) And, the Yankee influx notwithstanding, they continued to dominate the ranks of the city's lawyers, doctors, and newspaper publishers and maintained a very strong if not predominant presence in commerce and banking. They also retained their refined manners and gracious lifestyle and continued to expect, and receive, a measure of deference from the less exalted old citizens.[13]

The egalitarian impulse of the Jacksonian era had swept through the South as it had the North; but in the South it had not wholly expunged the heritage of social hierarchy. Southern elites, even into the postwar years, wielded moral authority over, and influenced the opinions of, the white common folk to a greater degree than their counterparts in the North. This is not to say that the common folk were servile or gullible or that Southern gentlemen strutted about issuing commands like grand seigneurs lording over the peasantry. (This is how many people in the North pictured the South.) Nevertheless, there was, in Memphis as across the South, a clear dividing line between the cultured, affluent few who had great influence and the many of plain manners, meager education, and modest means who had little or none.[14]

All Southerners were very conscious of the divide. Elite men and women habitually referred to themselves as the "better sort," the "better class of society," or "our best people." They repaid plain-folk deference with a good measure of paternalism and more than a little patronizing. An editorial comment in the *Memphis Appeal* about the annual ball of the local iron molders' association held in April 1866 typified the attitude of the elite. It "was a brilliant success," the writer observed benignly, "and we cannot do less than congratulate the mechanics of this city . . . on the chaste and admirable manner in which they conducted the evening's entertainment and pleasure. Not the slightest incident occurred to mar the sociability and courteous interchange of sentiment which characterized the cheerful conversation of the evening; and as to the dancing, although it presented not the glitter and the grace of more fashionable circles, [it] was yet in [its] simplicity and strict modesty almost bewitching."[15]

Elites directed their hauteur not just at the native whites of lesser status but also at the Irish. In their thinking about the latter, however, there was little trace of paternalism, no doubt because the Irish were notoriously undeferential. Memphis's "better sort," in fact, deemed the Irish (or most of them) not merely inferior but disgusting: crude, ignorant, undisciplined, drunken, untrustworthy, and violent—not to mention utterly incapable of running the city government responsibly.[16]

As the editorial remark about the iron molders' ball suggests, the Conservative newspapers of Memphis were in some respects mouthpieces of the city's elite. In the spring of 1866 there were six Conservative papers, all dailies: the *Appeal, Argus, Avalanche, Bulletin, Commercial,* and *Public Ledger.* Among the owners and editors of these, J. H. McMahon (chief editor of the *Appeal*), Matthew C. Gallaway (co-proprietor of the *Avalanche*), and Lewis J. Dupree (chief editor of the *Bulletin*) were especially prominent. McMahon, a fifty-four-year-old Tennessee native and longtime newspaperman, had lived in Memphis since 1838. On the eve of the war he was worth $25,000; when it began he put aside his journalistic career to serve with the Confederate army's quartermaster department. Gallaway, Alabama-born and forty-five years old, had been in the newspaper business since at least 1857, the year he moved to Memphis from Mississippi. A man of means before the war (but not rich—he was worth $12,000 in 1860), he had stayed in the city after the war started, exchanging newspaper work for service as a Confederate postmaster. When the Yankees arrived in 1862 he fled and joined the Confederate army, serving as a staff officer under General Nathan Bedford Forrest. Dupree, a thirty-six-year-old Georgia native, had moved to Memphis from Mississippi in 1850. He had amassed a large fortune before the war (he was worth $100,000 in 1860 and owned twelve slaves), but not in the newspaper business: the census taker listed his occupation as "auctioneer"—probably a euphemism for slave trader. His wealth was mostly in real estate, suggesting that he also speculated in that commodity. He left Memphis in June 1861, served on and off for four years as a voluntary Confederate army staff aide (not formally enrolled in the military), and returned to the city a few months after the war ended.[17]

In fact, all of Memphis's Conservative newspapers were run, in whole or in part, by men who had served in the Rebel army, nearly all of them as officers. These included (besides McMahon, Gallaway, and

Dupree) the local-desk editor of the *Argus*, one of the coproprietors of the *Public Ledger*, three of the *Avalanche*'s editors, one of the *Commercial*'s, and probably others. A notable exception was James B. Bingham, co-owner of the *Bulletin*, which he had bought around the time the war started. An unswerving Southern Unionist, he had suppressed his political sentiments until the Yankees took the city. He published his paper throughout the war, but by 1865 he had broken with the Radical Unionists of Tennessee and taken up the Conservative banner. All six of the Conservative papers firmly endorsed President Johnson's reconstruction policies and opposed the disenfranchisement of Rebels decreed by Tennessee's Radical government. The *Avalanche* and *Argus* were particularly vehement, not only in their political editorializing but also in their condemnation of Memphis's blacks and Yankees. The *Avalanche* had the largest circulation of any newspaper in the city.[18]

Of all the changes the war had brought to Memphis, none was more abhorrent to the old citizens than emancipation. They had been brought up to believe that the white race was inherently superior to the black, that the black race was incapable of improvement on its own and capable of only limited improvement in the best circumstances, and that servitude was the natural and best condition for blacks. They were convinced, in other words, that slavery as practiced in the Old South had been a benevolent institution. It had granted civilization and Christianity to people who would otherwise be heathen primitives in the African jungle, nurturing a hedonistic race unable to provide decently for itself. It had kept these people, whose animal instincts made them a potential danger to themselves and others, under tight control. Moreover, whites claimed, despite much evidence to the contrary, that blacks had generally been quite content as slaves and loyal to their masters during the war, and that they had certainly not desired freedom— it had been thrust on them by the Yankee invaders. Emancipation had thus been a dreadful mistake brought about by misguided Northerners. This mistake would only be compounded if Radicals succeeded in raising freed slaves to a level of legal, political, and social equality with whites.[19]

Some of the old citizens of Memphis tried to explain all this to the unbelievers. "The negro [is] by nature indolent & improvident," J. A. Williamson advised Freedmen's Bureau superintendent Nathan

Dudley in the fall of 1865, "living only for to day & permitting tomorrow to take care of itself—not influenced to any extent by the hope of reward but chiefly moved by the fear of punishment." In the absence of the whip, now regrettably banned by federal authorities, some rigorous method of coercing black workers—certainly not the free-labor contract system imposed by the Bureau—must be devised, Williamson said, to "insure order & discipline." The *Argus* editorialized in February 1866 on the folly of granting equality to the freed people: "The more 'rights and privileges' you accord to the negroes . . . the less industrious will they become. The higher they are elevated in the scale of society, by the politicians, the less will they work."[20]

Given the impossibility of resurrecting slavery (the white South understood at least that it was gone forever), what was to be done about the freed people? Some Rebels argued that emancipation had made it impossible for Southern whites and blacks to continue living together harmoniously. "Society . . . will ever be in a state of uneasiness," one prophesied in a letter published in the *Appeal* in late 1865, "feeling evils without hope of remedy, and anticipating greater evils." If the white South could be left alone to deal with the freedmen, he went on to say, things might be settled satisfactorily; but the meddlesome North would not allow that. "The presses, the legislative halls, popular meetings, conventions, organized societies, at the North, will be forever exciting a crusade against the whites of the South; and the halls of Congress will be laboratories for the manufacture and transmission of moral poison over the South; destructive alike to the health of whites and blacks. . . . There will be no peace."[21]

In the postwar months, Memphians frequently discussed the idea that the two races could no longer peacefully coexist in the South. There was much talk of recruiting foreign immigrants (again, Germans or other "dependable" folk, not Irish) to replace black laborers, which would presumably encourage blacks to leave the region. The letter published in the *Appeal* proposed a more drastic solution: the federal government should round up all the blacks in the South and ship them to Africa.[22]

Most Rebels, however, in Memphis and across the South, dismissed the notion of an all-white Dixie as chimerical: the freed people were there to stay and Southern whites must somehow manage to live with them. What was best for all concerned, many realists concluded, was a kind of peonage for the emancipated race under native-white control: blacks could not be bought and sold and would enjoy legal recognition of their marriages and parenthood but would not be entitled to the rights of free laborers or most other benefits of legal equality; nor, of course, would they be entitled to the franchise or social equality. (The Rebel-controlled state governments restored under Andrew Johnson's plan actually attempted to create such systems of peonage, through legislation known as Black Codes; these were struck down by the Civil Rights Act.)[23]

Other Rebels, many former slave owners among them, saw paternalism as the solution. In their view, the freed people were, for the most part, decent folk but also childlike, helpless, and easily led astray, and thus deserving of white pity and assistance. Paternalists saw themselves as the ex-slaves' friends and protectors, who would save them from the Yankees and their own foolishness and puerility. The *Appeal* frequently voiced this point of view. "Upon us of the superior race, rests a very fearful responsibility," declared one editorial, "[and] we shall not fail in doing whatever devolves upon us, to aid the freedman. . . . To let him sink down to sloth, idleness, profligacy and relapse into barbarism, for the want of a friendly hand to steady him, a kindly voice to encourage him, and good and wholesome laws to stimulate him . . . would be criminal." If the objects of this beneficence responded ungratefully, whites should be "patient and forgiving," for the freed people were not really responsible for their misbehavior: "It must not be forgotten that the negro is, in his nature, but a grown-up child, subject to the perversities of children. . . . [Whites should follow the same] course by which a wise father directs his perverse children into better ways—a course inflexibly firm and just, but invariably kind." Such sentiments were not necessarily hollow, self-serving rhetoric. Many former masters did generously if patronizingly offer aid and advice to blacks who came to them seeking these things.[24]

The paternalist view was sharply challenged by those who saw many or all of the freed people as dangerous semisavages who did not need coddling and encouragement but harsh restraint. The editors of the *Avalanche* and the *Argus* were particularly vocal proponents of this idea. Inherent in the black character, said the *Argus*, were "deceit, untruthfulness and ferocity." The *Avalanche* declared that emancipation had unleashed blacks' "beastly passion." The papers printed lurid accounts of every major incident—confirmed or merely rumored—of black crime in the city and surrounding region. FIENDISH ATTEMPT TO POISON AN ENTIRE [WHITE] FAMILY! read a headline in the *Argus* on February 7, 1866; THE MONSTER ESCAPES! An account in the *Avalanche* of "the hellish murder" of a white by a black man who was later caught reported that the perpetrator had "as villainous a countenance as the utmost depravity of his race ever possibly shows." Particularly dangerous, the *Argus* claimed, were the "big, stout, buck negroes" who regularly got drunk and lost all their money in gambling houses; emerging from these "dens [of] vice, idleness and infamy," they proceeded to recoup their losses through the "robbery and garroting" of "weak and defenseless" victims. Most menacing of all, armed as they were with muskets and federal authority, were the troops of the 3rd Colored Heavy Artillery: ANOTHER MURDER! the *Avalanche* excitedly informed its readers on January 14, A WHITE MAN SHOT AND BAYONETED BY NEGRO SOLDIERS!, only the latest outrage in "the carnival of [black] crime now holding high festival in our city." The papers attributed nearly every incident of suspected arson to "negro incendiaries" and even blamed the freed people for threatening whites with disease. Whenever smallpox appeared in the city, as it did in February, the black neighborhoods were identified as the source. "Indeed," said the *Avalanche*, "it is no uncommon circumstance to meet a negro on the streets with the pustules and disseminating the contagion of this loathsome disease."[25]

More than random mischief and violence, many whites feared a mass black uprising. This fear had a long history. Rebellion scares, almost always without foundation, had periodically gripped the South from colonial days through the Civil War. Emancipation magnified white anxiety. Late in the fall of 1865 terrifying rumors of a black uprising planned for Christmastime swept across many parts of the South, including Memphis; its supposed aims were pillage, arson, murder, and rape. Panicked whites pleaded with federal authorities to crack down on the freed people. On December 10, fifteen citizens of Memphis dispatched a petition to President Johnson claiming that "bad advisers have inculcated in the minds of the negroes a false and improper influence, to an extent that many in this vicinity feel that an outbreak may take place during the Christmas holidays that would be unprecedented in its consequences to helpless women and children";

they begged Johnson to order the military authorities to disarm and disband the black troops in the city. Nowhere did the army take pre-emptive action against blacks in or out of uniform, but in some rural districts white citizens acted on their own, invading the homes of blacks to search for arms and arresting many. There was no truth to the rumors, however, and Christmas passed quietly everywhere. But the specter of vengeful, lustful, armed black men rising en masse would not be altogether exorcised from the psyche of the white South for a long time.[26]

Any regular and uncritical reader of the *Avalanche*, the *Argus*, or certain other Memphis papers in the winter and early spring of 1866 could easily have become convinced that an orgy of black crime had brought the city to the brink of anarchy. Informing its readers on Feb-ruary 22 of ANOTHER FIENDISH OUTRAGE—in this case, the killing of a policeman by a black man in military uniform—the *Argus* asked, "When will the blood-thirsty spirit of the black population be ap-peased?" The voice of the *Public Ledger* swelled the chorus in April: "South Memphis has become notorious for negro outrages," it declared in reporting yet another "daring" robbery by a gang of black men who remained at large. "A few more such . . . and the [criminal] parties will get so bold that there will be no safety, either for life or property, for any place these marauders feel like plundering."[27]

The mustering out of the 3rd Colored Heavy Artillery at the end of April was hailed by Rebel Memphis with a great sigh of relief. But it did not dispel the fear shared by many that the city's freed population was dangerously out of control. Something must be done, they de-manded, to stem the tide of black villainy before it became a deluge.[28]

Another source of Rebel anxiety and anger in the postwar months was the city's Yankee population—specifically, the latter's power and influence. That their city continued to be occupied by U.S. Army troops vexed the Rebels. It was utterly unnecessary, they insisted, a gratuitous insult, for they had laid down their arms, bowed to defeat, resumed peaceful pursuits, and sworn their acceptance of emancipa-tion and national reunification. More vexatious still was the presence of the Freedmen's Bureau. There was no more need for the Bureau, Rebels argued, than for the army. As the *Appeal* put it in March 1866, the "status [of the former slave] as a free man, untrammeled, in the smallest degree, in the full exercise of his volition as to the manner and means of working out his new destiny, is firmly and forever established," and the white South had no intention of reenslaving or otherwise abusing him. Furthermore, the Bureau's "bad influences" stirred up black hostility toward Southern whites; race relations in the South would be far more harmonious without it. The *Avalanche* was, characteristically, more acerbic: "It has been said that nothing is all evil," it remarked in February, "but this was said before the Freedmen's Bureau was thought of."[29]

The old citizens of Memphis also hated and feared the Yankee missionaries, who, though they lacked formal power, were seen as insidious agents of black discontent. Their efforts to educate and uplift freed people would only tempt the latter away from their God-given role as servants of the white race. As the *Appeal* put it in November 1865, the Yankee teachers were determined to "seduce the poor negroes into the same course of unproductive, profitless, impractical and visionary habits and employments in which these fanatics pass their [own] lives and waste faculties and energies that might be employed in some useful avocation."[30]

It was not just the freedmen who were in danger of contamination by Yankee culture: Southern whites were threatened, too. In an editorial in January warning of the recent proliferation of "free and easys," saloons where workingmen frittered away their wages drinking and watching lascivious entertainments, the *Appeal* pointed out that this "sad blight on the morals of our city" was "of decided Northern origin." More sinister was the arrival of Northern textbooks and juvenile literature, which would only poison the minds of Southern youth. In April the *Avalanche* devoted the better part of a column to reprinting an editorial from a Kentucky newspaper on this matter. The South was inundated, the editorialist claimed, by Yankee-authored books and periodicals for children, nearly all of which "contain some base and cowardly stab or slur at the people of the South. The most open and causeless insults are offered [in these works]—glaring and cruel falsehoods." This was no mere coincidence but "a concerted effort" by Northerners, a campaign of cultural imperialism intended to warp the minds of Southern youngsters, induce them to adopt noxious Yankee notions, and turn them against the faith of their fathers.[31]

As they took their stand against the villainous freed people, army and Freedmen's Bureau authorities, and missionaries and other cultural polluters, the embattled Rebels of Memphis also rallied against the political threat of Radicalism. They waged this struggle on three fronts: national, state, and local. In Washington, congressional Radicals were working to undo the reconstruction policies of President Johnson and impose their own nefarious plan, which included legal equality for the freedmen. In Nashville, native Unionist Radicals dominated the legislature, held the governor's chair, and presided over the disenfranchisement of Tennessee's ex-Confederates. In Memphis, Yankee immigrants along with a few Southern Unionists had established two Radical newspapers and organized a local Radical party that aimed to seize control of the city and county governments. (It bears repeating that Rebels declined to acknowledge the distinction between moderate and Radical Republican; as far as the Rebels were concerned, anyone who opposed Johnsonian reconstruction, favored black legal equality, or approved the disenfranchisement of the former Confederates was a "Radical.")[32]

Although deprived of the ballot, the Rebels had two other weapons in their armory with which to wage political battle: press and party. With these they endeavored to discredit Radicalism and win adherents to the Conservative cause from among the enfranchised population of the city and county.

The city's Conservative newspapers maintained a steady barrage of anti-Radical editorials. A typical one appeared in the *Appeal* in early April, lauding Andrew Johnson's reconstruction plan and his recent veto of the Civil Rights bill. The president, it said, was a staunch defender of states' rights as guaranteed by the Constitution and a noble champion of "the cause of free, democratic institutions"; his defeat at the hands of the congressional Radicals would mean "the triumph of anarchy and despotism." The disenfranchisement of Tennessee's former Confederates, the paper commented on another occasion, was purely vindictive, evidence of the Radicals' "unmanliness," for peace now prevailed and the Rebels had humbly accepted defeat: *It strikes men who are down!*" Commenting in April on Governor Brownlow's recent message to the legislature justifying disenfranchisement, the *Appeal*'s deep bitterness was manifest: "We do not hesitate to say that for unprincipled inconsistency, reckless disregard of every idea of republican government, malignant mendacity in statement of facts, rapacity of personal greed in self-seeking, and scandalous absence of all proper dignity, this Message is the most discreditable to its author of any public document that has ever come under our notice."[33]

A small and loosely organized local Conservative party, comprised almost wholly of former Confederates, was active in the city by late 1865, holding occasional meetings and rallies. But in March 1866, no doubt provoked by the recent militancy of the city's Republicans, the Conservative movement surged. In a series of enthusiastic meetings that month and the next, Conservatives formally organized themselves into the Johnson Club of Shelby County, adopted a constitution and bylaws, proclaimed their purpose to the world, and dispatched a letter of thanks to their hero in Washington, praising him as a "defender of the Constitution and of Free Government under it, whose services in this regard it is no impiety to rank along with those of the 'Father of his Country.'" They also set about energetically recruiting new members.[34]

Rebels comprised the core constituency of the Johnson Club, its heart and soul, but they had considerable success in attracting men from outside their ranks—men who, unlike themselves, could vote. Among the club's members were Yankee immigrants of Democratic persuasion, Southern-born Unionists anxious to reconcile with the Rebels and horrified by the Civil Rights Act, some German immigrants, and many Irish, who needed little coaxing, having embraced Democratic politics and white supremacy practically from the moment they set foot on American shores. In welcoming them into the Johnson Club, many of the Rebels had to suppress their distaste for the sons of Erin as a matter of expediency.[35]

Rebel Memphis tried to induce Radicals to actually leave, but with little success. The boycotting of Radical merchants urged by the *Avalanche* never crystallized into a significant movement, for too many consumers were willing to ignore politics when they found a good bargain. Social ostracism was widely practiced: few army personnel, Bureau agents, missionaries, Radical businessmen, or their wives were received in Rebel homes, and there was a lot of turning up of noses, ostentatious averting of eyes, and contemptuous muttering by old citizens when passing Yankees on the street. But none of this seemed to bother the Yankees enough to drive them from the city. Only very rarely was an outright threat uttered by an old citizen, and then not by any respectable sort. If any actually contemplated violence, they were restrained by the fear of punishment by the army, if not the municipal authorities. Generally the Rebels had to content themselves with simply letting their Yankee nemeses know that they were despised and unwelcome.[36]

Treated thus by the old citizens, many Yankees concluded that true loyalty to the Union was a scarce commodity in Rebel Memphis, and real love for it nonexistent. And, indeed, there was plenty of other evidence that when the former Confederates claimed to accept defeat and reunion they were defining acceptance in their own terms, and that when they swore allegiance to the United States they did it no more enthusiastically than they would swallow a bitter dose of medicine.[37]

Few Rebels in Memphis or anywhere else in the South evinced the sense of guilt about the war that Yankees wanted to see proof of. The vast majority believed, as they had believed in 1861, that seceding from the Union was lawful and that in taking up arms they had been rightfully defending their homeland from enemy invasion. Their surrender in 1865 was no more than an acknowledgment that their armies had been overpowered; they still cherished the principles they had fought for, including white supremacy, states' rights, and self-determination. They were deeply proud of fighting for their short-lived Southern nation. In fact, the memory of their wartime deeds and sacrifices became a source of great comfort and inner strength to them as they endured military occupation, political subjugation, and social upheaval in the postwar world. As they rallied around the political banner of Conservatism, they rallied too around the ideological banner of the Lost Cause.[38]

In the spring of 1866, Memphis was awash in mementos, celebrations, and commemorations of the Cause. In homes and shops hung many a portrait of Robert E. Lee, Thomas J. ("Stonewall") Jackson, Jefferson Davis, and other Confederate heroes; indeed, there was a store in town that sold nothing but war memorabilia. The faithful could also purchase decks of playing cards featuring the engraved portraits of fifty-two Confederate generals. For sale, too, was a volume of poems and songs composed in the South during and right after the war, including such sentimental favorites as "The Lone Sentry," "The Tennessee Exile's Song," "Dirge for [General Turner] Ashby," and "The Conquered Banner." Whenever a band struck up "Dixie" in the city it evoked cheers; on at least one occasion, "The Star-Spangled Banner" and "Yankee Doodle" were greeted with hisses. Had the army authorities tolerated the display of Confederate flags, those would no doubt have vastly outnumbered the four U.S. flags that flew in the city (above General Stoneman's headquarters, the Freedmen's Bureau office, the post office, and the *Memphis Post*'s print shop).[39]

Among the sacred commandments of the postwar South's Lost Cause creed was the duty to aid those who had sacrificed for the Cause and now needed a helping hand. Rebel Memphis did not shirk that duty. In January 1866 a benefit concert at Greenlaw's Opera House raised money for the indigent widow and orphan of Stonewall Jackson, who had died of wounds in Virginia in 1863. "Remember the family of the patriot and Christian hero," the *Bulletin* urged in its announcement of the event. "Let the hall be filled to overflowing." In April local Rebels established the Branch Benevolent Society of Memphis to provide artificial limbs for Confederate army veterans who had endured amputation; the organization announced plans for a fundraising event at the Gayoso House on May 3. The Southern Soldiers Relief Society of Memphis, also dedicated to aiding the men who had worn gray, had been active since July 1865. By April 1866 it had raised $15,000 through benefit concerts, *tableaux vivants*, orations, fairs, horse races, and door-to-door solicitation. In its first months the society spent much of its money on meals, clothing, and transportation for the hungry and ragged veterans who passed through the city while making their way home after surrender or release from Northern prison camps. Since then, the bulk of the society's funds had gone to assisting the partially disabled indigent ex-soldiers living in the city (of whom there were sixty-eight in the spring of 1866) and providing full care for the wholly disabled (who numbered between thirty and fifty). The society owned and operated a hospice called the Southern Soldiers Home, where any needy disabled veteran was welcome.[40]

This benevolent work for the Cause was conceived, organized, and carried out almost entirely by women. It was a natural role for them, for Southern white women had always taken responsibility for caregiving, not only within their families but in the world outside, a duty many had performed selflessly in military hospitals and soldiers' aid societies during the war. The Lost Cause charitable associations of Memphis, like those everywhere else in the South, were dominated by elite women, who, blessed with wealth and servants, had ample money and time to devote to the work.[41]

Fannie Gallaway was the matriarch of Lost Cause benevolence in the city. Virginia-born and forty-two years old, she lived in a spacious house on Court Street, in the heart of downtown, with her three-year-old daughter, Lucile, and her husband, Matthew, coproprietor of the *Avalanche*. She had resided in Memphis with Matthew before the war but apparently fled, as he had, after the Yankees captured the city, for her daughter was born in Arkansas. A member of both the Branch Benevolent Society and the Southern Soldiers Relief Society, she was elected president of the latter in January 1866 and subsequently held its committee meetings in her house. (Meetings of the whole were held in the Cumberland Presbyterian Church, also on Court Street.) She devoted enormous time and effort to the Relief Society, not only chairing meetings, supervising personnel, and writing reports but also taking on the drudgery of solicitation: in the early spring she went door-to-door among the city's dry-goods stores pleading for donations of cloth and buttons with which to make summer clothes for the disabled veterans.[42]

Gallaway also played a prominent role in another sacred rite of the Lost Cause: honoring the soldiers who had given their lives in the war. In Memphis, the Relief Society took the lead in this work. On April 14, having learned that sister associations in other Southern states had chosen the twenty-sixth of that month to commemorate the fallen by decorating their graves, the society held a special meeting. Those attending voted to arrange a public ceremony at Elmwood Cemetery, located in the eastern suburbs two miles from downtown. In a specially designated section of that cemetery were the graves of eight hundred Rebel soldiers, most of whom had died of wounds or disease in one of the military hospitals established in the city during its brief Confederate period. The Conservative newspapers of Memphis publicized this Decoration Day event and called on the faithful to attend.[43]

Thursday, April 26, was a beautiful spring day—proof to the more than one thousand women and girls and nearly three hundred men who gathered at Elmwood that God had bestowed His blessing on the occasion. Many of the women were dressed for mourning. A wooden obelisk had been erected by the society; it was painted white and adorned with evergreen, laurel, a cross, and the words "To our Gallant Dead." (Plans were already under way to replace this with a stone monument inscribed with the names of the eight hundred martyrs.) Following the ceremonial placing of flowers on each grave, those in attendance gathered around the speakers' stand, built just for this occasion. In accordance with custom, no woman addressed the crowd: public speaking was the province of men. Two gave orations this day, while a third offered prayers. One of the orators was the Reverend S. H. Ford, who reminded his listeners that those being honored "went forth at the call of their States. They were prompted by a lofty sense of duty. Their courage and endurances were made glorious by principle. They believed they were defending *their* country against unjustifiable invasion. . . . They sleep in no dishonored graves. They are to us, and ever will be, the 'patriot dead.'"[44]

Confident that they had acted dutifully and honorably in the war, and determined to restore what they could of the cherished world they had lost, the old citizens of Memphis gazed Janus-like toward the past and the future. The past they saw was clear and comforting. The future they saw, by contrast, was murky and threatening, a foggy field on which new battles would be waged.

3

Irish Memphis

Almost all the police are Irish; all our public men, from the mayor downward, are for the most part Irish.

—Testimony of Martin Gridley, a Memphis resident since 1840

The Memphis police . . . [are] the worst police I ever saw in any city.

—Testimony of Benjamin P. Runkle

The whole thing grew out of a feeling of spite between the police and negroes. . . . It has been gradually growing up. I have heard it remarked that it would ultimately come to a riot, the way the thing was going on.

—Testimony of James H. Swan, deputy sheriff of Shelby County[1]

Saint Patrick's Day, 1866, witnessed celebrations all over the city, but none outshone the grand ball hosted by the Fenian Brotherhood. It was held in the elegant new Greenlaw Hall and Opera House, a few blocks from the Gayoso House. Printed invitations with complimentary tickets had been sent to some of the city's prominent citizens; lesser folk had been invited to purchase tickets at downtown stores or from members of the organizing committee. The *Avalanche* had predicted that the event, which was to include supper and dancing to the music of Professor Withers and his orchestra, would "do fitting honor to the natal day of [Ireland's] patron saint."[2]

The hundreds who attended were not disappointed. The weather was fine that evening, the hall gaily festooned in green and brightly illuminated by gaslight, and the music lively. The celebrants saw the most striking decoration as they walked into the hall. Suspended above the entrance, side by side, were an Irish flag and an American flag. The reverse side of the Irish flag, as described by an attendee, was emblazoned with two symbolic figures: "Columbia supporting a shield with the American arms" and "a daughter of Erin, who held a shield, . . . while her eyes were fixed upon a temple, behind which the sun was rising, the whole being surrounded with a wreath of shamrock, surmounted by a harp." The hall echoed with the sounds of dancing, singing, and toasting well into the night.[3]

The flag display embodied the blended identity of Memphis's Irish-American community, which warmly embraced its adopted land while remaining firmly attached to its native land. The community was a sizeable one, although nobody could say exactly how many Irish now lived in the city. The census taker in 1860 had counted a little over four thousand Irish-born Memphians. Taking into account the considerable influx of Irish since then, and counting the American-born children of the Irish-born, and including furthermore those who lived in the suburban neighborhoods, an informed observer in 1866 might have estimated that the Irish numbered six or seven thousand, perhaps one-fifth or one-sixth of the total population.[4]

Some had lived in America for several decades, others but a few years or months. Most, however, had arrived on U.S. shores in the 1840s or 1850s, driven from their homeland by famine and unemployment—engendered by the calamitous potato blight and exacerbated, as they saw it, by British misrule—and lured by the promise of work and democracy in the republic across the Atlantic. They and the hundreds of thousands of other Irish men, women, and children who immigrated to America in the middle decades of the century generally struggled in their new land. Most had been propertyless laborers or very marginal landholders in Ireland; they arrived in America utterly impoverished, poorly educated, devoid of skills save the simplest agricultural ones, and devoutly Roman Catholic in an overwhelmingly evangelical Protestant society. Congregating in cities, where unskilled jobs were plentiful, they worked hard for paltry wages, drank hard after the workday was done, and prayed hard in church on Sundays. They socialized

among themselves, flaunted their Irishness and Catholicism, and retained strong sentimental ties to the old country. At the same time,
they were eager to become American citizens. Once naturalized, they
embraced politics and were heartily welcomed by the urban bosses of
the Democratic Party. They also adopted an especially fierce strain
of the racism common among white Americans.[5]

Almost all Irish immigrants arrived in New York or another Northern seaport, and the vast majority stayed in the North. But some made
their way to the cities of the South. Many who went south before the
war adopted the sectional attitudes of the native whites, endorsing slavery, Southern rights, and eventually secession. Some fought in the ranks
of the Confederate army. At war's end they accepted defeat and willingly
resumed their loyalty to the United States while holding fast to Irishness, Democratic politics, white supremacy, and Southern identity. The
Irish who did not think of themselves as Southerners—those who went
south during and after the war—held cultural, political, and racial views
that were in every other respect the same as those of the Irish who did.[6]

American, Irish, Catholic, Democratic, white, and (in some cases)
Southern: the Irish residents of Memphis in 1866 proudly declared
themselves all of these. But whether they were *Memphians* was another matter. Many were longtime residents of the city, had married
and raised children there, and were thoroughly integrated into its social, political, and economic life even as they maintained their Irishness. But many other Irish made up part of what some Memphians
referred to as the city's "floating population," rootless and unsettled
men and women, in Memphis but not of it, who drifted in and would
soon drift away to some other place.[7]

The Irish were the city's largest ethnic minority, but not its only
one. The German-born and their children—Catholics, Lutherans,
and Jews—numbered several thousand. Like the Irish, they embraced
American citizenship while clinging to their native identity and tradi-
tional culture. The German Catholics had their own church, as did
the Lutherans, and together they supported a German Mutual Benevolent Society, a *turnverein* (athletic club), and various German political clubs. The Jews, although numbering only three hundred or so
families, supported two congregations—one Reform, one Orthodox—
and a number of fraternal, benevolent, and educational institutions,
including a B'nai B'rith lodge, a chapter of the United Hebrew Relief

Association, and a Hebrew school. Significant numbers of English, Scots, Scotch-Irish, French, Italians, and other European-born folk also made Memphis their home. Most of the non-Irish immigrants had come to America with a decent education, some money, and remunerative skills, and thus few had had to settle for low-wage, unskilled labor in the new land. The breadwinners among the German gentiles were mostly artisans (particularly shoemakers), shopkeepers (many of them grocers), store clerks, or salesmen for wholesale businesses. The Jews were almost all shopkeepers; they dominated the city's retail clothing, dry goods, and tobacco trades.[8]

Some of the Irish had managed, through hard work, shrewdness, and luck, to claw their way out of the ranks of unskilled labor. By early 1866, Mary Grady was doing quite well with the dance hall and groggery she operated in the area known informally as South Memphis (embracing the two southernmost wards of the city and the southern suburbs). She catered to a black clientele, offering not only music, drink, and good times but also prepared foods and rooms for rent. Another Irish entrepreneur, twenty-six-year-old John Callahan, had come to the city around 1861 and had served in the Confederate army. He now owned a grocery store in South Memphis. Like Grady he had a sizeable black clientele, and like many other grocers he served liquor in a back room. Another grocery store nearby, owned by twenty-four-year-old John Pendergrast, sold not only food but necessaries of all sorts, including pistol ammunition.[9]

Other Irishmen had mastered a skilled trade and made decent wages; Pendergrast's brother Michael was an iron molder prominent in the city's workingmen's movement. Still others found employment with the city or county government. Most of the city's policemen and firefighters were Irish, as were many of the higher local officials. A handful of Irish had risen to take a place, if not among the city's social elites, then certainly among its plutocrats. One was Eugene Magevney, who had left Ireland in 1828 at age twenty-two, spent five years in Pennsylvania, and then moved to Memphis. Much better educated than the typical Irish immigrant, he was a schoolteacher by profession; but he eventually turned to real estate speculation and succeeded terrifically. On the eve of the war his landholdings were worth $115,000, and by 1866 a good deal more.[10]

The great majority of Memphis's Irish, however, permanent residents and "floating population" alike, earned their bread through manual wage labor, and poverty was their lot. Many were mired in indigence not only because of their lack of trade skills but also because they were illiterate; some were further handicapped by language, for many of the Irish who came to America spoke only Gaelic and struggled to learn English. But even those literate and fluent in English rarely found work in Memphis that did not involve hard labor at low wages. Many of the men were employed—under the supervision of contractors, artisans, retailers, or wholesalers—in construction, railroad maintenance, porterage, steamboat lading, or other work that demanded strong arms and backs. Others drove hacks or drays, almost all of them for wages (a few owned their rigs). Irishwomen worked for wages, too. While married women generally tended to their home and children, most of the unmarried labored as servants or washerwomen.[11]

Well-off Irish families owned or rented nice frame houses; the poor crammed into run-down tenements or rough shanties. Single men and women generally roomed in all-Irish boardinghouses or lived with their employer or some Irish householder. The Irish who came to Memphis before the war had gravitated to the First Ward, on the city's north side, which gained the nickname of "Pinch" (supposedly short for "Pinch Gut," a reference to the undernourished appearance of the inhabitants). In 1866 the First was still home to over half the city's Irish, but Irish men, women, and children could be found in every part of the city, including mostly black South Memphis, where their dwellings stood, in many cases, side by side with those of freed people.[12]

Among the Irish of the laboring class were many unmarried men and fewer unmarried women, for the male Irish population of the city well outnumbered the female and the women tended to marry young. At the end of the workday, these bachelors, along with similarly inclined married men, crowded into saloons, grocery back rooms, gambling dens (especially keno parlors), and—for those with a taste for blood—cockfighting and rat-killing pits. In these places, the Irish rubbed shoulders with the native-born, and boisterousness, coarse language, and hard drinking were the rule. Especially popular were the "free and easys"—among them the Shamrock, the Basket, the Varieties, and the suggestively named Climax—which featured risqué song-and-dance performances and attractive "waiter girls." Men who lacked money for indoor entertainments congregated at night on downtown street corners and smoked cigars, spit tobacco, exchanged bawdy jokes, and ogled young women.[13]

Fighting was common in the hangouts of the laboring men, although most of it was harmless enough: spasms of alcohol- and hormone-fueled rage encouraged by a working-class ethos of masculinity (especially characteristic of the Irish but by no means confined to them) that prized physical strength and cocky self-assertion over polite manners and self-control. In that setting a man could get drunk and curse and brawl without sacrificing respectability in the eyes of his peers. But the Irish population of Memphis did have its share of truly disreputable sorts. The white hack drivers, most of them Irish, had earned a particularly bad reputation for their hair-trigger tempers even when sober, their frequent resort to violence to settle disputes on the streets, and their readiness to cheat customers.[14]

Of the actual criminals among Memphis's Irish, the young ones stood out. The city was plagued by juvenile delinquency, a problem much discussed and deplored by respectable folk but seemingly intractable. The worst offenders were an informal gang of parentally neglected and perversely clever eight-to-fifteen-year-old white boys (and a few girls), most but not all of Irish parentage, known as the Mackerel Brigade. Now and then they earned honest money as newsboys, but mostly they stole, having mastered to a remarkable degree the arts of shoplifting, pickpocketing, and burglary. On one occasion they outdid themselves by robbing a bank. When not committing larceny, this beardless brigade could often be found loafing on the riverfront, swearing, drinking pilfered liquor, vandalizing property, and throwing rocks at steamboat hands.[15]

The notoriety of the Mackerel Brigade, the hackmen, the street-corner loungers, and the free-and-easy carousers obscured to a degree the Irishmen who obeyed the law and spent their free time quietly at home or in productive public activities. A considerable number, for instance, joined the workingmen's movement that began in the city in the spring of 1866. Its chief goal, shared with many urban wage-earners across the nation, who customarily labored ten hours a day or more, six days a week, was an eight-hour workday. On the evening of March 26 a large number of white workingmen—mostly skilled, some semiskilled, a few unskilled—gathered downtown at the Exchange Building (city hall) to discuss what might be done to advance the cause. The Irish were represented by, among many others, iron molder Mike Pendergrast, printer F. A. O'Hara, tailor Terence Maguire, shoemaker William Mahoney, housepainter James Mulligan, and laborer William Fitzgerald. The assembled workers selected from among themselves a committee to establish a Memphis "eight-hour league," an umbrella organization in which the city's various trade associations would all be represented. Three nights later they reconvened and voted for the officers of the new league; Pendergrast was elected recording secretary. At a third meeting on April 9, the league—to be known formally as the United Mechanics' Association of Memphis—discussed its proposed constitution and bylaws. Those in attendance also discussed, as the *Appeal* reported, organizing "a grand celebration of all the Trades in Memphis" to be held on Monday, May 6, "the Painters Association . . . kindly offering to paint such banners and mottos as may be deemed necessary."[16]

The city's Irish community also supported a number of institutions all its own. The Memphis Hibernian Mutual Relief Society, a fraternal and benevolent association, had been founded before the war by Eugene Magevney's brother Michael, a tailor-turned-businessman who, like Eugene, had made a fortune in real estate. The Irish Literary Society of Memphis had likewise been established before the war. But the most important Irish institution in the city was St. Peter's Roman Catholic Church.[17]

The church was formally established around 1840, though not until several years later was a church building erected. The first mass was celebrated in Eugene Magevney's parlor. The congregation included both Irish and Germans until 1852, when the Germans withdrew and founded their own church. One of the early pastors of St. Peter's took the lead in establishing the St. Agnes Academy of Memphis, a girls' boarding and day school thereafter run by Dominican sisters and closely tied to the church. In 1858 a new St. Peter's building was consecrated, an imposing brick edifice on the corner of Adams and Third—a central location downtown, although a good fourteen blocks from the heart of Pinch.[18]

In the spring of 1866 the church was led by the Reverend M. D. Lilly, an Irish-born Dominican in his mid-thirties who previously had been president of a Catholic college in Ohio. In his current post Father Lilly had the help of four assistant pastors and a corps of devoted lay leaders. They had much to do, for the St. Peter's congregation was very large and many of the faithful needed not only spiritual guidance but charitable aid. By day and by night the church building echoed with brogue and hummed with activity, an unceasing round of sermons, masses, confessions, weddings, baptisms, and committee meetings. The pulsing heart of Memphis's Irish community, it was a place where even the loneliest newcomer to the city, the Irish stranger in a strange land, would find a welcome.[19]

The Memphis chapter (or "circle") of the Fenian Brotherhood was both less inclusive and more assertively Irish than St. Peter's. Fenians (named for the Fianna Eirionn, mythical warriors of ancient Ireland) were Irish Americans dedicated to the violent overthrow of British rule in their native land. The brotherhood had been founded in New York in the late 1850s and quickly spread to cities across the country. Its members (men only, as the name implied) took a sacred vow of loyalty to the cause and learned its ways in solemn, secret rituals. Their public activity consisted mostly of raising funds to send to freedom fighters in Ireland. But they also formed themselves into militia companies, conducted drills, and declared their readiness to return to Ireland to fight the British. Some did, in fact, return individually. Fenians also threatened to attack British Canada. The brotherhood did not appeal to all, or even most, Irishmen in America. Some thought its militancy excessive or futile. The Catholic Church officially opposed it, and the U.S. government condemned those of its activities that violated American neutrality laws. But its blustery rhetoric and vigorous public presence could not be ignored.[20]

The brotherhood's Memphis circle was active at least as early as 1864, and among its members were many of the city's prominent Irishmen. Michael Magevney served for a time as its head officer, or "center." In 1866, John. J. Butler, the city wharfmaster, held the position. The circle officers under him included Memphis's fire chief, Edward O'Neill. The circle met every Thursday evening and also held a Monday-night military drill.[21]

The eternal fire of Irish nationalism flared up startlingly in Memphis and across the nation in March, when news arrived of a British crackdown on revolutionary activity in Ireland that involved the abrupt suspension of habeas corpus and the rounding up and jailing of patriots. The Fenian Brotherhood's leaders responded with a call to arms. Circles everywhere began mobilizing in earnest. In Memphis, the Irish flag that had decorated the Fenians' Saint Patrick's Day ball was hoisted over the circle's headquarters and volunteers began enlisting there in the expectation of imminent service. On Tuesday, April 17, the brotherhood posted flyers around the city summoning all "friends of Ireland" to a special meeting of the Fenians at city hall the next night: "The time has arrived for Irishmen to prove their fidelity to their native land. The freedom of Ireland can be achieved NOW OR NEVER. The destiny of our country is in our own hands. . . . Awake! Arise!!" The meeting room was packed on Wednesday evening, the mood feverish. Speaker after speaker stoked the passions of the crowd. One proclaimed that a forceful, united effort at this critical moment would "surely hurl the bloody and tyrannical hand of England from the soil so dear to the heart of every true Irishman." Volunteers stepped forward and donations poured in.[22]

The Fenians, and indeed all Irish Americans, saw no contradiction in identifying with the cause of Irish nationalism while embracing Americanism. On the contrary: in supporting Ireland's liberation, Irish Americans insisted that they were simply carrying the torch of American-style freedom and democracy to the rest of the world as good Americans should. They were both proudly Irish and proudly American. There were few Irish immigrants who did not claim American citizenship as soon as they were entitled to it; the Memphis chancery court rarely held a session without devoting part of its time to naturalizing some of the Irish. Fenians ceremonially displayed their flag not only on Saint Patrick's Day but also on Washington's Birthday.[23]

Irish immigrants were in fact among the most jingoistic of Americans, in part because so many native-born Americans had doubts about their fitness for American citizenship. The 1850s had seen a surge of anti-Irish sentiment, embodied in the Know-Nothing Party (formally the American Party), which arose after the demise of the Whig Party and wielded impressive political strength for several years. Appalled by the clannishness, Catholicism, and flagrant bumptiousness of the Irish, and especially by their lively participation in urban Democratic politics, the Know-Nothings demanded restrictions on

Irish enfranchisement and tried to discourage Irish immigration. (German Americans were likewise targets of their scorn.) The Know-Nothing Party faded away before the decade ended, but nativist prejudice in America remained strong. Some of the native-born even questioned whether the Irish deserved to be considered white, or at least in the same category of whiteness as themselves. This was in part why the racism of the Irish was so vehement. Asserting their superiority to blacks was a way of claiming an equal place in white America.[24]

Irish participation in antebellum Memphis politics was lively, and remained so after the war. The difference now was that the city's electorate had shrunk considerably. By state law, anyone who had aided the Southern rebellion could not vote in the municipal general election in June 1865. Most of the Irishmen (and most of the German men) residing in Memphis when the war began had declined to enlist in the army or in any other way serve the Rebel cause, and the early capture of the city by federal forces ensured that Confederate conscription was never carried out there. The twenty-five hundred voters in June 1865 were predominantly foreign-born; a majority were Irish. Their ballots put into office a good many Irishmen, who then appointed a good many more to municipal positions. The mayor was Irish, as were at least thirteen of the other twenty-eight city executive officers and nine of the sixteen aldermen.[25]

The Memphis government's legislative authority was vested in the city council—formally designated the Board of Mayor and Aldermen—which met in city hall on the first and third Tuesdays of the month. (The suburban neighborhoods were governed by the Shelby County court, which met monthly in the county seat some miles from Memphis, although most of the county officials had their offices in the city.) At the city council meetings, the aldermen (two representing each of the city's eight wards) and the mayor heard reports from the various executive officers—the comptroller, register, property tax collector, privilege tax collector, treasurer, attorney, health officer, street commissioner, wharfmaster, market masters, police chief, fire chief, and others—and approved necessary expenditures and ordinances.[26]

Council meetings were not always conducted decorously. A disgraceful incident at the April 17 meeting, reported in the next day's

Avalanche, was far from unusual. The council was considering a proposal to compensate several policemen who claimed to have been wrongfully deprived of some of their wages. Alderman John Toof of the Seventh Ward opposed it, citing it as an example of the "mal-appropriation" that he considered all too common in council proceedings. Alderman Martin Kelly of the same ward took exception to this, noting snidely that "Alderman Toof had not always been opposed to such appropriations, he had voted for other appropriations in large amounts but now finds it in his heart to become suddenly circumspect upon the claims of some poor policemen." This provoked Alderman E. V. Mahoney (First Ward) to jump to his feet and declare that "he did not believe that Alderman Kelly knew what he was talking about," to which Kelly replied that "he was sorry to say that Alderman Mahoney was a fool." After more bickering, the matter was referred to the finance committee.[27]

Mayor John Park was present at all council meetings. A native of County Tyrone, he was fifty-three years old in the spring of 1866. His memory of the land of his birth was no doubt dim, for his family had immigrated to America in 1820, when he was only seven or eight. After nine years in New York, the Parks moved to Kentucky. Once John was grown, he began a career in business that took him to Nashville, Mobile, New Orleans, and finally Memphis, where he settled for good in 1839. Twenty years later he married a much younger woman, a native Southerner named Caroline, probably a widow, who had three young children. By that time he was prospering—his real estate investments were particularly lucrative—and he was able to hire two live-in servants to help Caroline with her housekeeping.[28]

Park succeeded in business because he was smart, hardworking, and affable. His success won him respect in Memphis, not only among his fellow Irish but also among many of the native whites. When he ran for mayor in June 1861 against three other candidates he got not only the Irish vote but also that of many natives, and won a narrow majority. He proved to be a good mayor, at least in the opinion of many, and he ran again, and unopposed, in June 1862, by which time the city was under Union military occupation and the Rebel men had almost all left. A year later he won yet again, this time by a large majority over two opponents, and in June 1864 he won a fourth term.[29]

By then, however, the military authorities had begun to question his loyalty. He had never overtly aided the rebellion (besides simply carrying out his municipal duties as a mayor in the Confederate States of America for one year) and he had willingly remained in the city under Yankee occupation and had taken the required oath of allegiance to the United States. But his Unionism was of a very conservative sort. There were rumors that in his heart he sympathized with the Rebels. In any event, he was no friend of the Lincoln administration and he cooperated only reluctantly with the Union army. No sooner were the ballots counted in June 1864 than the post commandant, fed up with Park, suspended the city government and ousted him. But Park simply bided his time. When the war ended and military rule was lifted, he again rode the Irish vote into the mayor's office.[30]

But he had become a deeply troubled man, drinking heavily. No one knew what tormented him, but the fact of his drinking was no secret; he often showed up in public drunk. On one occasion, in August 1864, he was even jailed for verbally abusing several army officers while on a binge. Those who knew him well noticed that his sober, lucid moments were becoming rarer with every passing month. By the spring of 1866 he was probably drunk more often than not.[31]

Drunk or sober, Mayor Park wielded significant power. The municipal executive officers were under his direct command. He was an ex-officio member of all city council standing committees. He could veto council measures, and his veto could be overridden only by a two-thirds majority. His appointive power and influence were considerable, extending even to the rank and file of city employees. The police and fire departments in particular provided a rich source of mayoral patronage.[32]

The fire department, under Chief O'Neill (Irishman and Fenian), had forty-six employees, forty of them Irish. They were divided into five companies (steamer companies one through four and a hook-and-ladder company), each with its own station house in a separate part of the city. Each steamer company had one horse-drawn, steam-powered fire engine equipped with hoses and a loud steam whistle that gave fair warning of the engine's approach but unfortunately tended to spook citizens' horses. The chief also had under his command two unpaid volunteer units of firemen, each consisting of about forty men equipped with a hand-pump engine drawn by human power.[33]

The city council tried to keep the firefighters well equipped. The pride of the department was its newest steam pumper, a rotary-engine machine built by a New York manufacturer. Put into operation in mid-April, it weighed over three tons, pumped six hundred gallons of water a minute, propelled a one-and-a-half-inch-thick stream more than two hundred feet, and cost the city $7,000. What the department did not have and needed badly, according to a report delivered to the council in February by Alderman A. M. Hitzfeld after a study of other cities' fire departments, was an intra-urban telegraph system that would connect the mayor's office, the fire chief's office, and the firehouses and thus avoid the delays involved in the use of messengers.[34]

Hitzfeld's report also urged that the proposed municipal telegraph system include the police department. Unlike the firefighters, the police operated out of a single station house, located on Adams Street in the Third Ward, at the heart of downtown. The police chief was a native Southerner and longtime Memphian in his mid-forties named Benjamin G. Garrett. Under his command in the spring of 1866 were seven detectives, a captain and a lieutenant of the day police, a captain and a lieutenant of the night police, seventy-eight day policemen, eighty night policemen, a jail keeper with six underlings, and a clerk. Of these 177 men, 162 were Irish.[35]

The day and night policemen had no official uniforms, although some habitually wore dark-blue frock coats as a kind of uniform. On duty, policemen displayed a numbered, star-shaped badge on their chest and carried a billy club. All or nearly all were further armed with a revolver, usually carried concealed. For their labors they received one hundred dollars a month, docked proportionally for any day of work they missed. Although there were no formal, printed regulations governing the department, the city council's police committee had decreed that no one should be hired as a policeman who was not sober, well behaved, dutiful, literate, and a Memphis resident for at least the past year.[36]

David Roach, a member of the day squad, was in some ways a typical Memphis policeman. Thirty-three years old in 1866, Irish-born and poorly educated, he had lived in the city since before the war. He had been hired as a policeman in July 1865 and was no doubt very glad to get the job; he had previously earned his living as a common laborer. His Irish-born wife, Bridget, stayed home to care for their children, of whom there were at least three, none over nine years old. They lived in a rented place on Pontotoc Street, a stone's throw from the northern end of Fort Pickering, and they were very poor. Roach's work for the police department was apparently satisfactory to his superiors, and in the spring of 1866 he was dutifully walking his assigned beat in South Memphis.[37]

Though David Roach may have lived up to the police committee's announced standards, many of his fellow officers did not. In the police ranks were no small number of incompetents, drunkards, loafers, thugs, and crooks. Chief Garrett did his best to professionalize the force but was often frustrated by his superiors. The police committee, consisting of the mayor and five aldermen, had sole authority to nominate men for the force; the committee presented its nominations to the whole city council, which had the final say on hiring. Considerations other than the nominee's fitness for the job—in particular, the councilmen's desire to reward friends and strengthen their political base—often prevailed. Garrett had the authority to fire the unfit, but on more than one occasion the council rehired a man he had discharged. Sometimes the councilmen did not even bother to inform the chief when they hired or rehired a policeman.[38]

Indolence was rife on the force. Many policemen spent more on-duty hours in saloons than they did patrolling the streets. Moreover, many officers would have failed the literacy requirement had it actually been enforced—no fewer than eight could not even write their name—and many were habitually rude, swaggering, and overbearing when dealing with the public. These were just some of the minor failings. In one three-week period in late 1865, nine officers were charged with serious criminal offenses: four with abusing prisoners, two with unjustifiable homicide, one with stabbing a man in a quarrel, one with shooting and wounding a fellow policeman, and one with counterfeiting. The police committee was supposed to investigate such matters and see that the guilty were discharged from the force and prosecuted, but it was sometimes lax in that regard.[39]

The woefully unprofessional police force united nearly all Memphians in disgust. Newspapers Democratic and Republican editorialized about it, and citizens of every sort remonstrated. Chief Garrett himself lamented the deplorable character of so many of his men. The complaints even made it to Nashville; by the end of April the state legislature was close to passing a bill that would take control of the

Memphis police away from the city government and vest it in a board appointed by the governor.[40]

When the police arrested a white person for a petty crime, he or she was tried promptly in the city criminal court, generally known as the police or recorder's court. (Accused blacks went before the Freedmen's Bureau court; whites charged with major crimes went before the district criminal court.) The courtroom was in the police station house, as was the office of the city recorder, an elected official who served as the court's judge and jury. In the spring of 1866, the recorder was a thirty-two-year-old Irishman and longtime Memphis resident named John C. Creighton.[41]

Creighton lived in Pinch with his wife and children. He had no formal legal training—indeed, on the eve of the war he had been making his living as a labor foreman. But he had an imposing personality and was intelligent, literate, and politically shrewd. During the war he remained in the city, manifesting neither Union nor Rebel sympathy, and in June 1863 was elected recorder. Reelected a year later, he was among the city officials deposed under the post commandant's martial-law decree; but, like Mayor Park, he bided his time and was again elected in June 1865. Soon after that he hoisted partisan colors, becoming active among the city's Democrats, praising President Johnson's stand against the Republicans in Washington and accepting a position as vice president of the local Johnson Club, in which Mayor Park also served as a vice president.[42]

Another thing Creighton had in common with Park was a drinking problem. Although less frequently drunk than the mayor, he was meaner when under the influence and sometimes got into fights. In late 1865 he had, in fact, killed a man in a fight (the district criminal court judge ruled it justifiable homicide and let him off). Despite his reputation for drinking and brawling, or perhaps because of it, Creighton remained popular among his Irish constituents; but many others detested him. The U.S. marshal in Memphis thought him disgusting, wholly devoid of dignity, morality, and self-control. That official, a Republican who had tangled politically with Creighton, perhaps allowed politics to influence his opinion, but others without an obvious bias echoed the marshal's sentiments. The city register, for one, a native Southerner who had known Creighton since he was a boy, thought him utterly unfit for the recorder's office or, for that matter, any other one.[43]

Law enforcement in the Memphis suburbs was the responsibility of the Shelby County government. But here, too, Irish influence was strong, for voters living within the city limits cast ballots in county as well as city elections. Thirty-year-old Irishman Patrick Winters was the county sheriff. His office was downtown, his home in Pinch. Before the war he had worked in Memphis as a labor contractor but had made little money at it. The 1860 census taker recorded that he owned no real estate and only a couple of hundred dollars' worth of personal property. The office of sheriff, which entitled the holder not only to a decent salary but also to substantial commissions and fees for collecting taxes, serving writs, and so forth, was a plum sought by many. To an impoverished but bright and literate and ambitious young contractor it must have been very tempting. Winters ran successfully for the office in March 1864 and won a second two-year term in March 1866. But he did not regard the job as a sinecure; he took it seriously and earned praise for his work. "Pat has made a good sheriff," declared the editor of the *Avalanche* when Winters announced his candidacy for reelection, adding that he was a "noble-hearted and gentlemanly" fellow.[44]

He was handicapped, however, by a dearth of manpower. The population of the Memphis suburbs alone was big enough to keep the sheriff and his four deputies quite busy, but they were obliged to cover the extensive rural areas of the county as well, with the assistance of only a single constable in each of the county's seventeen districts. Moreover, although Winters was competent enough in dealing with the routine business of the sheriff's office, he had never been tested in a major emergency.[45]

The most critical law enforcement problem facing the suburbs and city alike in early 1866 was the hostility between the Irish and the freed people, which had a long history. In the antebellum years, Irish workers in the city—especially draymen, hack drivers, and day laborers— had had to compete for jobs with slaves whose masters hired them out for such work. The Irish made no secret of their resentment, which they directed more at the slaves than at their owners. The slaves repaid Irish anger and contempt in full. Rabid antiblack sentiment pervaded not only the ranks of Irish laborers but also the city police force;

but it was held in check by the power of the masters, who would not tolerate abuse of their slaves by anyone but themselves. With emancipation, that restraint on Irish racial belligerence evaporated. At the same time, the black population of the city multiplied. The presence of black troops added a particularly volatile fuel to the fire.[46]

The Irish felt aggrieved not only by the labor competition from the freed people but also by their demands for equality, justice, and respect. The reaction of grocer John Callahan to a petty dispute with a freedman named Adam Lock exemplified the racial mind-set of many of Memphis's Irish. At some point before the war ended Callahan had employed Lock to haul sixteen cords of firewood. On taking delivery, Callahan declared that some of the wood was missing, accused Lock of stealing it, and refused to pay him. Lock protested his innocence and reported the matter to the army provost marshal, who ordered Callahan to pay up. Callahan did so, but later vented his rage by viciously assaulting Lock (who was in his sixties), hitting him in the back of the head and knocking him down.[47]

Irish victimized by black criminals often became venomous enemies of the freed people. Late one night in February 1866, John Pendergrast caught a gang of uniformed black men breaking into his grocery and managed to drive them off with pistol fire before they stole anything. Thereafter he remained deeply suspicious of black men in groups and stayed well armed in case of further trouble. The apparently unprovoked murder of policeman William Mower, gunned down in the street later that month by a black man in uniform, enraged the entire Irish community, particularly Mower's fellow officers, who turned out en masse for his funeral.[48]

A few of the Irish, such as dance-hall owner Mary Grady, seem to have been genuinely free of racial prejudice. Sheriff Winters may have been among them, too, for some of his official actions suggested that he thought the freedmen deserved justice. A number of other Irish thought it wise to hide their hostility and make an effort to get along with Memphis's blacks. Callahan, whose business was dependent in great part on black customers, was generally pleasant toward them; he even patched things up with Lock, whose services he relied on, and never again exchanged a cross word with him. And, too, there were some Irish, John Pendergrast among them, who exempted certain "good" blacks they knew personally from their general condemnation of the race. Pendergrast evinced a measure of paternalistic goodwill toward a few individual freed people even as he burned with rage at Memphis's black population as a whole.[49]

Most of the Irish, however, made no secret of their loathing of blacks—particularly those in uniform—and exempted none from it. Some Memphians who were familiar with Irish Negrophobia in other cities thought it more virulent in Memphis than in any other place they had seen. The intense antipathy of the Irish extended to Northern immigrants, especially missionary teachers and preachers, deemed too friendly to the freed people—"damned Yankee niggers," the Irish called them.[50]

By April 1866 many Memphians had concluded that a racial detonation was very nearly inevitable. On the streets and in the saloons of Memphis, Irishmen often made remarks that led others to believe they would welcome an excuse to unleash their full fury on the black population, and were perhaps even planning to provoke a riot. P. D. Beecher, a Northern-born physician working for the Freedmen's Bureau, heard policemen on several occasions saying "they wished every 'damn nigger' was killed, and soldiers particularly." William C. Hubbard, a Yankee minister, heard hack drivers and firemen vowing that "the damned niggers [in uniform] would be cleaned out as soon as they were mustered out of service." On Sunday, April 29, on Madison Street, Southern Unionist and Radical newspaper editor B.F.C. Brooks ran into an Irishman he knew vaguely. After an exchange of polite greetings, the Irishman abruptly announced, "I am ready for action. . . . I have got a regiment and, by God, I am going to kill these damned niggers."[51]

Brooks walked away from the encounter convinced that the man's outburst was nothing more than Irish blarney and bluster. But others who heard Irish threats took them seriously. As April gave way to May, public peace and order in Memphis seemed, to many, fragile and insecure, liable at any moment to be obliterated in an explosion of racial hatred.[52]

4

Black Memphis

Some of those [blacks] who complain [of being cheated of wages by white employers] are industrious and prudent, and some are of the other sort, but a colored man has to be humble to get along.
　　　　　　　—Testimony of James E. Donahue, a freedman

I have [observed the behavior of the city's blacks for the past few months]; it has been peaceable unless they have had too much whiskey aboard.
　　　　　　　—Testimony of John Oldridge, an English-born white

The negroes have always thought themselves better than the Irish. . . . I have seen a storm brewing between the negroes and Irish for a long time.
　　　　　　　—Testimony of H. G. Dent, white, a Memphis resident
　　　　　　　　　　　　　　　　　　since the early 1840s[1]

At daybreak, every morning save Sundays, the streets of Memphis came alive with black people going to work. Many of the men carried lunch pails; some carried also the tools of their trade. Few of the women carried anything; most were employed as maids, laundresses, or cooks in the home of a white family and could count on getting a noon meal there and using the family's broom and mop, washtub and iron, pots and pans. A little later in the morning, the cooks emerged from their kitchens, each carrying a large basket and a little money. They trudged to market and back, fetching a day's supply of fresh meat and eggs and vegetables for the white family.[2]

Black Memphians wrung their daily bread from the sweat of their brow. Many men earned their livelihood on the riverfront. The city stood atop a steep bluff, thirty feet above the river, and at the base of the bluff was a shelf of land known as the levee. Sometimes wide, sometimes narrow, depending on the river level, it sloped gradually down to the water. There was no embankment; only the city's elevation prevented flooding when the Mississippi rose dangerously high. Nor were there any wharves, for the river level fluctuated too much to allow their construction. Steamboats simply got as close to the levee as possible and then waited while a long gangplank was set in place, one end on the ground and the other on the boat's deck. Black stevedores lolled around the levee, springing into action six or eight or ten times a day when a steamboat appeared, chugging down from Cincinnati, Louisville, or Saint Louis or up from New Orleans, Natchez, or Vicksburg. Other black men drove many of the drays and wagons that hauled freight between the levee and the city, trundling up and down the steep paths cut into the bluff. The most important freight going down the bluff was cotton, in big four- or five-hundred-pound bales that the draymen and wagoners dumped onto the levee and that the stevedores then hauled up the gangplanks. This cotton, the product of the fertile plantations of west Tennessee and north Mississippi, was destined for the textile mills of the Northern states and England. Other black men climbed aboard the steamers not to load or unload freight but as deckhands or engine tenders.[3]

Above the levee, throughout the city and its suburbs, most black people were unskilled or semiskilled laborers whose hard day's work yielded a meager return. These were men such as Primus Lane, a brewery hand; women such as Hannah Colman, who prepared and peddled food at an "eating stall" in one of the markets; and children such as sixteen-year-old Taylor Hunt, a coachman for a wealthy white man. A minority were lucky enough to have a marketable skill. Among them was John Brown, a barber at the Gayoso House. A very few black Memphians, such as Mat Wardlaw, who owned a small fleet of drays and hired other black men as drivers, earned a living outside the ranks of manual laborers.[4]

These individuals were among the twenty thousand or so blacks (counting the U.S. Army garrison troops) who by April 1866 lived in Memphis and its suburbs. Blacks made up no less than half the total population, and very likely more. Only six years earlier, before war transformed the city, there had been fewer than four thousand black inhabitants, comprising less than one-fifth of the population.[5]

A variety of paths had led Memphis's black people to the city. Almost all had been slaves. Many, probably most of those in their thirties or older, had been part of the vast forced migration of the antebellum decades that brought enslaved people westward from the older states of the South to work the plantations of the expanding cotton frontier. Brown, the Gayoso House barber, was one. Around 1845, at the age of six, he had been taken from his home plantation near Richmond, Virginia, to another in Yalobusha County, Mississippi; he made his way to Memphis during the war, in 1864. Some, on the other hand, were already living in the city when the war began. Thirty-nine-year-old Julia Henderson had been brought there in 1851, culminating a decades-long journey that had taken her from one master to another in South Carolina, Alabama, and Fayette County, Tennessee, east of Memphis.[6]

Freedom had come to black Memphians in different ways and at different times. A very small number had been born free or emancipated before the war. Colman, eating-stall keeper and longtime resident, had gained her liberty around 1847, having been permitted by her unusually generous master to earn money on her own and eventually to buy herself from him. For the vast majority, however, freedom had come with the Civil War. Those fortunate enough to be living in Memphis when Union forces captured it in June 1862 benefited from the rapid disintegration of slavery that occurred in every federally occupied Southern town during the war. The servitude of Mary Allen, a Memphian since 1857, lasted only seven months after the Yankee army arrived; by January 1863 she had deserted her owner and was living as a free woman. Slaves in the countryside (who comprised the great majority of slaves in the South) had a harder time gaining freedom, but some took advantage of the fortuitous appearance of Union troops. Milton Jones was laboring on a plantation seven or eight miles from Memphis when, in late 1862, the 54th Ohio Infantry marched by. Seizing the moment, Jones followed the regiment into the city and proceeded to make a new life for himself there. Where no Yankee invaders appeared, some slaves took the risk of running off to an often distant federal post, dodging county patrols and Rebel army scouts along the way. On a Sunday in July 1862, Humphrey Morris, born and raised in Tipton County, Tennessee, north of Memphis, slipped away from his master, hopped into a dugout canoe, and headed downstream to the Mississippi River. Paddling desperately through the night, he arrived safely in Memphis an hour before dawn. Most slaves, however, found no opportunity to escape bondage until the war ended. Twenty-seven-year-old Richard Cuthbert, a South Carolina native, spent the war years accompanying his master, a Confederate officer, as a cook. Cuthbert came to Memphis only after the surrender of the Rebel army he had been forced to march with.[7]

Many of the slaves who attached themselves or fled to the Union army stayed with it in some capacity, working for wages as cooks, laundresses, or officers' servants or—once the U.S. government began recruiting black troops in 1863—enlisting. John Jones, a native of Madison County in west Tennessee and living there when the Yankees invaded, initially became a servant in the 119th Illinois Infantry. Later he enlisted in the 8th U.S. Colored Heavy Artillery, which was organized in April 1864 and mustered out in Kentucky in February 1866. His service at an end, young Jones (he was only seventeen or eighteen) went to Memphis to seek his fortune.[8]

Like other Southern towns garrisoned by the Union army during the war, Memphis was a magnet for runaway slaves. Until the Confederate government collapsed and its armies gave up the struggle, most of the Southern countryside remained a stronghold of slavery; only in the Yankee-held towns was freedom secure. U.S. Army authorities set up "contraband camps" in the towns to feed and shelter black fugitives unable to support themselves. There were several such camps in and around Memphis; the main one, located on a river island just below the city, housed as many as three thousand people. But even after the war's end and the closing of the contraband camps, Memphis and other towns continued to draw blacks from the hinterlands in great numbers, for although slavery had been abolished the rural South remained inhospitable to black freedom.[9]

For rural blacks, freedom meant a farm of their own. Their dream of yeoman independence was encouraged by a persistent rumor in the postwar months that the federal government intended to confiscate plantations and reward each formerly enslaved family with "forty acres and a mule." But the rumor proved false. Southern soil remained in white hands, and the penniless freedmen lacked the means to buy or rent any even if whites had been willing to let them. The planters, while grudgingly resigned to emancipation and the necessity of now compensating their black laborers, expected them to work the corn and cotton fields as they always had: men, women, and children alike toiling six days a week from dawn to dusk in gangs under the eye of a white overseer, retiring each night to the cluster of cabins formerly known as the slave quarters, behind the Big House. Moreover, facing a shortage of cash and credit in the struggling postwar Southern economy, and convinced besides that if freed people were paid regular wages they would simply disappear after payday and reappear for work only after they had spent their money, planters insisted on binding their workers with annual contracts and compensating them with a share of the crop—payable, of course, only after the harvest. In some areas planters banded together to deny blacks the benefits of the free-labor system by setting a cap on workers' compensation and agreeing not to entice workers away from other planters. Some planters assumed the right to discipline their workers with the whip or cane just as they had in the days of slavery.[10]

The freed people fought these developments at every turn. If they still had to work for a white man, they reasoned, they should at least enjoy the privileges that white laborers had always enjoyed. They made demands of their own: weekly or monthly cash wages, more time off, the right to bargain with employers, and no gang labor, slave quarters, physical abuse, or women and children in the fields. And they wanted schools set up on the plantations, so that their children might be educated. Angry disputes between planters and freed people became commonplace. Though arbitrated in some cases by the Freedmen's Bureau, these disputes rarely ended with what blacks regarded as a satisfactory deal.[11]

The turmoil in the countryside led many freed people to see Memphis as a beacon and a haven. While life there was hardly idyllic, the presence of the army garrison and the Freedmen's Bureau subdistrict headquarters seemed to offer more security against despotic white power than blacks enjoyed in the hinterlands. And, too, the schools run by Yankee missionaries in Memphis offered the educational opportunities the freedmen longed for. As planters bewailed the agricultural labor shortage and demanded that the Bureau do something about it, blacks continued to abandon the countryside for the city. Those already there dug in their heels against all attempts to return them to the plantations.[12]

Thus did Memphis lure and hold freed people by the thousands. But it was no easy place for them to get along. Unskilled laborers could earn two or three dollars a day—a good wage by prewar standards, but much devalued by the inflation resulting from (among other things) the city's population growth since 1861 and the soaring consumer demand that came with it. Rent was exorbitant in crowded postwar Memphis; a decent apartment cost twenty-five dollars a month, a cottage more than sixty. Food, clothing, and heating coal were dear, too. A few freedmen, mostly in the suburbs, were able to produce some of their own provisions. Brewery hand Primus Lane, for example, had enough of a homestead to raise a couple of hogs, some chickens, and a vegetable garden. But the self-sufficiency that rural folk could enjoy was generally impossible in the city. Most Memphis freedmen saw their earnings wholly and quickly consumed by the barest necessities.[13]

A few did better, making enough to live comfortably and even put away some savings. Andrew and Maggie Minter lived on the southern edge of the city in a two-room frame house. Andrew had paid cash for it in 1865, using the $500 he saved during his wartime service with the U.S. Navy. His job as a boiler stoker on the steamer *R. M. Bishop* took him away from home for days at a time and provided only a modest wage ($45 a month and board); but Maggie worked, too, as a seamstress, and they were apparently careful with their money. They furnished their home with a stove and a carpet and a good deal of furniture, they had several hundred dollars' worth of clothes, and among Maggie's treasured possessions were two diamond rings.[14]

Some who managed to save money deposited it with the Freedman's Savings and Trust Company—better known as the Freedman's Bank—a private, U.S. government-chartered institution founded to serve the former slaves (a branch was established in Memphis in December 1865). But most, distrustful of banks, carried their savings around or hid them. Some of these nest eggs were substantial. Shoemaker Albert Harris, for example, kept $350 locked in a trunk at home.[15]

At the other end of the spectrum were the black Memphians who lived in utter indigence. These were the aged, the blind, the crippled, the orphaned, and the desperately sick with no kinfolk or friends to care for them. Their numbers were not large. The Freedmen's Bureau and the missionaries assisted during April 1866 fewer than two hundred—only a hundred or so on average on any given day. Of those, fifty were children in the Colored Orphan Asylum.[16]

Between the helpless few and the comfortable few were the great mass of black Memphians, scratching out a living and getting along the best they could. Many lived in their employer's home, especially unmarried domestic workers. But most, like most of the Irish, crowded into tenements or shanties. The tenements, owned by white landlords, were cheaply constructed and poorly lit, ventilated, and heated buildings divided into small single-room apartments. A typical one, as described by a U.S. Army officer investigating the living conditions of black soldiers' families in the city, was a two-story building, eighteen by thirty-five feet, divided into four or five claustrophobic apartments in which seven families crammed themselves. In some cases a half-dozen or more such structures were shoehorned into a single city lot, for there was little or no municipal regulation of construction in the interest of public health or fire safety. Conditions were generally no better in the shanties, which sprouted like mushrooms wherever a vacant lot offered a little space. Some of these were built by the lot owner and rented out or sold, but most were built by the freed people who inhabited them, some of them squatters who paid no rent. They were generally one-room plank structures, windowless and leaky, providing little more than sleeping quarters. Most shanty and tenement dwellers lacked the wherewithal to cook their own meals, subsisting instead on prepared food purchased at the eating stalls and groceries scattered around the city.[17]

Many shanties were clustered into informal neighborhoods recognized among Memphians by nicknames. There was Happy Valley, for example, in the area of Poplar Street near one of the bayous (the term local folk applied to the two sluggish streams that wound through the city), and Lickskittle, in the southern suburbs. Densely populated, poorly drained, and often reeking with refuse, these shanty warrens were fertile breeding grounds for disease, as were the tenements. Smallpox and measles were ever-present threats. Warm weather brought cholera, malaria, and yellow fever.[18]

Wretched as they were, the shanties and tenements of black Memphis nevertheless nurtured a rich family and community life. While many black men and women in the city were partnerless—widowed or never wed—the majority were married and lived with or very near their spouse. Their marriages mostly dated back to the days of slavery—informally avowed and legally unrecognized unions then, but since the war recognized by federal authorities and in some cases confirmed in formal ceremonies. Most of the younger couples had children living with them. The city in fact teemed with black children; those twelve and younger alone accounted for roughly a quarter of the black population.[19]

Until emancipation, black families in the South had faced long odds, for they could be abruptly dissolved at the whim of a master. Such heartbreaking separations were common. A sizeable portion of the freed people living in Memphis in early 1866 had endured the forced severance of family ties. Martha Canand was one. Born in Missouri about 1849, she had no memory of her father, who was sold away when she was a baby. At age eight, she herself was sold, to a master who brought her to Memphis. Her brother and sister were sold at the same time to different masters and taken away to parts unknown, leaving her mother alone in Missouri.[20]

Some freed people were involved in intimate relationships less formal than marriage. Elvira Walker, a twenty-six-year-old laundress, lived with a man who was not her husband. A few defied custom and law by cohabiting openly with a white person. Charles Harris and another man lived with two white women in a shanty in South Memphis—until April 17, when a policeman, tipped by an informant, raided the shanty and hauled Harris and the women off to jail (the other man escaped). While such blatant cohabitation was rare, nobody in the city could have been shocked by this evidence that blacks and whites were having sex with one another. Miscegenation in the South was as old as Dixie itself and as common in Memphis as anywhere else, although usually confined to society's shadows and discussed only in muted tones. The unmarried freedwoman Mollie Davis, for example, had a white lover whom she saw regularly but discreetly; she spoke of him demurely as her "friend." Many Memphians were themselves the product of an interracial relationship, among them laborer Patrick Ford, born of an enslaved mother and a white father.[21]

To an extent unusual for a military unit in the occupied South, the regiment of U.S. troops that garrisoned Memphis in the early months of 1866 was embedded in the city's family and community life. The 3rd U.S. Colored Heavy Artillery had been formed in Memphis in June 1863, had recruited most of its enlisted men from among the city's black populace, and had never served anywhere else. Many of its soldiers had wives, children, or other kinfolk who lived in the city, mainly in the neighborhoods near Fort Pickering. These families were financially dependent on the soldiers' pay and emotionally dependent on the visits they made whenever they could get away from camp.[22]

Henry Hunt of Company D was a typical soldier of the 3rd. Born in 1843 in Crawford County, Missouri, he had been separated at age eleven from his parents and siblings, transported to a Memphis slave market, and put on the auction block. His new master took him to Panola County in north Mississippi. During the war he escaped and made his way to Memphis. On July 3, 1863, he enlisted at Fort Pickering. His company's descriptive book recorded that the newly enrolled Private Hunt was five and a half feet tall and very dark-skinned. Although illiterate like nearly all his fellow enlisted men, he struck his superiors as an able and responsible soldier and in 1865 was promoted to corporal. By the spring of 1866 he had married. His wife, Lucy, maintained a home in the southern suburbs.[23]

The 3rd was one of several Union regiments, black and white, that garrisoned Memphis during and right after the war, but by early 1866 all the others had been transferred away or mustered out. It numbered nearly sixteen hundred men, divided into twelve companies. Despite its official designation, it never did duty as artillery; from first to last, it was armed and equipped as infantry and served as such. Like all black units it was officered by whites. And like most black units it had never seen combat, for during the war the U.S. Army authorities preferred to relegate black troops to garrison, guard, or fatigue duty and leave the fighting to whites.[24]

That was not the only sort of discrimination faced within their own army by the men of the 3rd and other black soldiers. The rations, equipment, and medical care provided to the U.S. Colored Troops were generally inferior, and pay was often slow in coming. In December 1865 the 3rd's commander, Colonel Ignatz G. Kappner, had complained angrily about the rations his men were receiving from the commissary department: half the bread allotted was hardtack instead of fresh loaves; the amount of rice issued was only half what it was supposed to be; the beef was "inferior in quality, badly butchered and the necks and shanks not excluded, and in some instances almost unfit to eat"; and rather than coffee the troops got mostly tea, which they were unused to and could not stomach. That same month Kappner's immediate superior, also headquartered in Memphis, reported that the black troops there "have not been paid during the last six months, and cannot provide for their families, who [are] destitute."[25]

In the spring of 1866 the army ordered the 3rd to muster out. On April 17, Colonel Kappner issued a formal farewell to his men, which was read to them that day at their last dress parade. "The chances of war have not brought us into actual conflict with the enemy," he proclaimed somewhat wistfully, "and we have had no opportunity to show our determination to uphold the flag or die; but we have done our duty." Paperwork and other formalities dragged out the regiment's existence for a while thereafter, but in the last days of the month the men turned in their muskets and equipment and finally, on April 30, were officially mustered out of the United States service. Most remained in uniform, however, because they had no other clothes. Moreover, because no paymaster had yet arrived to settle accounts, nearly all the men stayed around awaiting the back pay due them. Those like Henry Hunt who had a family in the city joined their loved ones at home; the rest remained in the barracks at Fort Pickering.[26]

No less vital than family and work to most black Memphians was the church. Whether a native of the city or a rustic newcomer, the typical freed woman or man had been spiritually raised in the arms of evangelical Protestantism and devoutly affirmed its creeds of sin, rebirth, and salvation. As slaves, black people had generally attended their masters' church (although in Memphis and other cities there were a few autonomous black congregations). But with emancipation blacks across the South began withdrawing from white-controlled churches and founding their own, staking out full independence in one of the few spheres where whites wielded no coercive power.[27]

Postwar Memphis pulsed fervently with the activities of black brothers and sisters in Christ. Two of the city's black churches predated emancipation, boasted substantial physical facilities, and thrived now in the vibrant environment of freedom. The Baptist church on the corner of Main and Overton, in the First Ward, was a two-story brick building with seventy-five pews and two heating stoves. Collins Chapel, affiliated with the Methodist Episcopal Church, South, was on Washington Street near the city's eastern edge. A brick-and-wood structure thirty feet tall, it boasted carpeting, two stoves, and pews seating eight hundred.[28]

Other black churches in the city were the fruit of freedom, new communities of faith with only the crudest of facilities and as plain and unassuming as the untutored preachers who led them. Fifty-one-year-old Africa Bailey, a Baptist, former slave on a Mississippi plantation, and Union army veteran, had begun gathering a flock and preaching in the city soon after the end of the war. He delivered the Good News each Sunday in a sawdust-floored brush arbor not far from Fort Pickering. Another Baptist man of God, sixty-four-year-old Morris Henderson, had lived in the city since 1849. His owner had used him as a carriage driver, but Henderson had served the Lord, too, informally spreading the gospel among his fellow bondsmen. In 1864, now freed by the Yankees and the grace of God, he gathered a real congregation and was formally ordained. Although he could not read and could write only his name, he proved a formidable and visionary leader. Energetic fund-raising, especially by the congregation's women, who organized a sewing society and held a series of fairs and other events, enabled Henderson's church to make a down payment in 1865 on a vacant lot on Beale Street, in the southern part of town. There the minister oversaw construction of a crude plank shelter where he preached to hundreds every Sunday. His goal was to pay off the mortgage on the lot as quickly as possible and then begin work on a real church building. Henderson's ministry reached beyond his congregation to embrace the whole black community of Memphis. He was much involved, for example, with the Colored Orphan Asylum, providing helpful information about the children, rounding up volunteers to aid the institution, and preaching there whenever called on.[29]

Sunday services at the black churches were joyful gatherings, marked by spirited singing and hand-clapping, rhythmic swaying of bodies, and impassioned preaching that spoke to the heart. Not so the services conducted for the freedmen by the Northern missionary ministers, who frowned on exuberant worship and generally delivered from the pulpit either solemn disquisitions on scripture or patronizing homilies. The missionaries tried hard to draw freed people on Sundays, but their churches were rarely crowded. Even Ewing Tade's Lincoln Chapel, consecrated with great fanfare on January 1, 1866, struggled to attract a congregation, though its Sunday school, which offered Bible readings, picture books, and other things the city's illiterate and impoverished black-church folk could not, did better. So many parents sent their children to the Lincoln Chapel Sunday school that the missionaries had to hold two classes, one before and one after the sparsely attended church service. Among the various activities, the students especially enjoyed the singing. Passersby would often pause by the chapel door to listen to "Far Out Upon the Prairie" and "Rock of Ages" sung by sweet young voices. The freed people's distaste for the sermonizing of Northern ministers extended in some cases even to the handful of black ones. The Reverend T. N. Stewart, for one, came down from Columbus, Ohio, in 1865 with a decent education and great hopes, only to find that black Memphis preferred its own rough-hewn evangelists.[30]

Lincoln Chapel's school was one of a number of missionary schools in Memphis; by the spring of 1866 there were twelve in the city, staffed by twenty-two teachers. More were needed. The schools offered the only formal education a black Memphian could get, and about twelve hundred students were enrolled. Still, this was a minority of the black school-age population. Poverty meant, for many Memphis children, either that they had to work to help support their families or that their parents could not pay the dollar-a-month tuition that was generally (and regretfully) charged to keep the schools solvent. The missionaries did accept as many nonpaying students as they could—indeed, about half the students fell into this category—but there was a limit to the number who could be accommodated, given the shortage of teachers.[31]

Among the twenty-two teachers were two black men and one woman, all educated at Oberlin College in Ohio. One was a forty-one-year-old widower named Horatio Nelson Rankin. He had come to Memphis from Ohio by steamboat in the fall of 1863, leaving his two young children behind in the care of his sister. Supported by the Western Freedmen's Aid Commission, he first conducted a school at Fort Pickering for the men of the 3rd. By 1865 he had turned his attention to the freed children, teaching in a well-furnished schoolhouse owned by Collins Chapel, the black Methodist church, of which he had become a trustee. Unlike the Northern preachers, Rankin was embraced by Memphis's black community. Indeed, he quickly became one of its own, and emerged as a spokesman.[32]

The girls and boys who attended Rankin's school or one of the others were taught reading, writing, and arithmetic, along with some history and geography, according to the precepts of Yankee pedagogy. Teachers emphasized memorization and recitation, enlivening the classes with the singing of patriotic songs and some physical recreation. The children were avid learners and many made excellent progress. One who showed particular promise was a fourteen-year-old girl in Rankin's school named Rachel Hatcher. Enslaved as a child in west Tennessee and north Mississippi, she had come to Memphis in 1862 or 1863. She lived a half-mile from Fort Pickering with her mother and her stepfather, a disabled veteran of the 61st Colored Infantry. Distinguished by her superior intelligence and dedication to her studies, she was rewarded by being allowed on occasion to oversee the other students' recitations in Mr. Rankin's stead. She seemed destined for a career as a teacher.[33]

The missionary schools welcomed adult students, but only a handful enrolled. Few black men or women in Memphis enjoyed the luxury of free time to pursue education. The vast majority would be illiterate for life. They could not read or write a word, their arithmetic was limited to simple addition and subtraction, and most could not tell time. Many had only a rough idea of how old they were. Literacy was rare even among those regarded as leaders of the black community. Rankin could read and write, of course, but few of the black preachers could. Nor could many of the barbers, a group that enjoyed considerable prestige in black Memphis (John Brown could not so much as write his name). Most of the black business owners were likewise unlettered, including the prominent saloon keeper Robert Church. So were most members—including the officers—of the Memphis chapter of the Sons of Ham, an exclusive black men's benevolent association active in the city since 1859. The few literate black leaders were for the most part men who had been free before the war.[34]

Literate or not, the leaders of the black community held the church offices; oversaw the charitable work and public functions such as parades that were sponsored by the Sons of Ham, the black Masonic lodge, and other associations; and served as the ears and the voice of black Memphis when the missionaries or Freedmen's Bureau agents wanted black cooperation on some matter. But they were in no true sense an elite. Not only were they generally as uneducated and un-polished as other black Memphians, but they were also predominantly men of very modest means, most of them in fact quite poor.[35]

This is not to say, however, that black Memphis was a monolith, an undifferentiated mass. In fact, a significant divide ran through it (be-sides that of gender, which separated black Memphians no less pro-foundly than it did the rest of humanity). This was not a social divide between elites and the rest but a cultural divide between the "respect-able" majority and a minority that defied the canons of respectability.[36]

Some of the defiant ones were outright predators, disdaining hon-est labor and instead living on what they could steal. Among them were thieves who crept out of the city to the surrounding farms, re-turning with hogs and cattle that they sold to butchers and with horses and mules that they sold to livestock traders. There were others who preyed on the city folk, white and black alike, and some of these indi-viduals were not just larcenous but vicious. A young black man named Needham Collins was one of their victims. Around nine o'clock on the night of April 14 he went to a grocery to buy candles. Three black men loitering around the store watched him make his purchase and then followed him as he headed home. At the corner of Beale and Orleans one of them pulled a pistol and fired a bullet into Collins's back. As he lay helpless, the three went through his pockets, relieved him of the candles and the little cash he had—twenty-five cents—and then dis-appeared into the night. Collins died two days later.[37]

There were other black Memphians who lived outside the bound-aries of law and respectability and yet could not fairly be branded as predators because they provided goods and services much in demand. These included prostitutes, of whom there were many. They plied their trade openly at night on the sidewalks and around the clock in brothels. Periodically the city police would declare war on prostitution, black and white, round up some of the women, and turn the black ones over to the Freedmen's Bureau court; those convicted would pay the modest fine or serve a short term in the city workhouse and then return to business. Likewise the blacks who operated gambling houses or sold liquor to soldiers in violation of military decree: the occasional crackdowns on these entrepreneurs by the police, the army, and the Freedmen's Bureau interrupted business only temporarily.[38]

The great majority of those deemed unrespectable in black Memphis were guilty of nothing more serious than rowdiness. The liquor-soaked patrons of the grogshops, gambling joints, and dance halls that catered to blacks offended the sensibilities of those living within earshot with their unrestrained merriment, frequent profanity, and occasional fights. The most notorious of these establishments was Irishwoman Mary Grady's groggery–cum–dance hall in South Memphis. Hardly a day went by that the police did not arrest a few of the patrons of these places. Found guilty in the Bureau court of drunkenness or disorderly conduct, they paid their fine or served their term and then returned to their customary haunts. A good many of these black rowdies carried concealed knives or pistols, and their fights occasionally drew blood. But the pistols were brandished more often in merriment than in mayhem. Mary Grady's customers, in particular, routinely fired pistols into the air for fun.[39]

The 3rd Colored Heavy Artillery, distilled as it was from the black community of Memphis, had its share of rowdies and criminals. There were probably no more proportionately than in the civilian black male population of the city, but their uniforms made their misconduct more conspicuous. Moreover, discipline in the regiment was lax—a fact frequently bemoaned by Memphians and admitted even by the army authorities.[40]

Some of the soldiers' misbehavior was confined to Fort Pickering. There was a good deal of fighting and petty theft in the barracks. (Even Henry Hunt, a model soldier for thirty-two months following his enlistment, eventually got into trouble. Charged in March 1866 with fighting, he was convicted by a regimental court-martial, stripped of his corporal's rank, and sentenced to thirty days in prison. He was released just two weeks before the regiment mustered out.) But soldiers also got unruly outside the fort—where they could often be found, having either obtained a pass or sneaked out past the guards at night. Military orders notwithstanding, the men could readily get liquor. Some patronized places such as Grady's and joined in the carousing. Others bought their whiskey by the canteenful and hung out in groups on street corners and in shanty neighborhoods, growing more and more boisterous and profane as the canteens were emptied. And, too, although the men were forbidden to carry their muskets or bayonets when off duty, and forbidden to possess any other weapons, some acquired pistols surreptitiously and took them along whenever they left the fort for a night on the town.[41]

More serious than these transgressions were the stealing and fencing of army supplies, the burglary of houses, and the robbery of shopkeepers perpetrated by soldiers. In some cases these were the work not of hardened predators but of desperate family men whose wives and children were suffering because the army was so far behind in paying them. Moreover, many of the crimes blamed on soldiers were actually committed by black civilians wearing articles of army clothing. Nevertheless, there was a measure of substance to the complaints frequently heard in the city about the troops of the 3rd.[42]

Almost all these complaints came, not surprisingly, from the white population, as did the unceasing chorus of grumbling about the city's freed people as a whole. While the Yankee portion of the populace generally welcomed black freedom and endorsed—up to a point—black equality, other white Memphians did not. They not only condemned the idea of black equality but to the extent of their power prohibited its realization.

The freed people of the city were very much second-class citizens. Indeed, until the federal Civil Rights Act was passed in early April 1866, they (along with every other black person in America) were not citizens at all. Although Tennessee—alone among the former Confederate states—was controlled politically by Southern Unionists rather than former Rebels, the state government did nothing to secure the equality of blacks in the immediate postwar period except to ensure that they were not reenslaved. Tennessee blacks could not vote, hold political office, or serve on a jury; they could not even testify in a Tennessee court.[43]

Social inequality compounded legal inequality. When freed people boarded a train in Memphis, they took their seats in a car designated for blacks. When they traveled by steamboat, they fended for themselves on the open deck while white passengers relaxed in their cabins and ate in the dining room. When the circus came to Memphis, blacks sat under the big top in a separate section of the stands. Black visitors seeking lodging did not go to the Gayoso or any other white-owned place but to the Talley House on Beale Street, the only hotel that accepted black guests. When Memphis freedmen died, they were buried in a segregated cemetery on the corner of Jackson and Lauderdale in the southern suburbs, the only place in town where their remains were welcome.[44]

Racial segregation was of course not absolute. Far from it: black and white Memphians rubbed shoulders every day. Most blacks worked for white employers, and many resided with them. Of those who lived on their own, almost all were in racially mixed neighborhoods. While the freed population was concentrated in South Memphis, that section was also home to many whites; and thousands of blacks lived in other parts of the city, where whites predominated.[45]

The relationship between blacks and the Southern-born whites whom they lived and labored alongside in postwar Memphis was complex, for the freed people's feelings about them were deeply ambivalent. There was, on the one hand, the righteous wrath of the oppressed. Most blacks had bitter, indelible memories of slavery and of the Rebels' fierce defense of their slaveholding republic. And now, even after their defeat on the battlefield, the Rebels continued to insist on their right to rule over the black race.

One wartime event in particular was etched in the consciousness of black Memphians, especially the soldiers. On April 12, 1864, a Confederate force commanded by General Nathan Bedford Forrest had surrounded, attacked, and overrun a Union bastion named Fort Pillow, on the river just thirty miles north of Memphis. It was garrisoned by a mixed force of black and white units. Many of the black soldiers were murdered after they surrendered. "Remember Fort Pillow" became a rallying cry for the U.S. Colored Troops throughout the South. The men of the 3rd were especially touched by the massacre, for in the late winter and spring of 1866 a number of them were sent to Fort Pillow with picks and shovels to reinter the bodies of those who had died there, which had been hastily buried where they fell. This task was a solemn reminder of the sacrifices black Southerners had made in the war for their emancipation, and of the ferocity of the Rebels in their struggle to deny blacks freedom. Another reminder was a badly scarred black man who walked the streets of Memphis in the spring of

1866. His name was Arthur Edmonds, and he had been one of the Fort Pillow garrison on that fateful day two years earlier. His survival was something of a miracle, for Rebel bullets had pierced his wrist, his shoulder, and his head.[46]

Black anger toward Southern whites was tempered, however, as it had been during the days of slavery, by instances of white kindness. The sentiments of two freedwomen with whom an English visitor spoke on the Memphis levee in November 1865 were in many ways typical. The Englishman, who was planning to write a book about his American tour, approached one of them and engaged her in conversation. Suspicious and guarded at first, she eventually opened up enough to answer his questions about slavery and race relations. She was bitter about slavery. "There's been a heap of money made in this country," she said. "They've made it out of us." Her sister, she told him, had been literally worked to death on an Alabama plantation. She herself had once been beaten so severely that her head hurt to this day. It was not her master who had done that, however, but another white man, to whom she had been hired. About her master she had no bad word to say: he was "kind, and never gave me a lick." The other woman then joined the conversation. She and her fellow slaves had hated bondage, she said, and during the war they had prayed fervently for Yankee victory. But she too had fond memories of her master and his family: "they treated me like one of themselves." She directed her anger at the institution of slavery rather than those who had profited from it: "They were kind to me, but my children were sent cotton-picking, and they might have been sold away any day."[47]

There were many such black people in Memphis, and in some cases their close relations with the whites who had owned them continued after emancipation. Prince Moultrie, who had lived in the city since the mid-1850s, had been well treated by all four of his former masters and in the spring of 1866 was still living with the last one. So was another freedman, Jack Harris Walker, who praised his last owner and current employer as an indulgent, fair-minded, honest man. Many other black Memphians established relationships of this sort with paternalistic Southern whites after emancipation, relying on them not only for employment and lodging but also for advice and sympathy and the occasional loan of a few dollars to get through hard times. Such relationships were so common that most blacks were reluctant to condemn white Southerners as a class, however much they oppressed the freed people. The balm of personal ties soothed relations between the two, although friction and black resentment were never absent.[48]

Ambivalence of a different sort marked the attitude of the freed people toward Northern-born whites. There was heartfelt gratitude toward the U.S. government and the Yankee people—epitomized by the revered figure of "Massa Lincoln"—for their role in smashing the chains of bondage. Even those who ascribed their liberation to God gratefully acknowledged the Yankees as His agents. Avowing himself "a true frend," one black Memphian told a Union army officer in a letter that "my peple . . . is thankful to god for thare deliverence from slavery which is a high blessing. . . . It were the yanky peple that was the instruments thro god of giving pore slaves thare Liburties." The freed people were likewise thankful for continuing Yankee aid as they struggled to make their way in the postwar world. The missionary teachers who brought the gift of literacy were much praised. Blacks appreciated the presence of the U.S. Army, which provided, as one put it, "the protection of the bayonet," and of the Freedmen's Bureau and its court, where blacks could get redress when cheated or assaulted by whites.[49]

Yet here, too, there arose friction and black resentment. The teachers, while selfless and devoted, could also be (like the Yankee preachers) exasperatingly didactic, judgmental, and condescending. The U.S. Army authorities provoked anger with their discriminatory treatment of the U.S. Colored Troops; one more infuriating injustice was added when, citing a legal technicality, the War Department reneged on a promise to pay sizeable bounties to black troops on mustering out. The Freedmen's Bureau aroused the bitterest complaints for its periodic roundups of black "idlers," most of whom were forced to sign work contracts with planters. In the fall of 1865, Anthony Motley, a barber and spokesman for the black community, wrote a letter to the Bureau that seethed with rage at this policy. "The great Slave trade Seems To be Revived In Memphis," he said. Freedmen were being "hunted down Like Brutes . . . and taken to a Corall Like Beasts to be hired or Sold to the highest Bidder."[50]

There was, by contrast, little ambivalence in blacks' attitude toward the Irish. The freed people were just as contemptuous of the Irish (with a few exceptions, such as Mary Grady) as the Irish were of them. The police, who it seemed could not arrest a freedman without beating him senseless, were particularly despised—especially by blacks in uniform, who were frequent victims of police brutality. Hardly a day passed that some black soldier, his courage perhaps fortified by liquor, did not confront a policeman and damn him as an Irish scoundrel and a son of a bitch. The policeman would invariably react violently, and a scuffle would ensue.[51]

By the spring of 1866 some soldiers were primed for all-out resistance to the police. An incident in South Memphis on April 18 was a sign. Policeman J. F. Sweatt, off duty and unarmed, was taking an evening stroll when a white woman came up to him, claiming that a black woman had stolen something from her. Sweatt agreed to help her and she directed him to the house of the alleged thief, whom he arrested. But at that point, as a newspaper account related, "he was met by a party of negro soldiers, who, with many oaths, declared he should not arrest any one in *their part* of the city." When he started to reply, they rushed him and knocked him down. The black woman got away. Sweatt managed to escape with only a cut on his head.[52]

A few days later, in a nearby section of the city, there was another omen. Five policemen arrested a soldier for no apparent reason. As they led him away, he repeatedly asked for an explanation. They answered by clubbing him savagely on the head. He fell facedown into the muddy street and lay there, his body twitching spasmodically. The policemen summoned a dray, loaded him onto it, and sent him off to jail. Other soldiers were close by, watching. They made no move to interfere but became very agitated and cursed the police loudly. One was heard to say, "By God, if I catch a policeman arresting one of our men in that way again I will resist him."[53]

Not all black Memphians were willing to speak out against the abuse they suffered at the hands of the police, nor against the disenfranchisement, discrimination, vilification, fraud, and violence inflicted by other whites. Some believed that the best way to get by was to accept it all without a murmur of complaint. Austin Cotton, a carpenter, bitterly resented the mistreatment of freed people but hid his feelings behind a mask of deference and bent over backward to stay on good terms with the whites he dealt with. As far as he was concerned this stratagem paid off: he never had any difficulties with them. "You are [all] right, Uncle," they would tell him; "you are humble just like a slave."[54]

Very different from Cotton were the few black Memphians who burned so fiercely with racial anger that they scorned any kind of accommodation with whites. Their rage was directed not just at the Irish or the Rebels or the Yankees but at the whole white race, against which they seemed at times to be waging a personal war. Since joining the 3rd in August 1863, twenty-six-year-old private Charles Nelson had repeatedly earned the notice of his officers for his disinclination to follow orders. He had already served a couple of terms in the military jail when, a little before noon on January 14, 1866, he was accosted by city policeman John Kelly as he was (in Kelly's words) "parading Beal[e] St with a large knife in his right hand and a club in his left. He was going along beating at peoples doors and swearing that no white livered Sons of Bitches should arrest him." When Kelly intervened, Nelson fended him off with the knife. It took the combined efforts of Kelly, another policeman, and an officer and two black soldiers of the provost guard to finally subdue Nelson, relieve him of his weapons and the bottle of whiskey in his pocket, and march him to the military jail. Struggling all the way, Nelson repeated his claim "that no white livered son of a bitch had any controll [sic] over him or could arrest him." As he was dragged into the jail, he vowed "that he would kill the first white son of a bitch he met after he got out."[55]

The great majority of black Memphians were more willing than Nelson to come to terms with whites but less willing than Cotton to meekly accept injustice. Some had an expansive vision of the future, foreseeing a time when the black race might enjoy not just freedom and justice but full equality. Sergeant Henry J. Maxwell of the 3rd had traveled to Nashville in August 1865 as a delegate to the first State Colored Men's Convention of Tennessee. There, in the presence of 139 other delegates (barber Anthony Motley and teacher Horatio Rankin among them), he delivered the keynote address. This convention, Maxwell declared, was a step on the "march to victory. We shall be heard before Congress and before the legislature. We came here for principles, and there will be no dissension. We want the rights guaranteed by the Infinite Architect. For these rights we labor; for them we will die. We have gained one—the uniform is its badge. We want two more boxes besides the cartridge box—the ballot and the jury box. We shall gain them. Let us work faithfully unto that end."[56]

In Memphis in early 1866, those pondering the future of their people could discern rays of light on the horizon, none brighter than the federal Civil Rights Act, which granted blacks citizenship and forbade states from treating any citizen unequally under the law (although it did not enfranchise blacks). On April 12, three days after its passage, the *Memphis Post* printed a letter from a person signing himself "A Colored Friend." The writer decried the continuing abuse of black laborers, but he went on to say that Congress's recent enactment encouraged hope that "this injustice and cruelty—relics of slavery—will soon become numbered among the things of the past." The time was at hand, he thought, when "justice [would be] done between man and man, irrespective of the color of his skin."[57]

No sooner had Congress forged this powerful new weapon than a Memphis freedman went forth to do battle with it. Robert Church, who owned a billiard saloon, had been indicted for operating it without a municipal license. Church had never obtained a license for the simple reason that under existing state law only white people could do so. Such cases were common—although they typically involved a black-owned groggery in a shanty, a far cry from Church's upscale establishment—and they were invariably handled in the Freedmen's Bureau court and decided according to state and municipal law (with the exception that black testimony was accepted). But now, armed with the Civil Rights Act, Church challenged this legal inequity. Bypassing the Freedmen's Bureau court, he hired two white lawyers who pleaded his case in the district criminal court, where on April 16 the judge agreed that the Civil Rights Act did indeed outlaw racial discrimination in the granting of licenses. The charge against Church was dismissed, and the district attorney general declared a halt to the prosecution of any more such cases pending a state supreme court ruling on the criminal court's decision.[58]

This was, to be sure, only a small victory. But it was a significant and heartening one for the freed people of Memphis. It reinforced their faith in the city as a place where they could enjoy a measure of justice, protection, and opportunity. As April 1866 drew to a close, much of black Memphis faced the future hopefully.

PART II

THE RIOT

5

An Incident on the Bayou Bridge

Monday, April 30, Midafternoon to
Tuesday, May 1, Late Afternoon

The sky is slate gray. Rain has been falling, on and off, for more
than twenty-four hours and the mud is thick on the streets and
levee. The river has been rising fast, considerably narrowing the levee;
but it hardly matters, for business has been dull there today, with few
steamboats arriving or departing and thus little work for the stevedores and draymen.[1]

On Causey Street, near the city's southern boundary and half a
mile from the river, Rachael Dilts peers out an open window of the
house she shares with her husband, Johnson, and two relatives, a married couple named Ellen and Samuel Dilts. All four are Northern immigrants. Ellen and Samuel are in the house with Rachael, but Johnson
is not home.[2]

Rachael's attention has been caught by an incident across the
street, sixty feet away. Three black men in military uniform, walking
south on the sidewalk, have encountered four policemen going in the
opposite direction. The blacks have given way to the officers, but
words have been exchanged, the two parties have halted, and there is
trouble of some sort. One of the blacks dashes into the muddy street,
trips, and falls. A policeman follows, collides with him, and also falls.
Both get up and return to the sidewalk. All the men are angry, whites
and blacks cursing one another. The officers pull out revolvers.[3]

Ellen is also watching. She and Rachael see the black men try to break off this encounter, sidestepping the whites and moving down the sidewalk in the direction they had been headed. But then one of them turns and taunts the officers, daring them to follow. One accepts the challenge, advances, and clubs one of the blacks with his revolver. It is a hard blow, so hard that the gun breaks in two and falls out of the policeman's hand. The black man cries out in surprise and pain and claps his hand to the side of his head where he has been hit. He is stunned but stays on his feet, bleeding badly from the wound and from his nose. One of his companions picks up a stick from the street—it looks like a discarded broom handle or perhaps a cane—and strikes the policeman. The bleeding man, regaining his senses, becomes belligerent. He dares his assailant to fight. The policeman backs away. Another officer picks up a stone or brickbat and throws it at the blacks, hitting one in the back of the head and drawing blood. The adversaries exchange more taunts and curses.[4]

Now Samuel comes to the window to watch, but the incident is nearly over. The black men keep moving south, still hurling challenges and insults, and are soon out of sight. One of the officers retrieves the broken revolver from the sidewalk and the four resume their northward course. The street is quiet again.[5]

Some time later, during the evening, Captain Arthur Allyn of the 16th U.S. Infantry is troubled by the sound of pistol fire. He is with his detachment in the north end of Fort Pickering, several blocks west of the Diltses' house. He has been hearing such fire for a week or so, most of it between six and eleven o'clock at night. He is not sure where it is coming from or what it means, but he worries that it might endanger his men.[6]

He decides to investigate. Accompanied by another officer, he leaves the fort and walks east and a little south, following the streets toward the sound of the guns. Eventually he learns that they are being fired into the air by soldiers of the 3rd Colored Heavy Artillery—former soldiers, that is, for they have just been mustered out today—who have been drinking at Mary Grady's place on Clay Street near the bayou, less than half a mile from the 16th Infantry's barracks. Allyn returns to the fort, determined that if he hears gunfire again tomorrow he will send a squad to Grady's and put a stop to it.[7]

Around midnight Ellen Dilts hears something going on in front of her house. She looks out and sees several policemen huddled in conversation. The storm clouds have moved on and the moon is up, just one day past full. There is enough light for her to recognize the men as the regular night-beat patrol. She cannot make out their words, for they are whispering; but she notices that they seem unusually agitated.[8]

Two hours later Ellen and Rachael are awakened by another disturbance in front of their house. A group of black men, at least seven and perhaps as many as ten, are having a loud, excited discussion. Some of them seem to be drunk. They are talking about the fracas between the police and the blacks the previous afternoon. One points out the place on the other side of the street where it happened. Rachael hears him say something about wanting the group to go fight somebody, but it is not clear whom. Ellen hears them agree among themselves that the trouble is not over, that there is sure to be more. After fifteen minutes they move along, heading south. As they go, some fire pistols into the air.[9]

The sun rises above the horizon a few minutes after five. As the day progresses—it is Tuesday, May 1—word of yesterday's altercation spreads throughout South Memphis. By midafternoon there are probably very few people in that section of the city, black or white, who have not heard about it.[10]

On the south side of South Street, about five hundred yards from Fort Pickering, several dozen black men are gathered. They have been carousing there all afternoon. They are former soldiers of the 3rd celebrating yesterday's mustering out. All are still in uniform, and about half are noticeably drunk. Their whiskey has been supplied by the groggeries in the vicinity, but rather than drinking indoors the men are sitting or standing around on the street and sidewalk, for the weather is pleasantly cool and breezy, the sun is screened by light clouds, and the ground has dried after the rains of the previous two days.[11]

The ex-soldiers are yelling and laughing boisterously, to the consternation of nearby residents and shopkeepers. S. J. Quinby, a Northern-born druggist who is at work in his store on South Street, counts about a hundred noisy celebrants, but others who see and hear them think there are fewer, perhaps seventy or fifty or only thirty. At least once during the afternoon Quinby steps out of his store to see what the revelers are up to. He concludes that they are doing no real harm and returns to his work.[12]

It is getting close to four o'clock. Near the corner of Causey and South, two or three hundred yards east of where the rowdy ex-soldiers are congregated and very close to the Diltses's house, four policemen are walking their beat. They are James Finn, David Carroll, John O'Neill, and John Stevens, Irishmen all. A buggy pulls up next to them. In it is John C. Creighton, the city recorder. Somehow he has gotten wind of the disturbance down the street and has decided to do something about it. He orders the four to go disperse the crowd. One protests that that area is beyond his beat. (The city's southern boundary runs down the middle of South Street, and the south side of the street is thus beyond the city limits.) Creighton replies, "I do not care a damn whether it is your beat or not, I want you to go there."[13]

The four policemen may also have doubts about Creighton's authority to order them around, for he is a judicial officer, not part of the police department's chain of command. But Creighton is a powerful municipal official and a prominent and popular member of the Irish community, and he has a forceful personality. The policemen obey him. Heading west on South, they cross a short bridge that spans the bayou. A short distance beyond that they confront the black crowd.[14]

Recognizing one of the blacks, a policeman asks what he and the others are doing. "Just drinking and going on," is the response. "This will not do," the officer tells him; they must cease their carousing and get off the street. The black men ignore this order. Some begin taunting the policemen, calling out "Hurrah for Abe Lincoln." One officer tells them to shut up; another taunts them in return: "Your old father, Abe Lincoln, is dead and damned."[15]

The verbal sparring goes on for several minutes, growing nastier. The ex-soldiers stubbornly refuse to disperse; some tell the policemen to go away. Tempers are rising on both sides. It is very likely that one or more of the policemen, and perhaps some of the black men they are arguing with, were involved in the altercation yesterday.[16]

One man in the crowd is particularly excited and angry. He is Charles Nelson, inveterate enemy of the white race, who had been dragged to the military jail in January swearing that he was going to "kill the first white son of a bitch he met after he got out." He was arrested on that occasion by an Irish policeman, whom he tried to stab, and the military authorities subsequently decreed that he pay for his sins with sixty days of hard labor encumbered by ball and chain. Recently he tangled with another Irish policeman, who, after arresting Nelson on a false charge of arson, beat him up. Nelson has just recognized one of the four policemen standing before him as that very man, and he has flown into a rage. Brandishing a club, he curses the officer and moves toward him. He is restrained by some of his comrades.[17]

The policemen are growing uneasy, for these unruly, belligerent black men overwhelmingly outnumber them. It is obviously pointless, and perhaps dangerous, to stand here arguing any longer; breaking up this disorderly gathering will require reinforcements. The four back away from the crowd and begin retreating up the street.[18]

A few in the crowd follow on their heels, the rest at a distance. Nelson is among the larger group, still wielding his club, growling threats of vengeance, and being held back by comrades. Others have clubs, too, and some have picked up rocks. Shouts are heard from the crowd: "stone them," "club them," and even "shoot them" and "kill them." One of the blacks closest to the policemen comes up and gives one of them a shove, but the officers just keep moving east.[19]

Many bystanders are watching on the sidewalks or from doorways or windows, druggist Quinby among them. Seeing a couple of the uniformed black men moving along very close to the policemen, he and others infer that these men have been arrested and are being taken to the station house downtown. But it is not so; the policemen have arrested no one.[20]

The four reach the bayou bridge, still trailed closely by a few ex-soldiers and at a distance—twenty-five yards or more—by many others. Parked just this side of the bridge is a cart loaded with firewood. One of the blacks nearest the policemen takes a piece of wood from the cart and throws it at them. One or two others do the same.[21]

Up to this point no weapon more dangerous than a stick or rock has been displayed. But now a pistol shot rings out. One of the more distant black men, intending no doubt to scare the policemen and speed them along on their retreat, has pulled out a revolver and fired into the air. A few others follow his example. The policemen, thinking they are being shot at, halt on the bridge and turn. Three of them reach for their revolvers. Two of them draw, level their weapons at the crowd, and open fire. The black men who are shooting into the air immediately lower their guns and fire at the policemen. Others pull out revolvers and likewise shoot at the policemen. Within moments, twenty or more black men are firing.[22]

One of the officers, thirty-two-year-old John Stevens, falls. A shout goes up from the crowd: "He is shot." He has in fact been shot, but not by any of the blacks. In his panicky attempt to draw his weapon and return fire, he has pulled the trigger prematurely, putting a bullet into his own leg. It is a bad wound: the bullet goes deep and shatters his right thighbone. All who see him go down assume he has been hit by gunfire from the blacks.[23]

The fusillade is quickly over. The firing has all been hasty and inaccurate. Dozens of rounds have been discharged, but no black person and no policeman but Stevens has been hit.[24]

As the whitish powder smoke dissipates, officers Finn and O'Neill—the two who have fired at the crowd—flee up South Street, turn onto Causey, and continue northward, heading for the police station downtown. Some in the crowd cross the bridge and chase after them. The rest either stay where they are, milling around excitedly and talking about the shootout, or drift back to where they had been drinking. No one molests officer Carroll, who has not drawn a gun and who has remained on the bridge with the wounded Stevens. Eventually Carroll is able to enlist the aid of a couple of sympathetic black men—perhaps members of the crowd, perhaps onlookers—who help him carry Stevens into a nearby grocery.[25]

A few minutes later one of those who has gone after the two fleeing policemen returns, crying, "They have killed one of our men." Some who hear him quickly reload their guns and head up South and onto Causey. They do not find O'Neill, but on nearby Avery Street they encounter Finn. One calls out, "Kill the God damned white livered son of a bitch." As Finn desperately tries to reload his revolver—he fired four rounds on the bridge and more as he fled—he is shot in the back. He falls to the ground and lies motionless. The wound is serious—the bullet has entered just below his left shoulder blade and lodged in his side—but not fatal. His pursuers come up and look him over. Certain that he is dead, they head back toward South Street, leaving him where he lies.[26]

O'Neill, hurrying on up Causey, passes the scene of yesterday's altercation. Samuel Dilts is there. He has heard a rumor of some sort of trouble nearby, and no doubt has heard the gunfire. As O'Neill passes, Dilts recognizes him as one of the regular day-squad patrolmen, hails him, and asks what is going on. O'Neill's reply is rushed and incoherent. He says something about "the damned niggers," advises Dilts to get inside his house and stay there, and moves on.[27]

The men who have gone after Finn and O'Neill return to South Street and tell their comrades that they have killed a policeman. One has brought along Finn's billy club, which has blood on it. Contrary to the earlier report, none of the pursuers has been killed; but three have been slightly wounded by pistol fire from Finn or O'Neill or both.[28]

The crowd of ex-soldiers—perhaps sobered by the seriousness of what has happened and surely worrying about the consequences now that the confrontation is over, tempers have cooled, and there is time to reflect—begins to disperse. A few stay in the area of South Street. Many head for Fort Pickering, where they are still quartered although officially mustered out of service. One of their former officers, Lieutenant B. F. Baker, has appeared on South Street, having been nearby when the shooting erupted, and he is telling every uniformed man he sees to go to the fort; some twenty-five or thirty follow him there. No one bothers David Carroll or his wounded fellow officer John Stevens, who are still holed up in the grocery.[29]

Recorder Creighton has kept himself out of the line of fire but has stayed in the vicinity long enough to ascertain that two policemen have been shot. Now he hastens northward in his buggy, heading for the police station on Adams Street, a little over a mile away. On the way, he meets an acquaintance, a man named Sterling. He tells him quickly what has happened in South Memphis and hurries on.[30]

At the station house Creighton again tells of the shootout. The police chief, Benjamin Garrett, is there. Sheriff Patrick Winters is there, too, by coincidence; he has come by on some matter of county business. Before long, policeman O'Neill arrives and confirms Creighton's story. No one really knows what to do. There is no reserve force of police at the station; all the day-squad officers are out walking their beats and all the night-squad officers are off duty and not scheduled to report to work for some time. The police department has no contingency plan to deal with a major civil disturbance.[31]

One is hastily improvised. Garrett will assemble whatever policemen he can at the station and lead them to South Memphis to confront the black rioters. Because it is by no means certain that the police will be able to bring the situation under control, Winters and Creighton will go to the headquarters of General Stoneman, ten blocks north, and ask him to provide troops to assist the police. The sheriff climbs into the recorder's buggy and the two ride off at a fast clip.[32]

There is little need, as it turns out, for Chief Garrett to expend any effort rallying the police force. Word of the violence between policemen and black ex-soldiers on South Street is spreading through the city with seemingly electric speed, aided no doubt by the reports that Creighton and O'Neill passed on as they hurried from the scene to the station house. Policemen around the city, on duty and off, begin making their way to the station house or head directly for South Memphis.[33]

They are joined by white citizens, many hundreds of them. The downtown streets are soon thronged with white people. With rumors flying, most are just anxious to know what is really going on. Was this just another scuffle of the familiar sort between black soldiers and the police, or something more serious? Some, however—almost all of them working-class Irishmen—have heard all they need to know. They are preparing to march to South Memphis with the police. Most are carrying guns.[34]

The wounded Stevens has been moved to a house on Causey just around the corner from South. A physician who lives nearby, Dr. Robert McGowan, has been summoned to treat him. McGowan dresses the wound but sees that it is very serious; amputation may be necessary. He tells those helping Stevens that he should be taken to the city's charity hospital, and offers to lend them a stretcher.[35]

———

Twenty-five or thirty policemen have collected at the station house and Chief Garrett now leads them southward. Ahead of, behind, and alongside Garrett's band march scores of citizens, all or nearly all Irishmen. On Beale Street, a white grocer named C. M. Cooley watches as they pass. He hears some of them say they are on their way to South Street, where the blacks have "raised a riot."[36]

Another large crowd of policemen and white citizens has coalesced two or three blocks to the east. It has no leader; but it, too, moves southward. A white house painter named Henry Taylor tags along with the crowd. Questioning those around him, he is told that there has been a fracas involving policemen and blacks in South Memphis, that some policemen have been killed, and that their fellow officers have sworn revenge. He hears some of the policemen near him say that they intend "to shoot down the damned niggers." But he notices that the great majority of those in the crowd seem to be men like himself, unarmed and not looking for trouble, just curious. Men with weapons in their hands and vengeance in their eyes seem to Taylor to number perhaps fifty. They include citizens as well as the policemen.[37]

Near the head of the crowd Taylor has joined is a twenty-six-year-old Irishman named Henry Dunn. He lives nearby with his wife and two children and is a member of the fire department, an engineer with No. 2 steamer company. No doubt he is off duty, for this crowd has been nowhere near his fire station, which is down near the river, close to the Gayoso House. He is among the fifty or so who are marching southward with a grim purpose.[38]

On Causey Street, Chief Garrett has ceased to exercise whatever control he may have had over the policemen he has brought from the station house. They are anything but a cohesive, disciplined force: they and the citizens moving along with them are now thoroughly intermingled, spread out along the street, and in no mood to take orders.[39]

As this crowd passes the Dilts house, Samuel, Ellen, and Rachael are watching from inside. Some of the policemen Ellen sees appear to be those who were involved in the incident at this same spot yesterday afternoon. She notices, too, that nearly all the citizens accompanying the police seem to be Irish "rowdies." Rachael observes that everyone in the crowd, policeman and citizen alike, is carrying a pistol.[40]

As the Diltses look on, two black men come up Causey from the direction of South Street and encounter the crowd. The two are carrying lunch pails, no doubt on their way home from work. Some of the policemen immediately attack them, slugging them with billy clubs or pistols. Ellen hears a policeman call out, "Kill every nigger, no matter who, men or women." The crowd passes on, leaving the two blacks in the street. A few moments later, another black man comes up Causey past the Dilts house. Apparently he too has run afoul of the crowd: his face is covered with blood.[41]

It is now close to five thirty. The second crowd of whites reaches South Street, turns right, and moves toward the scene of the shootout at the bayou bridge. The Causey Street crowd nears the intersection with South, between the bridge and the other crowd. By now both are in the grip of a feverish excitement. They are no longer walking but running. They are not just angry crowds now: they have become homicidal mobs.[42]

Samuel Dilts leaves his house and goes down toward South Street to see what is happening. Ahead of him, the policemen and their citizen allies are emerging from Causey onto South, shouting and firing their pistols in every direction. Bullets zip by close to Samuel. He has no stomach for this sort of thing. He turns and goes back to his house.[43]

6

"You Have Killed Him Once, What Do You Want to Kill Him Again For?"

Tuesday, May 1, Late Afternoon to
Wednesday, May 2, First Light

Recorder Creighton parks his buggy at the headquarters of General Stoneman, and he and Sheriff Winters hurry inside and state their business. The general, who is upstairs in his private quarters, is told of the visitors and comes down to hear what they have to say.[1]

Winters does the talking. He tells Stoneman what has happened in South Memphis and asks him to deploy troops to suppress the black rioters. He is dismayed when Stoneman responds that he has no troops to spare. His small infantry force—185 officers and men, less those unavailable for duty for various reasons—has its hands full guarding U.S. government property. And besides, he says, white Memphians have repeatedly demanded the withdrawal of federal troops from the city, claiming that the civil authorities are perfectly capable of maintaining order on their own; let us see, says Stoneman, if that claim can now be substantiated. He asks Winters if he has exercised his power to summon a posse. Winters says no. Stoneman advises him to do so.[2]

The sheriff makes his disappointment obvious but does not argue. He and Creighton return to the buggy and head back to the police station.[3]

A mile and a half south of Stoneman's headquarters, the second mob of policemen and citizens is running west on South and approaching the Rayburn Avenue intersection with weapons in hand. The mob numbers fifty or so; the curious citizens like Henry Taylor are hanging back, aware by now of what is happening and anxious to stay out of it.[4]

One part of the mob continues down South Street, the other veers left onto Rayburn. Many black men and women are in the vicinity of the intersection, going about their business. They have no idea of what is happening until the shooting erupts.[5]

On the southwest corner of the intersection stands the shop of Irish grocer John Pendergrast. He is undoubtedly aware of the shoot-out that occurred nearby an hour and a half ago, and has been prepared for action ever since. He has in fact been prepared to deal with black hooligans since at least last February, when he ran off a gang of burglars at gunpoint. Now, as police officers and other white men rush past his store shooting at blacks, Pendergrast arms himself with a pistol in each hand and heads out the door. His mother, who lives with him, urges him to stay inside and not get involved, but he ignores her. He steps out onto Rayburn and becomes one of the mob.[6]

Many of the blacks being shot at are fleeing down Rayburn or across the eastern branch of the bayou. Pendergrast sees one who appears to be lagging behind the rest; the man is running down Rayburn just twenty feet ahead of the mob. Pendergrast can see only his back. He takes aim at him with one pistol and fires. The man pitches forward and sprawls facedown on the street. Pendergrast goes up to him and turns him over on his back. To the grocer's astonishment he sees that his victim is white. "God damn it," he exclaims, "I am sorry I shot this man, I thought he was a God damn yellow nigger."[7]

The man is fireman Henry Dunn, who in his eagerness to wreak vengeance on blacks raced ahead of the rest of the mob. He is alive but unconscious, and obviously cannot live long. Pendergrast's bullet has entered the back of his head, plowed through his brain, penetrated the skull on the other side, and lodged under the skin of his forehead.[8]

Pendergrast now seeks atonement for his error by claiming a black victim. Leaving Dunn, he goes down to the bayou and spots a short young man in army uniform who is trying to get away. The man is Lewis Robinson, a former corporal in the 3rd. He is too far off to get a good shot at but is within shouting distance. Pendergrast calls to him, telling him to come back, that he will not be harmed. Robinson takes Pendergrast at his word. He halts, then begins making his way back toward the grocer. When he is close enough, Pendergrast raises a pistol and fires into his face. The bullet hits Robinson in the jaw. A policeman nearby also fires, hitting Robinson in the side.[9]

Robinson falls to the ground on the bank of the bayou. As he lies there bleeding from the two wounds, his tongue severed and his body jerking convulsively, Pendergrast comes up to him, hammers his head with a pistol, and walks away.[10]

Except for Dunn, the mob's targets are men wearing federal uniforms or parts of uniforms. Other black people are not harmed, even those in the very path of the mob. One is James Mitchell, who is standing with his wife in front of their rented house on Rayburn, just fifty paces from where Dunn has fallen. Mitchell is a veteran of the U.S. Colored Troops but is wearing civilian clothes.[11]

Looking on from a residence on Rayburn is a black woman named Penny Le Muir. She has seen Pendergrast shoot Lewis Robinson and beat his prostrate body. After the grocer walks away, she hastens down to the bayou to help Robinson but finds that he is dead.[12]

A third black witness residing on Rayburn is a middle-aged woman named Cynthia Townsend. She is thankful that her husband and son are not here now; they have taken temporary work out in the country. Her son served in the U.S. Colored Troops. Townsend is shocked by Pendergrast's savagery, for she has always known him as a man friendly to blacks, or at least certain blacks—including her, whom he calls "Aunt Cynthia." Her impulse now is to flee, but she worries about leaving her house vacant with the mob running rampant. She seeks out Pendergrast's father, who lives with his son and whom she calls "Mr. Pender," and begs him to keep an eye on her place while she is gone. He advises her not to leave, saying that her reputation as a "good old" Negro will protect her and that, in any event, he thinks this outbreak of violence is "all done with now."[13]

Besides Robinson, at least two other black men in federal uniform have been shot down near the Rayburn-South intersection. No white besides Dunn has been hurt. No black has fired a gun, or offered any resistance at all.[14]

The black bodies remain where they have fallen, ignored by the mob. Dunn, however, soon gets attention, although it can do him no good. Ten or fifteen minutes after his wounding, a hack is procured and he is loaded into it, still breathing but comatose. The hack carries him away toward downtown.[15]

One or two hundred yards northwest of where Dunn has fallen, the mob of several dozen policemen and Irish workingmen under Chief Garrett's nominal command has emerged onto South Street, on the run and with a shout. They quickly spread east and west along the street, shooting and beating black people. Here, too, the victims are taken wholly by surprise as they are going about their business. The moment they realize what is happening they flee, or try to; none offers any resistance.[16]

These rioters are less discriminating than those on Rayburn: although men wearing any part of a federal uniform are particularly targeted, no black person is exempted. A young servant named Adeline Miller is killed by a gunshot as she stands on the sidewalk in front of a grocery store talking with a friend. A thirteen-year-old boy is wounded by a bullet.[17]

Tony Cherry is luckier than many. Until yesterday a private in the 3rd's Company H, he is still wearing his uniform. He was among the angry crowd of ex-soldiers involved in the shootout on the bayou bridge an hour and a half ago, but unlike many of them he has continued to hang around South Street. Now, as firing erupts, Cherry takes off running toward Fort Pickering. He is not ahead of the rioters but surrounded by them. As he desperately flies past them, some fire at him. Two bullets pierce his cap, but he is unhurt and makes it to safety in the fort.[18]

His comrade Isaac Richardson, who was also a private in Company H and served by Cherry's side for thirteen months, is not so lucky. He too runs for his life, but he is twenty yards behind Cherry and the bullets fired at him do not miss. Richardson falls in the street.[19]

The rioters moving east on South Street can see other rioters approaching them. These are the men of the second mob who bypassed Rayburn. Caught between the two is a uniformed veteran of Company

L of the 3rd, a thirty-year-old private named Allen Summers. He has just left the house on South where he and his wife live and is walking to a nearby store with twenty-five dollars that he has borrowed to buy some provisions. Summers spent the last three months of his military career in Fort Pickering's penal stockade at hard labor for the offense of absence without leave. Mustered out and released from confinement on April 30, he has enjoyed but one day of freedom before suddenly finding himself between two swarms of armed, murderous white men.[20]

Summers runs back to his house and crawls under his bed. His wife, who works as a laundress, is not home. Several white men follow him into his house. One, a brawny policeman with a red mustache, drags him from under the bed and into the street. Summers manages to break away, but the whites fire at him with pistols and he runs only twenty yards before he is hit. He is not felled by the bullet, which enters his right shoulder, but he gets only a little farther before being knocked to the ground by a big Irishman. This man stabs Summers in the side with a knife, takes the money from his pocket, and kicks him repeatedly in the face. He is joined by a policeman who clubs Summers with his billy. Summers is still conscious but is lying motionless with eyes closed. Around him he hears men vowing to kill every one of "the God damned nigger soldiers."[21]

Summers's life is saved by the intervention of a Yankee doctor who lives nearby and has witnessed the attack on him. He is J. N. Sharp, employed by the Freedmen's Bureau as a surgeon at the Freedmen's Hospital. Heedless of his own safety, Sharp goes up to the rioters who are pounding Summers's prostrate body, tells them that their victim is dead, and asks them sarcastically if they intend to keep abusing the corpse. The men desist, then move on to seek other victims. Sharp enlists the aid of a black man who is likewise brave enough to risk the flying bullets and the mob's fury, and the two help Summers to his feet. Each taking him by an arm, they walk him back to his house and get him undressed and into bed, where the doctor treats his injuries.[22]

Not far away, another Yankee immigrant also witnesses the carnage on South Street. Illinois-born William Brazier, an agent of the Aetna insurance company who has lived in Memphis only four months, sees a dozen blacks who have been shot down. One, a man in army uniform who is lying in the street with bullet wounds in his head and chest, conscious but barely clinging to life—he is perhaps Isaac Richardson—is being taunted by some of the rioters: "It is good enough for you, you God damned son of a bitch."[23]

Brazier notices that there are many whites besides himself looking on from the sidewalk or the stores and houses along the street, taking no part in the violence but doing nothing to stop it. He is horrified by the bloodshed, but the onlookers around him do not seem to share that sentiment; the comments he hears suggest they approve. Seeing another black cut down just twenty feet from where he is standing, Brazier protests loudly enough for others to hear that it is "damned barbarous to shoot a man in that way." Several white men turn and glare at him; one growls, "It is right." Brazier, suddenly aware that his own life might be in danger, resolves to keep his mouth shut.[24]

Not every white bystander on South Street is bold or foolish enough to remain there watching the gruesome spectacle while bullets fly. Many seek refuge in the back rooms of houses and stores, as far from the street as they can get. Many others flee South Street altogether, scattering to the north or south. Some take shelter, without invitation, in the Dilts house on Causey. Ellen Dilts is there as her front room suddenly fills with frightened, breathless men babbling about what they have seen on South. As they catch their breath, some regain their courage: "Do not let us be such cowards," they tell the others; "let us go back again."[25]

Ellen looks out the window and sees the street and sidewalk crowded with black refugees from South Street. They look dazed and scared; some have bloody head wounds and are covered with the dust of the street.[26]

Having concluded another day of ministry and teaching at Lincoln Chapel, the Reverend Ewing O. Tade and his wife, Amanda, are strolling along Beale Street near the city market. Word of the attack of the white mobs on Rayburn and South has not reached this part of town, and blacks and whites here are going about their customary business. There is a bit of trouble, however, but of a very common kind in Memphis: a traffic accident. Two hacks, one driven by a black and the other by a white, have collided, the drivers have jumped down from their vehicles and gotten into a nasty argument, and a crowd has gathered to watch the show. As the Tades look on, the hackmen are separated before they come to blows. The Tades continue westward on Beale, but the crowd does not disperse.[27]

The Rayburn Avenue mob has completed its murderous work and joined Garrett's mob on South Street. When South no longer offers any targets, the rioters move on, mostly trooping northward in small bands. With pistols and cudgels they attack nearly every black person who crosses their path, venting particular fury on those in uniform.[28]

A little after six o'clock, as Willis Jones, a blacksmith, is closing up for the day and preparing to head home for supper, a group of policemen and citizens appears, coming up Main from South. One spots Jones, aims his pistol at him, and fires, hitting him in the right eye. When Jones turns and runs, the man fires at him again but misses. Jones escapes with his life but is severely injured.[29]

Among that band of rioters passing the blacksmith shop is policeman David Roach. It is perhaps he who has shot Willis Jones. If so, it is not the first time today that he has shed a black person's blood. A few minutes ago on South Street he shot a man named Coleman Default. Badly wounded but alive, Default begged Roach not to kill him. "Yes, God damn you, I will," was the reply. "You, and all the balance of you." Roach was accompanied by several other policemen, one of whom put a second bullet into Default. They then pistol-whipped him, robbed him of thirty dollars and his army discharge certificate, and left him for dead.[30]

Walking south on Main Street is a veteran of the 3rd named Frank Williams. He is coming from downtown, where a little while ago he heard rumors of the rioting in South Memphis and decided to investigate. He does not have to go far before he sees all he needs to know. Ahead of him on Main is a crowd of policemen and white citizens attacking black people; as he watches, two are shot, one of them a man he recognizes as a comrade in the 3rd. Williams, who is in uniform, decides to seek safety in Fort Pickering, where he is still quartered. He runs down a cross street to Shelby, but there he finds another crowd of rioters and sees more black victims fall. He manages to evade this mob, too, and makes his way to the fort.[31]

Williams reports what he has seen to an officer of the regular troops and then spreads the word among his comrades in the barracks of the 3rd. His news confirms what the men have no doubt heard from Tony Cherry and others who have made it to safety in the fort: that in the streets outside the fort mobs of policemen and white citizens, all or nearly all Irish, are slaughtering black people.[32]

These reports have stirred up great excitement and anxiety among the men in the barracks, many of whom have kinfolk living in South Memphis. Some now voice their determination to leave the fort and go to the aid of their families. Word of this reaches Colonel Ignatz Kappner, who like most of the other ex-officers of the 3rd has remained in the fort following mustering out. Fearing that the presence of more black soldiers on the streets will only stoke the violence, Kappner calls his former officers together and tells them to keep the men in their quarters.[33]

They try to do so but fail; they have no formal authority now and can only plead, not command. About a hundred men ignore the pleas and rush out of the fort in a group. None is carrying a musket or bayonet, for the regiment turned in all government arms before mustering out. But many are carrying concealed pistols.[34]

The men spread out along South Street, which has by now been mostly abandoned by the white rioters. Their presence emboldens other black men to come out of hiding and join them; many of these, too, are armed. Soon clusters of gun-wielding black men, almost all in full or partial uniform, are making their way northward along the streets that intersect South, following the tracks of the rioters. They intend to drive the white mobs from South Memphis. Wherever they encounter policemen or other armed whites, they open fire. If the whites retreat, they give chase, crying, "Halt, you white son of a bitch."[35]

At 444 Main Street, where physician R. W. Creighton has his office and home, Dr. Creighton is inside chatting with a visitor. He has lived in Memphis for twenty years and is not related to the city recorder. A hack pulls up outside. Two policemen jump out and rush into the doctor's office. They are very agitated and have pistols in hand. They tell Creighton that there has been "a hell of a fight" between the police and blacks and that one of their number has been wounded. He is in the hack and needs the doctor's attention.[36]

The wounded man is brought in, moaning loudly. Creighton examines him and finds nothing more than a small flesh wound on one finger where it has been nicked by a bullet. As Creighton bandages the injury, one of the other policemen, who appears to be in a frenzy of rage over the wounding of his comrade, abruptly announces, "I'm going out to kill a nigger." He steps outside, spots a black man carrying whitewashing equipment who is apparently headed home from work, cocks his pistol, and fires at him; the man is not hit.[37]

Within a few minutes three more hacks pull up to Creighton's office bearing two more wounded policemen and two injured white citizens. The citizens have not been involved in the rioting, Creighton learns, and their injuries are accidental: one has been grazed on the shin by a stray bullet, the other kicked by a horse. But the two wounded policemen, like the first, are casualties of the black counterattack. One, an Irishman named D. F. Slattery, has been hit in both thighs by two different bullets. The injuries seem serious at first glance, but Creighton finds that both are mere flesh wounds; he binds them up and assures the patient that they will heal. Slattery, who was carried in from the hack, leaves the doctor's office on his feet.[38]

Downtown, Sheriff Winters and Recorder Creighton have ridden back to the police station. Winters has decided to take General Stoneman's advice to form a posse and lead it to South Memphis to quell the black unrest. He hopes to find a force of policemen at the station who can bolster the posse, but there are none: Chief Garrett has already gathered all those available and taken them southward.[39]

Winters goes ahead with his posse-recruiting anyway. He and the recorder head south to the city market. Along the way, they halt the buggy whenever they come across any able-bodied white men, and the sheriff attempts to enlist them in the posse. He has little success. Most of those he summons beg off with some excuse or simply refuse to cooperate. The sheriff, who is unarmed, does not try to compel the shirkers.[40]

The few who agree to do their civic duty follow behind the buggy as Winters and Creighton move along. By the time they get to the market they number about twenty, some armed with pistols, some weaponless. Winters leads this motley assemblage southward from Beale along Saint Martin Street. It is now a little after six thirty, almost dusk. As they near Morris Cemetery they are fired on by black men several hundred yards ahead of them. Only two or three shots are discharged and no one is hit, but this is sufficient resistance to extinguish the sheriff's enthusiasm. He halts his men, turns them around, and leads them back the way they came.[41]

The rioting policemen and their citizen allies who are under counterattack by the armed blacks do not, for the most part, make a stronger stand than Winters and his posse. But some return fire, and in a few instances they countercharge and repel the blacks. It is in one such engagement that policeman Slattery is wounded; he falls near the bayou bridge on South Street as he and his comrades are driving the blacks back. But these white successes are short-lived. By quarter to seven, when the sun sets, a general retreat of the white mobs toward downtown is under way.[42]

Even in retreat, however, the white rioters are still dangerous. As one band of twenty or thirty passes the Freedmen's Hospital, its members spot two patients sitting by the entrance. Several open fire with pistols. The patients are taken by surprise and have no chance to get out of the way. One of them, a man named Robert Davis, could not get away even if he had warning, for he is a paraplegic. He and the other patient are wounded by the gunfire, badly but not fatally. The assailants continue their retreat up Main.[43]

Ewing and Amanda Tade have turned north onto Second Street from Beale, intending to go to the post office downtown. As they pass Gayoso Street, an excited crowd of white men approaches them from the opposite direction. Some have knives or pistols in their hands or waistbands. Reverend Tade's first thought is that these men are going to investigate the encounter between the hack drivers on Beale. He speaks up, telling those nearest him that that incident is over, that there is nothing to see now. No one pays him any attention. The Tades step out of the way as the crowd goes by.[44]

A few feet away, a black man is likewise standing on the sidewalk and watching. The Tades see a policeman in the crowd approach him, grab him by the collar with one hand, and pummel him on the head with the other. He then shoves the man against a wall, pulls out his revolver, points it in his face, and curses and threatens him, vowing to blow his brains out. "You damned niggers ought to be shot," he says. "You ought to be all driven out." Reverend Tade glares at him. The policeman notices this, releases the black man, and moves on with the crowd.[45]

Sheriff Winters and his posse have retreated from the cemetery to the corner of Vance and Causey. Winters is still riding in Creighton's buggy with the recorder at the reins. A crowd of fifty or more white men is gathered at the intersection, some of them policemen.[46]

The sheriff takes this opportunity to try to reinforce the posse. He speaks to the crowd, calling on the men to join him. Creighton then takes a turn, putting to use his formidable electioneering skills. "Gentlemen," he says, pulling a pistol from his pocket, "I am a brave man, by the God, and this is the best piece of metal in the state of Tennessee. We are not now prepared but let us prepare to clean every nigger son of a bitch out of town." Arm yourselves, he says, and we will march in a body through the black neighborhoods and kill every "God damned nigger" in Memphis.[47]

It is a rousing speech. When he concludes, his listeners reward him with three cheers and declare their intention to vote for him in the next election. Neither his nor Winters's oratory, however, succeeds in swelling the ranks of the posse. The crowd drifts away, to the north, east, and west.[48]

At city hall, in the Second Ward, the mayor and aldermen assemble for their regular biweekly council meeting. The excitement in the city has kept some members away: Mayor Park is present, but only eleven of the sixteen aldermen are. Park is drunk. Everyone assembled there

with him realizes it and is disgusted. No one wants to talk about anything but the rioting in South Memphis and the refusal of General
Stoneman to help; all scheduled business is ignored. No sooner is the
meeting called to order than Alderman S. T. Morgan moves that it be
adjourned until two o'clock tomorrow afternoon. The motion quickly
passes. But no one leaves, because the mayor immediately calls a special meeting of the board and reads a prepared statement: "I find . . .
that the disturbance between the blacks and whites this evening
requires prompt action on our part. In the absence of proper military
aid, therefore, please authorize me, as Mayor, to secure such aid as may
be required to quell and suppress all disturbance, and I will do it."[49]

The ensuing discussion leads nowhere. Park is unsure what emergency powers he possesses or might be granted. The assistant city attorney, who is present, opines that the mayor should be allowed to take
whatever steps he thinks necessary. Alderman John Toof, preferring to
keep this matter out of the mayor's hands, moves that an ad hoc committee be appointed to handle it. Alderman Michael Burke asks the
mayor to comment on this motion before a vote is taken. Park abruptly
decides to take direct action: "I now order the doors of this hall closed,"
he announces, "and summon you all as a p———." He stumbles over
the term. A voice calls out, "A posse comitatus." "Yes," the mayor continues, "a posse comitatus." He intends to lead this little force of city fathers to South Memphis and deal with the unrest.[50]

The aldermen have no taste for this. One promptly moves adjournment of the special meeting, and all but one of the rest concur. They
begin exiting the room over the mayor's protests. Alderman A. P. Bur-
ditt confronts Park: "Sir," he says, "I am sorry and astonished to see
you drunk in an hour of peril like this to the safety of the city. Sir, I am
astonished."[51]

White rioting has by now broken out at several points on and around
Beale Street. This violence, to which no blacks offer any resistance,
has been encouraged by news of the skirmishing between whites and
blacks to the south, and has likely been triggered by the encounter
between the hack drivers witnessed by the Tades.[52]

Irish grocer John Hollywood, whose store is on the south side of

Beale a little west of the city market, is frightened by the tumult on the street. He has no desire to join the rioters; he is concerned only for the safety of his store, which is also his home. He considers locking up the building and hunkering down inside, but some of his neighbors urge him not to, for that might only encourage a mob to break in and loot the place. Hollywood accepts this advice, keeps the store open, and makes his presence there known.[53]

A little before dusk, a black carpenter named Austin Cotton steps onto Beale on his way home from work. He is unaware of the danger. As he nears Hollywood's grocery, he passes a small crowd of white men, several of them policemen, who are talking together on the street. One of the policemen yells, "Halt! you damned nigger, or we will knock you on the head," and the group begins to chase him.[54]

Cotton runs to the grocery; he trades there frequently, knows Hollywood well, and lives in a place on Saint Martin directly behind the store. But he is caught by one of the pursuers just as he gets to the grocery's doorway. The man grabs him around the waist and holds him. Two policemen come up, pull out revolvers, and club Cotton on the head with them. He struggles desperately, protesting that he has done nothing wrong.[55]

John Hollywood is watching, horrified, from inside the store. He knows Cotton as a humble, ingratiating man who never causes trouble. The grocer cries out to the assailants, pleading with them to "have mercy" on Cotton and not murder him "in my own house." They ignore his pleas.[56]

Cotton, although badly injured, manages to break free. He runs through the store, escapes out the back, and makes it to safety in his own home.[57]

Within moments the crowd finds another victim. Jackson Godell, a drayman, devout Baptist, and veteran of the 55th U.S. Colored Infantry, has just left his home, a rented basement in a house two doors from Hollywood's store. He is carrying a pan in which he intends to bring home some cornmeal from the grocery for his supper. His wife, Lavinia, would have run this errand but she is unwell. There has been no shooting in this neighborhood, nor any other commotion loud enough to give warning to people indoors. Godell does not know that the cluster of white men he sees ahead of him is thirsting for black blood.[58]

The crowd, numbering a dozen or so, pounces on Godell as he nears the grocery, beating him on the head. He tries to escape but gets no farther than the sidewalk in front of the store, where the blow of a club brings him to his knees. Another blow fells him completely; he collapses into the gutter.[59]

As the crowd continues to beat him, other white men and boys passing along the street come up to watch. Someone says, "Shoot him." One of the policemen pulls out a revolver and fires a bullet into Godell at close range. Godell groans loudly.[60]

Some in the crowd, including the policemen, walk away. But one policeman, having gone only four or five steps, abruptly stops and turns. He walks back to within a couple of paces of Godell, points his pistol at him, and puts a second bullet into him. Godell emits another loud groan.[61]

The crowd disperses, leaving Godell where he lies. His wounds are very bad, but he is still breathing.[62]

Nearby, a black woman has witnessed this attack. She lives next door to the Godells and attends the same church they do. To leave her house now is obviously dangerous, but she must tell Godell's wife what has happened. She runs next door. "Sister Lavinia," she cries, "Jackson is killed."[63]

Lavinia rises from her sickbed and rushes to her husband's side. He is barely clinging to consciousness. She puts her hand to his chest and speaks his name, but he does not respond. She kneels in the gutter and cradles his bloody head in her hands.[64]

Three white men walk by. Lavinia hears one say, "Here is a damned nigger; if he is not dead we will finish him." One of the others replies, "You have killed him once, what do you want to kill him again for?" They pass on.[65]

Another white man comes by. This one is sympathetic: he urges Lavinia to get her husband home, where his wounds can be treated, and offers to stay there with him while she gathers some friends to assist her. She accepts this offer, but cannot find any blacks willing to risk their lives by coming out onto the street and carrying her husband home. Not knowing what else to do, she returns to Jackson's side and sits there with his head in her hands.[66]

———

Inside Fort Pickering, Captain Arthur Allyn has decided that he must act. The disturbing reports brought to the fort by Frank Williams and others and the continuing gunfire in the streets can no longer be ignored. Allyn has received no orders from General Stoneman regarding this trouble in South Memphis, but yesterday he made up his mind, after investigating the pistol-firing at Mary Grady's place, that if shooting broke out again today he would put an end to it.[67]

Two squads of Allyn's troops are detached and given arms, and officers are appointed to command them. First Lieutenant Walter Clifford takes charge of six men: five privates and a noncommissioned officer. Captain William Smyth takes charge of twenty-five men, three of them sergeants. Because Allyn's understanding of what is going on in the streets is vague, his orders to Clifford and Smyth are very general. He tells them simply to patrol South Memphis, put down disturbances, halt the shooting, disarm any citizens found with weapons, and break up large gatherings.[68]

It is close to sunset when the fort's north gate opens and the two officers lead their squads out onto the streets, each following a different route. The rest of Allyn's force remains in the fort under arms.[69]

The former soldiers of the 3rd who have stayed in their barracks are by now consumed with anxiety about the fate of their families and comrades outside the fort. The only thing keeping them from joining the fray is a lack of weapons. But they know where their recently surrendered muskets, cartridges, and percussion caps are stored: in the fort's armory, which stands nearby and is guarded by some of the regular troops. A cry goes up in the barracks: "We must have our arms." One or two dozen men rush out in a group and descend on the armory.[70]

Captain Thomas Durnin of the 16th is ready for them. He has a party of troops protecting the armory with loaded muskets and fixed bayonets. As the black ex-soldiers approach, Durnin orders his men to fire—but to fire high, well over the heads of the blacks. The volley thus inflicts no casualties, but is enough to scare off the would-be raiders, who retreat and return to the barracks.[71]

———

Lieutenant Clifford leads his small squad of regulars to Main Street and then moves northward. Along the way they hear intermittent gunfire; here and there they find armed men, some black, some white. Clifford scrupulously follows his instructions to disarm these men—those, that is, who do not elude him—and orders them off the streets. By the time he and his squad reach Beale they have collected a derringer, a revolver, a double-barreled shotgun, two muskets, and a repeating rifle.[72]

On Beale they find a large crowd of white men. Clifford seizes a musket from one and a pistol from another. The pistol owner protests that he is a policeman, and opens his coat to show the badge he has until now kept covered. Clifford returns the pistol to him.[73]

Captain Smyth and his much larger squad go eastward on South and then northward on Causey. Until he reaches the corner of Causey and Vance, Smyth finds little or nothing requiring him to invoke Captain Allyn's orders. At the intersection he encounters a group of white men. One comes up to him and identifies himself as Sheriff Winters. He and his posse have remained here following the failed attempt to recruit more men. Winters asks Smyth to assist him in putting down the disturbances, and Smyth agrees to cooperate.[74]

As they talk, gunfire erupts nearby. Smyth breaks off the conversation and leads his men at the double-quick in the direction of the firing. The sheriff's courage now fails him, as it did earlier near the cemetery. Unarmed as he is, and with a posse of questionable dependability, he decides to leave riot-quelling to the military and get out of danger. He gathers his men and leads them northward, away from the firing, which soon ceases. Winters concludes that Captain Smyth has handled the matter.[75]

Ewing and Amanda Tade have returned to Beale, which has quieted down as blacks flee the street, leaving the rioters with no more targets. The only blacks to be seen are Jackson and Lavinia Godell and another woman—perhaps the Godells' next-door neighbor—who has bravely come to help Lavinia tend her dying husband. The Tades approach Lavinia, who is still cradling Jackson's head in her hands as he lies semiconscious in the gutter. The twenty-seven-year-old Jackson is so disfigured by his head wounds that Ewing mistakes his age, taking him for an elderly man.[76]

The Tades want to help, but there is nothing they can do. They find that no blacks strong enough to carry Jackson home can be prevailed on to venture into the street. They leave Lavinia and continue eastward. Other sympathetic whites eventually persuade her to abandon her husband for her own safety; the rioters, they tell her, are determined to kill every black person they find. Reluctantly, she lays Jackson's head down and goes home, where her friend remains with her to comfort her.[77]

As night descends on the city, the armed black men on the streets of South Memphis bring their counterattack against the white rioters to an end. They are satisfied with their success: the enemy has been repulsed. By seven thirty almost all have put away their weapons and made their way back to the fort or to their homes. As far as they are concerned, the trouble is over.[78]

The bands of white rioters disperse as they retreat northward from South Memphis. Some of the citizens go home, others linger on the streets. Two or three dozen of the policemen post themselves along Gayoso Street at the intersections of Shelby, Main, and Second, intending to offer resistance if the armed blacks threaten to advance farther north. Most of the other policemen head for the station house on Adams. In their custody are a number of black men whom they have, for some reason, arrested rather than killed. These prisoners have not escaped the wrath of the rioters altogether, however: most have been badly beaten.[79]

By the time Sheriff Winters reaches Beale Street his posse has dwindled to a dozen or fewer men. They have so far accomplished nothing; but as they trudge westward on Beale, Winters spots Jackson Godell lying in the gutter and takes this opportunity to make his men useful. He summons a hack and has them put Godell into it, intending to send the injured man to the police station downtown, near which is a doctor who can treat him.[80]

Before the hack can set off, Lieutenant Clifford and his small squad of regulars appear. Clifford orders Winters's men to surrender whatever weapons they are carrying. Winters protests, but only feebly. Clifford tells those he has disarmed that they can reclaim their guns at Fort Pickering after order is restored in the city.[81]

Seeing Godell in the hack and being informed of the sheriff's intention, Clifford suggests sending him to the Freedmen's Hospital in South Memphis instead of the police station. Winters confesses that he did not know there was such a hospital. This discussion leaves the matter unresolved, and eventually the hack driver, having gotten no further instructions, rides off to the police station with his bruised, bleeding, and barely conscious passenger.[82]

By now white rioting has spread northward from Beale, through the Fifth Ward and into the Fourth and Third, the heart of downtown Memphis. Mobs of whites coalesce spontaneously here and there and then march along the streets, shooting or beating every black person they catch. Among the rioters are a number of boys, members of the notorious Mackerel Brigade, who have armed themselves with sticks and rocks. The city's gas streetlamps provide light for the mobs' work during the hour and a quarter between nightfall and moonrise.[83]

A black man is shot in the face right in front of the Gayoso House. Another is killed by gunfire close to Court Square. A third is savagely clubbed on Adams Street. A fourteen- or fifteen-year-old boy barely survives a beating near the corner of Jefferson and Main. Besides these there are many other victims. Nowhere do any blacks resist. Those who manage to escape the mobs abandon the downtown streets and seek safety in whatever hiding places they can find.[84]

United States marshal Martin T. Ryder witnesses some of this violence. Thirty-three years old and Scottish-born, he has been a Memphis resident since 1857. But he lived in the North before that, his wife and two children were born there, he spurned the Rebel cause, and he considers himself a Northern man. He is also a politically active Republican, and has thereby made himself obnoxious to many white Memphians.[85]

Since the rioting began Ryder has ridden on horseback from downtown to South Street and back, unable to do anything to halt the violence but gathering what information he can about its origin and progress. He has passed on this information to the editors of the *Memphis Post* and the *Memphis Commercial*.[86]

As he finishes delivering his news at the *Commercial* office, on the corner of Second and Adams near the police station, Ryder hears a commotion in the street. Leaving the building, he sees that there has been an accident. A carriage has overturned, the driver has been unable to halt his team, and the vehicle is being dragged noisily along the street. Passersby have stopped to watch. Among them is a black man apparently unaware of the spread of rioting into this ward. The white onlookers abruptly turn on this man. One grabs the carriage driver's whip and strikes the man with it while others pummel him with fists or weapons. The man eventually breaks free and runs for his life; some of the whites chase him.[87]

One of those who has not given chase spots Marshal Ryder and comes up to him, a pistol in his hand. "I know who you are," he says menacingly. The marshal and his ilk, this man continues, are responsible for stirring up the blacks in Memphis and ought to be killed for it. Turning to the other people standing around, he denounces Ryder as a "damned Yankee abolitionist," "worse than a nigger." He then turns back, raises his pistol, and slams the marshal in the head with it. Ryder is staggered but stays on his feet. He is carrying a pistol but fears that if he goes for it the man will shoot him. He retreats from the scene, gets on his horse, and rides away.[88]

A few minutes later he runs into a man he knows, the editor of the *Memphis Argus*. The two are inveterate political enemies, but now the emergency brings them together to share news and thoughts. The editor is deeply worried. Memphis, he says, is "in a very dangerous condition": the mobs are out of control, innocent people are being killed, and he fears the city might be destroyed. He urges the marshal to go see General Stoneman and try to persuade him to use his troops to restore order. Ryder asks, "Where is the Mayor?" The editor replies, "The Mayor is intoxicated."[89]

Ryder turns his mount northward and goes to Stoneman's headquarters. Escorted into the general's presence, he tells him what he has seen and heard. Stoneman asks him if he thinks the city officials can handle the crisis with the police force. No, says Ryder, matters have "passed that stage"; the police are in fact part of the mobs. Those rioting alongside the police, Ryder adds, are the dregs of white society: hack drivers, draymen, butchers, gamblers, and the like.[90]

This is indeed regrettable, the general replies; but he will not call out his troops. He proffers the same arguments that he gave Sheriff Winters earlier today: his force is too small to do more than guard government property and, besides, Memphians have long insisted that the federal garrison is unnecessary, that the civil authorities can maintain order on their own. Stoneman does suggest, however, that he might act if the city officials think it absolutely necessary; but he has received no request from them. Marshal Ryder, satisfied that he has done what he can, departs.[91]

Sheriff Winters's disarmed and thus wholly useless posse has melted away altogether. The sheriff, however, has again mustered his courage and resolved to do his duty. He and Recorder Creighton leave Beale Street and head downtown in the buggy, determined to recruit another posse.[92]

At eight thirty, near the corner of Adams and Main, where a crowd of white men is milling about in front of the Worsham Hotel, Creighton halts the buggy to make a speech. Again he calls on his listeners to arm themselves and march on South Memphis. He vows that if any white man is brought before his court for violating the city ordinance against carrying firearms he will dismiss the charge. He exaggerates his experiences today to dramatize the threat of armed blacks: he has been shot at four times by black soldiers, he claims, one bullet coming close enough to clip his horse's harness.[93]

In the crowd is Alderman Martin Kelly. He is unmoved by the recorder's impassioned rhetoric. He remarks to another bystander that it is a bad idea to whip up a crowd with violent intent like this. The alderman does not, however, make any attempt to pacify the crowd.[94]

At General Stoneman's headquarters a small party of white citizens comes calling. They represent the Board of Mayor and Aldermen, they tell Stoneman, and they entreat him to authorize the use of his troops to suppress the rioting. The general finds an excuse to turn these supplicants away. Questioning them, he learns they have no official status. He tells them stiffly that he will not deal with "irresponsible persons," only those formally empowered to speak for the municipal authorities. Furthermore, he says, he will not honor any mere oral appeal. If the city fathers want his help, let the mayor make a request "in black and white." Such a petition, he promises, will "receive due attention."[95]

Some time after this party leaves, a messenger arrives at Stoneman's headquarters with a letter addressed to the general and signed by Mayor Park. Its correct, formal, legalistic prose suggests it comes from the pen of the city attorney or assistant attorney, not that of the rather unpolished and quite drunk mayor:

> General: There is an uneasiness in the public mind, growing out of the occurrences of to-day, which would be materially calmed if there was an assurance of military co-operation with the civil police in suppressing all disturbances of the public peace. I should be happy to have it in my power to give this assurance at once. It would intimidate the lawless, and serve to allay the apprehensions of the orderly. I therefore request that you will order a force of, say, two hundred men, commanded by discreet officers, to be held ready to co-operate with the constabulary force of the city in case of any further continued lawlessness.[96]

Stoneman can no longer dodge the issue. If the rioting is as serious, and the civil authorities as impotent, as he has been told, he could be severely censured for inaction. He sends a reply to the mayor approving the use of the regular troops to restore order. But he tries to avoid any further direct engagement with the matter by telling Park to decide for himself if troops should actually be called out and to apply directly to Captain Allyn for whatever force he wants, and he discourages Park from expecting or demanding too much from the troops.[97]

That done, Stoneman dispatches an order to Allyn, his first since the rioting began. He is unaware that Allyn has already intervened to the extent of sending out two patrols to disarm rioters. Not wanting to be bothered further about this matter by Allyn any more than by Park, he grants the captain broad authority and tells him to make his own decisions. Later he sends Allyn another order, directing him to guard the fort's armory well and have Colonel Kappner disarm any of the former soldiers of the 3rd who might still have their muskets.[98]

By ten o'clock there is not a living black person to be seen on the streets of Memphis from downtown to South Street. Most who reside in those wards are holed up fearfully in their homes; others have sought refuge elsewhere. Some have fled to Fort Pickering and have been given shelter there. From Beale southward the streets are pretty much deserted by whites, too. But downtown, crowds of excited white men are milling about.[99]

Captain Smyth and Lieutenant Clifford consider their task accomplished. The area they have patrolled, from South to Beale, is quiet now. They lead their squads back to the fort and report to Captain Allyn, who is satisfied that they have followed his orders and that the violence is at an end.[100]

Allyn is wrong about the violence. As Smyth and Clifford bring their troops back to the fort, the city police are making another descent on South Street.

Chief Garrett will not rest until the blacks in South Memphis are thoroughly under control. To accomplish this he has assembled, downtown, twenty or thirty of his officers. Also under his command is a posse of about the same strength, recruited by Sheriff Winters and Recorder Creighton. Winters has simply turned this posse over to Garrett; neither he nor Creighton choose to accompany it to South Memphis. The posse members are all or nearly all Irish, and all have guns.[101]

Garrett leads his combined force southward around ten o'clock. As they pass Beale and move on toward South they narrowly miss the retiring patrols of Smyth and Clifford. Garrett intends to keep his men under firm control: he does not want to preside over a homicidal mob like that he accompanied to South Street five hours ago, but rather to establish a police presence in South Memphis that will maintain order and suppress black unrest. There is plenty of light for this mission, even on the streets unlit by lamps, for the waning gibbous moon is high and still nearly full and the clouds have dissipated since this afternoon.[102]

Reaching South Street, Garrett finds it utterly quiet. He divides his force into small squads and orders them to patrol South and the streets nearby. Setting out noisily, they rouse some of the residents. One, a Yankee immigrant named J. S. Chapin, is bold enough to investigate. He steps outside, approaches some of the patrollers, and asks what they are about. We have come "to keep the peace," they tell him. But then he hears some of them say something about killing every black person they can find and burning down every black shanty on South Street. Alarmed, Chapin returns to his house and stays there.[103]

As the policemen and posse members disperse along the streets and disappear from Chief Garrett's view, whatever control he has exerted over them evaporates. Their lust for vengeance is unleashed. Finding no black people on the streets, they turn to those indoors.[104]

Twenty-four-year-old Lucy Tibbs hears a noise at the door of her home, a one-room shanty on Rayburn close to John Pendergrast's grocery. Her husband, a steamboat hand, is away. Her two children, ages one and four, are in bed asleep. She is pregnant with a third, conceived around last Christmas. Earlier today she saw Pendergrast murder Lewis Robinson.[105]

Several white men force open the door, enter the shanty, look around, and demand to know where her husband is. She tells them he is not home. "Please do not do anything to me," she begs; "I am just here with two little children."[106]

Her vulnerability excites one of the men. He pushes her down onto a bed. Another, who has noticed her swollen belly, tries to dissuade him, saying, "Let that woman alone . . . she [is] not in any situation to be doing that." The man ignores this admonition, and none of the others interfere as he rapes her. Fearing that the men will kill her if she resists, Tibbs submits quietly.[107]

The others stand around the bed watching or search the room for things to steal. One breaks into a locked trunk and finds $300 belonging to Tibbs's brother, a former soldier in the 59th Colored Infantry who has entrusted his savings to her care. Eventually the intruders leave, taking the money.[108]

The rest of Chief Garrett's peacekeepers are meanwhile breaking into other black homes and assaulting and robbing the occupants. In some cases they claim to be acting under orders to confiscate weapons, but mostly they do not bother to give any excuse.[109]

A gravely ill man named Shadrach Garrett is rousted from his bed by intruders, taken out to the street, and questioned. They accuse him of having been a soldier in the U.S. Colored Troops. It is not true, he protests; but he admits to being a civilian employee of the U.S. government. These are the last words he ever speaks. As his wife watches in horror, one of the whites raises his revolver and fires three bullets at close range into Garrett's head. Garrett falls to the ground, but is somehow still alive and conscious. As he writhes in the dust, one of the men tells him that if he does not hurry up and die they will shoot him again. Eventually one of them does, putting another bullet into his head that ends his suffering.[110]

Around midnight the sound of gunfire somewhere on South Street—perhaps the burst that has felled Shadrach Garrett—reaches Fort Pickering. Again Captain Smyth and Lieutenant Clifford are sent out with armed squads to restore order. Smyth goes to South Street, finds nothing amiss, and returns to the fort. Clifford encounters a crowd of fifteen or twenty armed white men on South. He confiscates a double-barreled shotgun from one, but when he orders the others to surrender their weapons they protest. Some claim to be policemen and display their badges; others insist they are members of a lawful posse that the sheriff has mustered to assist the police.[111]

Clifford relents, leaving all except the shotgun-wielder in possession of their weapons. Then, having heard no more gunfire, he leads his soldiers back westward on South and returns to the fort.[112]

The housebreakings, robberies, and assaults go on for hours before petering out. Chief Garrett goes back to the station house, leaving sixteen or eighteen policemen on South with directions to "preserve order." The posse members, dismissed or simply abandoned by Garrett, return to their homes.[113]

The sun breaks over the horizon a few minutes after five and slowly spreads its illumination. The scene is starkly different from other Wednesday mornings in Memphis. From downtown southward, the sidewalks and thoroughfares are devoid of the usual throngs of black people going to work.[114]

The public spaces in those districts are not altogether deserted by blacks. There are, in fact, quite a few to be seen—but they are dead, their friends and loved ones too scared to carry them away for burial. Lewis Robinson has grown cold on the bayou bank near Pendergrast's grocery. Shadrach Garrett lies crumpled on the street in front of his house. The rest occupy their own little plots, attended only by the flies that buzz around them. How long they will remain there, and whether they will be joined by others, no one can say.[115]

7

Fire

Wednesday, May 2, Early Morning to
Thursday, May 3, Dawn

As soon as Lavinia Godell rises she hurries to the gutter in front of Hollywood's grocery, where last night she had to abandon her badly wounded husband, Jackson. But he is not there; she finds only his hat. She picks it up and goes back home, distraught and unsure of what to do.[1]

A little later a friend of hers, a church sister, comes to her door. She tells Lavinia what she has learned of Jackson: he was put into a hack last night, still clinging to life, and taken away somewhere for medical treatment. She advises Lavinia to go to the police station downtown to see if anyone there knows where he is. It is possible that he was taken there, and that a doctor was summoned. Lavinia immediately sets out for the station house.[2]

As the sun climbs into a clear sky, Beale, South, and the other streets where the rioting occurred yesterday and last night remain quiet. Cautiously a few black people emerge from their places of shelter, hoping the terror is finally at an end. Some of the former soldiers of the 3rd who have stayed overnight in Fort Pickering now decide to take their chances outside. One is Tony Cherry, who was present yesterday afternoon at the shootout on the South Street bayou bridge that set off the rioting and barely escaped with his life when a mob appeared an hour and a half later. He is tired of holing up in the barracks. He tells one of his former sergeants that he intends to go out and the sergeant says he has no objection, for there seems to be no danger now. Some who leave the fort with Cherry plan to search for the bodies of their fellow soldiers who have been murdered.[3]

A few blocks east of the fort a freedman named Henry Porter watches from his residence on Rayburn Avenue near South Street, very close to John Pendergrast's grocery store, as a group of seventeen or eighteen black men in federal uniform approaches. They are looking for slain comrades, some of whom, including Lewis Robinson, still lie along the bayou nearby.[4]

Pendergrast has emerged from the store and as the men pass he stands brazenly on the porch watching them. The men, who are aware of Pendergrast's murderous role in the rioting, make some remark to him. Henry Porter cannot hear it, but he does hear Pendergrast's reply: "You had better go and get in your holes."[5]

The men walk down to the bayou and begin looking around. Pendergrast's mother calls to him from the house a few yards away where she, Pendergrast, and his father and one brother all live; his breakfast is ready, she says. He steps down from the porch and goes to the house. His mother comes over to tend the store. As Pendergrast is eating, the ex-soldiers come back. Two or three now have pistols in their hands. One calls out, loudly enough to be heard inside the store, where they assume Pendergrast is, "You have murdered our soldiers, and we intend to get you."[6]

There is no response, and the men soon move on. Henry Porter watches them go. He is certain that if Pendergrast had appeared at that moment they would have killed him.[7]

As the early morning hours pass, more black people appear on the streets of South Memphis. A few young ones even show up as usual at eight o'clock for their daily lessons at Horatio Rankin's schoolhouse on the corner of South and Causey. Among them, very probably, is star pupil Rachel Hatcher, who lives practically next door. Rankin, a black missionary from the North, is there to greet his students but immediately sends them home, telling them not to come back until tomorrow, for he fears there might be more rioting today. He then locks up the building and leaves.[8]

Lavinia Godell hurries northward toward the police station a half mile from her home. She enters the station building, which houses not only the police headquarters but also the city jail, the recorder's court, and the Freedmen's Bureau court. Both courts are in session, the former presided over, as usual, by John Creighton.[9]

At the desk inside the station entrance is assistant station-keeper and jailor W. G. McIlvain. Lavinia goes up to him and explains why she is there. His reply indicates that an injured black man was in fact brought in last night, and she begs him to let her see the man. McIlvain asks her to describe her husband. She does so, noting his short stature and his chin whiskers and the clothes he had on when he was attacked. McIlvain tells her that the man who was brought in fits that description but she cannot go downstairs to the jail in the basement, where the man lies, without permission from the chief station-keeper and jailor, M. H. Rieley, whom he points out. She goes over to Rieley. He says no. She pleads with him, but the answer is still no. She gives up and leaves the station.[10]

An Irishman who is there on some business has witnessed all this and taken pity on Lavinia. As she exits the building, he approaches her and says, "Aunty, you wait a little while, and I will see if you cannot go in." He disappears, and a few moments later calls to her from around a corner of the building. She follows his voice and finds him standing by a barred window at ground level through which a portion of the jail is visible. He indicates that she should look through the window. She peers in and sees Jackson's corpse.[11]

She returns to McIlvain's desk and tells him that she now knows that it is her husband in the basement and that he is dead. She wants to retrieve his body, but McIlvain refuses to let her. She asks him what the police intend to do with it. McIlvain continues to put her off. Desperate with grief and anger, she drops her humble demeanor and snaps at him: "After you have killed him you ought to give me the body." McIlvain is unmoved, and Lavinia leaves the station.[12]

On her way home she passes the Freedmen's Bureau headquarters. Black people have been coming here all morning, singly and in groups, pleading for protection in the event rioting breaks out again today. Superintendent Benjamin Runkle has had to tell them over and over that he is powerless; he has not a single armed soldier at his command.[13]

A Southern white man of Unionist sympathy was among Runkle's first callers this morning. He too expressed fear that rioting would erupt again today, and he urged Runkle to ask General Stoneman to mobilize troops to head off trouble. He also advised Runkle to get Stoneman to post a guard around the Freedmen's Bureau headquarters. Runkle was taken aback by this: surely, he replied, the mobs would not attack a place over which the United States flag flies. Indeed they might, the man responded; the flag would offer no protection from the kind of mobs he saw yesterday.[14]

Alarmed by this conversation, and sick at heart over having to turn away the helpless freed people whose welfare is entrusted to him, Runkle concludes that appealing to Stoneman is his best course. He mounts up and rides a mile north to the general's headquarters. As he enters he sees Stoneman come down the stairs from his private quarters and speak to his adjutant.[15]

The general has reconsidered matters since yesterday and decided that he must act more forcefully to suppress disorder. He tells his adjutant to dispatch two messages to Fort Pickering, one to Captain Allyn and one to Colonel Kappner. Allyn is to be instructed to maintain a patrol of fifty men, day and night, in the area from Beale to South streets, and to use the rest of his troops (those, that is, not needed to guard government property) to keep the ex-soldiers of the 3rd inside the fort. Kappner is to be told not to let any of his men out of the fort today.[16]

When Runkle is summoned to state his business, he tells Stoneman what he has seen and heard this morning and asks the general to assign him a force of soldiers with which he can protect the city's freed people, guard the Bureau headquarters, and apprehend lawless whites. A thrice-wounded combat veteran who ended his three years of active service as a brevet brigadier general, Runkle has no doubt of his ability to command troops in perilous circumstances. But Stoneman demurs, citing—as he did repeatedly when appealed to yesterday—the paucity of troops and the large amount of government property to be guarded. And now he proffers yet another argument: many of the soldiers of the

16th are of doubtful dependability in this situation, he tells Runkle, for they despise the freedmen no less than the rioters do.[17]

Runkle does extract from the general a promise to assign a sergeant and ten men to guard the Bureau headquarters. Runkle returns to his office, where more black people are waiting anxiously to see him. He tells them he can do nothing to protect them. Just go home, he says, and stay off the streets. Surely, he adds, the U.S. government will "at least redress [your] wrongs after the riot [is] over."[18]

The morning newspapers have dramatic accounts of yesterday's violence—mostly inaccurate, in some respects wildly so. The *Argus* and the *Avalanche* hold the freed people and their Radical friends completely responsible. What happened was an unprovoked black assault on innocent whites, as those papers tell it. "There can be no mistake about it," says the *Argus*, "the whole blame of this most tragical and bloody riot lies . . . with the poor, ignorant, deluded blacks," who "have been led into their present evil and unhappy ways by men of our own race." Under the headline THE LAW OUTRAGED BY NEGROES, the *Avalanche* declares that "the police deserve the very highest credit for the gallant conduct they exhibited in enforcing the majesty of the law when the messengers of death were hurled at them on all sides. . . . Our noble policemen are towers of might and purpose and courage."[19]

Around midmorning rumors of more trouble in South Memphis begin circulating downtown. They are baseless, for the area has remained quiet, but most whites are willing to believe them. One rumor has it that blacks are gathering with belligerent intent, determined "to resist the police to the death." Another says two white men have been shot by blacks while walking down South Street; a variant identifies the two as policemen. Yet another rumor claims that blacks have taken control of Fort Pickering's armory and seized four hundred muskets. Sheriff Winters is told at nine o'clock that armed black men have emerged from the fort and are "killing everybody."[20]

The downtown streets begin filling with excited white men, some carrying weapons. All the courts in session are abruptly adjourned. In the Greenlaw Building on Second Street at Union, which houses the offices of the county government officials, Judge Thomas Leonard orders Sheriff Winters to recruit a posse of five hundred to put down the black uprising. Winters begins enlisting men. The first twenty-five he gathers he turns over to one of his deputies, J. T. Sanford, and tells him to lead them to South Memphis and arrest everyone engaged in rioting. Winters subsequently rounds up another thirty or forty men and turns them over to district attorney general William Wallace with the same instructions. Few if any of the men in either of these posses are armed.[21]

Inside Fort Pickering, Captain Allyn is assembling forty of his soldiers for guard duty at the navy yard, a mile and a half to the north. Stoneman's order to patrol the streets from South to Beale has not yet reached him, but he has decided on his own that it would be a good idea to look around that area on his way to the navy yard.[22]

At nine twenty he mounts a horse and leads his infantrymen out of the fort. They go east on South Street as far as Causey, where they turn left and proceed northward, past the Diltses' house. Rachael and Ellen Dilts watch as they march by. Reaching Beale Street, the soldiers turn left. It is now about quarter to ten. At no point along the route has Allyn seen any hint of trouble.[23]

As the soldiers head west on Beale, a man on horseback rides up and tells Allyn that black rioting has erupted in South Memphis and that the mayor wants to see him about it. Allyn is skeptical; he knows that that area was quiet a few minutes ago. He wonders if the city's whites are planning to provoke trouble. Whatever the case, he needs to consult with the civil authorities. Turning the troops over to a sergeant with orders to go on to the navy yard, he gallops off toward city hall.[24]

The rumors of black violence have reached police chief Garrett, too, and he has hurriedly assembled all the members of his force he can round up, amounting to two or three dozen. As soon as they are gathered, he marches them toward South Memphis.[25]

As this police squad and the posses under Sanford and Wallace move from downtown southward, other white men gravitate in the same direction. Most are just curious, but some are intent on mayhem.

B.F.C. Brooks, a Southern Unionist and editor of the *Memphis Republican*, is watching as they pass. One of them, a man whom Brooks knows and regards as a dangerous sort, comes up to him and asks tauntingly how many "niggers" he has killed. Brooks replies stiffly that he is not involved in that. "By God," says the man, "I have killed five." Pulling some buckshot from his pocket and displaying it in his hand, he adds, "This is the kind of balls I do it with." Before moving on with the crowd, he tells Brooks that he is "going to kill some more of them."[26]

Tagging along behind Chief Garrett and his policemen now are four or five citizens on horseback and fifteen or more on foot; many of these men, perhaps all, are armed. Rachael and Ellen Dilts are still watching from their house. It is close to ten o'clock. The policemen, Ellen notices, appear to be angry and are talking excitedly among themselves. She notes, too, that it has been just twenty minutes since the force of U.S. troops passed by, marching in the opposite direction.[27]

When Chief Garrett arrives at South Street a couple of minutes later, quite a few black people can be seen there, going about their business. Garrett's followers break up into small bands and spread out, weapons in hand. He quickly loses whatever control over them he may have intended to exercise, just as he did yesterday afternoon and last night. As they fan out, they call to each other and point: "There's one . . . there's another." Volleys of pistol fire ring out with every call. The blacks who are not gunned down run for their lives. One is Tony Cherry, who flees back to the fort after seeing a black man shot and clubbed.[28]

Some of the armed whites make their way a short distance east to Rayburn Avenue. Among them is policeman David Roach. A friend of his is with him, a drayman named Galloway. Both are carrying revolvers. Watching from inside her shanty is Lucy Tibbs, who was raped last night. Also watching from inside his home is Henry Porter, who witnessed the verbal encounter between John Pendergrast and the black soldiers earlier this morning.[29]

Roach and Galloway spot two black men in uniform and go after them. One escapes, but the other they catch and hold. Roach shoves him up against the front gate of a house and accuses him of being one of the "damned rascal[s]" involved in the shootout with the police at the bayou bridge yesterday afternoon. "I was not in it at all," the man replies desperately; "please don't kill me." Roach—who was not present at the shootout—says, "Yes, you were," and fires a bullet into the man's leg. The man does not suffer long: Galloway comes up to him, puts the muzzle of his pistol to his head, and fires a bullet through his brain.[30]

Galloway and Roach leave their victim where he falls and go off in search of others. Henry Porter slips out of his home and makes his way to the fort along with some black soldiers who have managed to evade the mob.[31]

Inside a dwelling next door to Lucy Tibbs's is forty-year-old Fayette Dickerson, a former slave and a veteran of the 15th Colored Infantry. He lives there with his wife, but she is not with him now: she left yesterday to take refuge in the fort. Dickerson has hidden from the rioters who have suddenly appeared on his street, but some of them know he is there. They gather outside his door and call to him to come out. Among them are the men of the Pendergrast clan, who have emerged from their nearby house and grocery at the sound of gunfire.[32]

Dickerson obeys the summons, but no sooner does he step outside than he darts away, running into the yard of another home nearby. He gets no farther: gunshots ring out and he falls. "Damn you," says one of the whites, "that will show you [not] to leave your old mistress and master." His assailants search him, take twenty-five dollars from his pocket, and move on. He is alive, but a bullet has pierced his abdomen— an almost certain sentence of death.[33]

Captain Allyn has met with some frustration in his attempt to see the mayor. Park is not in his office at city hall. Allyn finally tracks him down at the Greenlaw Building, where he has gone to consult with county officials. Their meeting is unfruitful: Park makes it clear to Allyn that the situation demands a forceful response by the civil authorities, but he insists that the trouble is all south of South Street, beyond the city limits and therefore out of his jurisdiction. Sheriff Winters must take charge.[34]

Having thus absolved himself of any official responsibility, the mayor heads off to South Memphis to see what he can do unofficially. Allyn goes to see the sheriff, who is in the building. Winters asks him to provide troops to help restore order. Allyn is willing to do so, having been granted that authority yesterday by General Stoneman; but he wants a written request, for the record. The sheriff scribbles a one-sentence petition on a piece of paper and hands it to him.[35]

Stoneman's order of yesterday instructed Allyn to deploy troops only at the request of the civil authorities and "mainly to assist" them. Allyn therefore considers himself to be acting now under the sheriff's command. Winters does not want Allyn's troops to go directly to the scene of the rioting, probably because he is not sure exactly where that is. He tells Allyn to dispatch them instead to the Beale Street market, where he will meet them in one hour and give further orders. Allyn leaves the building, mounts up, and gallops away toward Fort Pickering.[36]

Tony Cherry has made it safely to the fort. He goes up onto the northern section of the parapet and looks out to the east. The rioters have by now spread several blocks southward from South Street and westward as far as the Mississippi and Tennessee Railroad track. They are roaming among the black cabins and shanties with guns in hand. Every sighting of a black man brings cries of "Halt!" and "Shoot him!" usually followed by gunfire. Blacks lucky enough to evade the bullets are scattering in every direction.[37]

The policemen and citizens led to South Memphis by Chief Garrett have by now been reinforced by other armed white men. At a point just south of South Street and close to the Mississippi and Tennessee depot, a crowd of fifty or more has surrounded a uniformed black man. He has tried to escape, but now, seeing that that is impossible, he turns and moves toward his pursuers with his arms outstretched in surrender and supplication. A white citizen steps up and slams him in the head with the butt of a pistol. Then a policeman comes forward wielding a carbine as a club and hits him in the head so hard that the gun's stock shatters. The man falls. Four or five other men in the crowd step up and fire their pistols into the prostrate body.[38]

Deputy Sheriff Sanford has arrived with his posse near South Street. He sees and hears the mob going about its bloody work and decides instantly that there is nothing he can accomplish with his two dozen unarmed citizens. He dismisses them and returns downtown to tell the sheriff of his aborted mission.[39]

Attorney General Wallace is not yet on the scene with his posse, for he recognizes the pointlessness of trying to suppress disorder with an unarmed force and is determined to go to South Memphis with some firepower. Making his way to Folsome and Company, a downtown store well stocked with guns and ammunition, he calls on the proprietors for help. They are happy to cooperate. When Wallace's posse marches away down Main Street some time later, each man is equipped with powder, lead, and a rifle or double-barreled shotgun.[40]

By now the fort's northern parapet is crowded with several hundred former soldiers of the 3rd, watching the slaughter in the streets. Some decide they must do something. Nine men slip over the parapet and down to the ground and then move eastward. Two have somehow gotten hold of muskets, and the others have revolvers. Reaching a point about halfway between the fort and the railroad depot and taking position behind a fence, they open fire on the white rioters within their view. Tony Cherry, who is not among the nine but is watching from the parapet, sees the whites run for shelter as they realize they are being shot at. He and the others on the parapet cheer.[41]

This counterattack is short-lived, however. In a few minutes the nine run low on ammunition. They retreat back to the fort, firing the last of their bullets as they go. There is no further firing by any blacks. No whites have been hit.[42]

Captain Allyn has arrived at the fort and has hurriedly set about mustering the men of his regiment. Only about forty-five are available, for the day-guard squad has gone to the navy yard and the night-guard squad has not yet returned from there. Allyn has decided to exercise direct command of this little force. It is about ten thirty when he leads it at the double-quick toward the Beale Street market, where the sheriff has promised to meet them. There are no soldiers of the 16th left in the fort now except some officers.[43]

Not all the whites who have made their way individually to South Memphis have joined the mob. Several hundred have come simply to see what is going on. The mayor and some other city officers are with them. Park has been drinking, but is less drunk than he was yesterday.

He is strutting around, telling those in the crowd to "let it alone," that he will "straighten out the whole thing" and "make it all right." His blustering has no apparent effect.[44]

The brief spate of firing by the nine black soldiers outside the fort has sparked fear among the spectators that those in the fort are about to launch an all-out assault on white Memphis. A rumor is going around that the white troops have turned over their muskets to the blacks. The mayor decides to intervene. Accompanied by a few other officials and some armed citizens, he approaches the fort's north gate. The presence of hundreds of black men on the parapet persuades him that entering the fort would be unwise; instead, he sends a message requesting that Colonel Kappner meet him outside.[45]

Kappner soon emerges from the gate, driving a buggy. Captain William Smyth of the 16th accompanies him on horseback. The mayor greets Kappner brusquely: "I want to know if you have any control over your men," he demands, "and if the firing will be stopped or not." Kappner replies that he no longer has any formal authority over the men of the 3rd and that they are seething with anger over the white mobs' assaults on their friends and families; he is not sure he can control them. "That will not do," says Park; "you must go there and stop this; I cannot keep the people back unless you stop this." As they talk, a drunken man accompanying the mayor points his rifle at Captain Smyth; another man in the mayor's entourage silently reaches over and pushes the barrel down. The brief meeting concludes with a promise by the colonel to do what he can to prevent any more shooting by blacks and to keep the men inside the fort, and a promise by the mayor that if Kappner succeeds there will be no more white violence.[46]

Kappner returns to the fort and endeavors to keep his word. Besides the black soldiers on the parapet there are a thousand or so in the fort, along with hundreds of other black Memphians—men, women, and children—who have fled their homes to escape the mob. They are clustered in groups, talking anxiously. Kappner tells them of his agreement with the mayor and pleads with them to remain in the fort. Some of the men protest: give us weapons, they say, with which we can rescue our brethren outside or at least defend ourselves if the mob attacks the fort. But Kappner insists that taking up arms "could do no good" and that the violence will cease if they will just "keep quiet."[47]

Only now does the order from General Stoneman's adjutant to Captain Allyn, instructing him to keep the black soldiers in the fort, arrive at Allyn's headquarters. Captain Smyth receives it and responds promptly. He urges those on the parapet and on the grounds to return to their barracks and stay there. They do so without further protest, even though Smyth has no authority over them and no troops with which to enforce obedience. By eleven o'clock or so all the black soldiers are in their quarters.[48]

The rioters have not finished their work, and the mayor is powerless to stop them no matter what he has promised Kappner. Near the corner of South and Rayburn, two pistol-wielding men enter a shanty where a married freedwoman named Harriet Armour lives. Claiming authority to confiscate weapons, they search the place. Where is your husband? they ask. In the fort, she answers. "Is he a soldier?" "Yes." One man says to the other, "Shut the door." They take turns raping her. One of them, a man of about twenty apparently named Dunn, rapes her twice. She submits quietly, fearing that if she tries to get away or calls for help they will kill her. Finishing his second assault, Dunn brandishes his revolver and tells her to suck him. She begins to cry. That is no use, says Dunn; there is no avoiding it, you "must do it." She continues to cry, and eventually the men leave.[49]

Captain Allyn and his force of regulars stand around uselessly at the Beale Street market for forty-five minutes waiting for Sheriff Winters. He finally arrives, on horseback. Together they march to South.[50]

Winters sees no evidence of the black rioting he has been hearing rumors of for the last two and a half hours. The first trouble he encounters is a crowd of whites on South Street crying "Shoot him, shoot him" as an unarmed, uniformed black man is led toward them by a policeman and a citizen. Winters rides up to the crowd and announces that he is there to preserve order and protect innocent parties and will arrest anybody, white or black, who disturbs the peace. He then takes custody of the black man, escorts him to his home—a cabin fifty yards away—and tells him to stay inside.[51]

Allyn devises a plan for his troops to sweep the area and requests that the civil authorities keep the crowd of spectators north of South Street. But before he can put his infantrymen in motion he receives Stoneman's order to send a detachment of one sergeant and ten men to guard the Freedmen's Bureau office. He obeys promptly. The departure of these men reduces his force to about thirty-five.[52]

Attorney General Wallace and his rifle- and shotgun-armed posse have arrived at South Street. The sheriff takes command of this force and tells Wallace to collect men in the crowd of onlookers who are carrying pistols and form them into another posse. Wallace musters thirty or forty and takes charge of them.[53]

With two armed sheriff's posses and Allyn's regulars on the scene, Chief Garrett and Mayor Park decide to get the police out of there. Garrett gathers up all the policemen he can, and he and Park lead them away toward the station house downtown.[54]

It is now about noon. Allyn gives First Lieutenant Walter Clifford command of twelve of the men and assigns him the area between the fort and the railroad. Both his squad and Clifford's start to move. They find no armed blacks, only the dead bodies of black men, at least eight of them, and a number of black women, children, and old men huddled in terror inside their dwellings. Many of the children are crying.[55]

Few rioters are to be found by now, for most of the policemen have departed with Garrett and Park, and many of their citizen allies have fled at the sight of the heavily armed infantrymen. Allyn and his squad encounter no rioters at all. Meanwhile, Clifford and his men come upon a group breaking into black people's homes. When Clifford confronts them, all but two claim to be policemen acting under orders to search for weapons. He tells these men to leave, then arrests the other two and seizes the shotguns they are carrying.[56]

As the soldiers execute their dragnet, Sheriff Winters orders the large crowd of spectators hanging around the intersection of Main and South to go home. He then leads his posse east on South, intending to patrol the area beyond that being swept by Allyn's troops. Reaching Hernando Street, he spots trouble. A group of ten whites has surrounded four black men, one of whom they are beating on the head. Winters gallops up and orders the whites to desist and to release the blacks. He then directs two members of his posse to escort the blacks to a tract of woods some distance away and let them go.[57]

Clifford takes the two men he has arrested to the intersection of

Main and South, intending to turn them over to the civil authorities as ordered. He looks around for the sheriff but fails to find him, unaware that Winters has left with his posse; nor are the police chief and mayor to be found, for they have returned downtown. Attorney General Wallace is close by, but Clifford either does not see him or does not recognize him as a civil official.[58]

Eventually Clifford encounters a tall man on horseback who appears to be in a position of authority and who identifies himself as Recorder Creighton. Clifford produces the two prisoners. Creighton looks at them and declares that they are in fact policemen. He accepts custody of them and promptly lets them go.[59]

As Clifford starts to make his way back to his troops, Creighton rises in his stirrups and delivers an impromptu speech to the crowd gathered around. The recorder promises—as he did before another crowd yesterday—that no white man brought before his court for carrying weapons will be punished. He then declares his intention to kill every "God damned nigger" he can find. The crowd cheers. Lieutenant Clifford listens, then returns to his troops.[60]

As Captain Allyn's squad completes its sweep, Allyn receives a message to report to General Stoneman's headquarters. He rides to the corner of Main and South. Nearby, Attorney General Wallace is speaking to a crowd of men, telling them to arm and organize themselves. Spotting Allyn, Wallace comes over and asks if the area south of South Street is now quiet. Allyn assures him that it is and urges Wallace to disperse the men assembled here. Allyn himself announces to the crowd that the trouble is over and advises everyone to go home.[61]

It is now about one o'clock. The throng of spectators gradually breaks up and drifts back toward downtown. Wallace leads his posse away in the same direction. Captain Allyn stays around the intersection of Main and South until he is satisfied that the trouble is over, and then rides to Stoneman's headquarters.[62]

Sheriff Winters, at the corner of Hernando and South, has concluded that that area is pacified and that his duty is done for now. He tells his posse to go home. But fearing that nightfall will bring another outbreak of violence, he instructs the men to reassemble at his office in the Greenlaw Building at six o'clock.[63]

All of the city north of South Memphis has remained free of violence so far today, unlike yesterday and last night, and the hysteria whipped up by this morning's rumors has dissipated. People downtown, white and black alike, are by now going about their business pretty much as usual. At the Frank Saloon in Bank Alley, the proprietor, a German-Swiss immigrant named John Myers, is busily serving his customers, some of whom have undoubtedly just returned from South Memphis, where they were among the spectators, posse members, or rioters.[64]

Spotting a black man he recognizes who is passing by outside, Myers hails him and invites him in for a drink—meaning a drink of water, for Myers knows that the man is working and in any event he would not welcome a black into his place as a customer. The man's name is Reuben; he is a barber who has a shop a few blocks away, and he occasionally does odd jobs for Myers. Reuben accepts this opportunity for a bit of rest and refreshment and enters the saloon.[65]

Soon after, a white man named Ben Dennis comes in and steps up to the bar. He too knows and likes Reuben, and the two begin chatting. Dennis is a Maryland native but a longtime resident of Memphis. He made a living as a millwright before the war, served in the Confederate army, and lately has worked as a steamboat hand. As the two men talk, Dennis, who is drinking something considerably stronger than what Reuben is drinking, grows jolly and expansive. Patting Reuben on the back, he tells some of the other patrons that this "boy . . . has shaved me many a time. I have as much confidence in him as I have in any one, and were I compelled to ask a favor to-morrow, he is the first I should go to."[66]

An Irishman named Michael Kenan is seated nearby eating a meal. He is a fireman, a member of the hook-and-ladder company. Overhearing Dennis's remark, he rises abruptly from his seat and confronts him. "What did you say?" he demands. "I did not mean any harm," Dennis replies. "This is no time to be talking to niggers," Kenan tells him. "This is no bad man," Dennis insists; "I've known him for years." "By God," says Kenan, "this is no time to be talking to niggers." He pulls out a pistol, slams Dennis in the head with it, and then fires a bullet into his chest. As Dennis collapses to the floor, he manages to call out to the proprietor, "John, I am shot."[67]

Kenan flees out the door and disappears down the alley. The bullet has penetrated Dennis's heart. He lives only a few minutes.[68]

Not long after two o'clock Ellen Dilts sees a small group of white men pass her house on Causey, going northward. They are close enough for her to hear their conversation. One remarks to another, who looks to Ellen like an Irishman, that he appears to be quite warm. Indeed, the man replies, he has "been at warm work." The others ask him what he means. He tells them he has been "setting a nigger school-house on fire."[69]

As the men continue on up Causey, Ellen leaves her house and goes in the opposite direction, toward South, to investigate. There, on the corner, she sees Horatio Rankin's school engulfed in flames.[70]

A crowd of whites and blacks gathers at the scene. Among them is Rankin himself, who has rushed there on learning of the fire. Nothing can be done now, however; the fire is too far advanced to be put out. As Rankin stands there watching, a white man comes up to him and asks tauntingly what he is going to do now that he has no school.[71]

The building is owned by the black Methodist church, but the furnishings and textbooks inside have been paid for by Rankin and his Northern patrons. Also being devoured by the flames is a set of lighters and ladders used to light the gas streetlamps each evening in this part of town; Rankin allows the city authorities to store them in the schoolhouse. The only light on the streets of South Memphis tonight will be that provided by the moon—unless there are more fires.[72]

The flames emanating from the schoolhouse are igniting nearby houses and shanties, or threatening to, and frantic efforts are under way to save them. Most endangered is the house of an elderly freedman named Adam Lock only eight or ten feet from the school. Lock's son-in-law, some black neighbors, and several white men in the crowd come to his aid. Women fetch buckets of well water; men get up on the roof to douse the flames. The men also tear down and remove the wall of the house nearest the school to keep the fire from spreading farther. As they work, Lock hauls his belongings out of the house and piles them in the street.[73]

Joining the efforts to save other nearby structures around the school is a squad of the 16th regulars, a dozen men commanded by Captain Smyth. They were sent out from the fort a little while ago by Allyn with orders to keep white men out of South Memphis, and were not far from the school when Smyth noticed the column of smoke and decided to investigate.[74]

Allyn, whose meeting with Stoneman was of no consequence, is now back in the fort. He has just learned of the fire, and orders Clifford to muster the rest of the troops and hurry to the scene. He then mounts up and rides there himself, finding the schoolhouse burned nearly to the ground. Several of the nearby dwellings have also been destroyed; but others, including Lock's, have been saved.[75]

By three o'clock or so the danger from the fires has subsided and the crowd disperses. Lock moves his belongings back into his house. But fearing more trouble tonight, he bundles up the smaller items in sheets and blankets, ready for quick removal. Eventually a fire engine arrives at the schoolhouse. There is nothing for the firemen to do now, of course, except dampen the smoldering rubble. But they cannot do even that, for there is no useful source of water here. The nearest public cistern is several blocks away.[76]

Few firemen are actually on duty this afternoon, for nearly all have turned out for the funeral of their comrade Henry Dunn, who died yesterday after being shot through the head on Rayburn Avenue. The firemen have assembled in uniform at Dunn's house, just south of the Beale Street market, where a hearse waits with the coffin. Joining them are many policemen, a good number of aldermen and other city officials, and a large assembly of ordinary citizens. Led by a band playing solemn music and accompanied by Dunn's grieving wife and children, the cortege leaves the house at about four o'clock and proceeds to the cemetery. There, with eulogies, dirges, and prayers, Dunn's body is interred.[77]

Few if any of those at the funeral know that the bullet that killed Henry Dunn was fired by John Pendergrast. It is taken for granted that Dunn died at the hands of black men. The afternoon newspapers have reported this as fact; indeed, like the morning papers (except the *Post*), they depict nearly all of yesterday's and last night's rioting as unprovoked black assaults on innocent whites who were forced to defend themselves. The *Public Ledger* gives details of the violence and urges that the city's freedmen be disarmed. The *Appeal*, decrying the "lawless aggression on the part of the vicious negroes infesting South Memphis," insists that "more stringent measures [be] adopted to either force them to behave themselves or leave the city."[78]

Rumors are going around that there will be more trouble tonight. These differ significantly from the rumors that agitated the city yesterday and this morning. Tonight's violence, it is said, will be perpetrated by whites—particularly firemen and policemen, who are reportedly seething with rage over the killing of their comrades yesterday. Black neighborhoods will be destroyed by fire, and freedmen slaughtered. Blacks will not be the only victims: their Yankee friends, too, will be murdered or driven from the city. The office of the *Memphis Post* will be torched or blown up.[79]

The Reverend Ewing O. Tade is taking these reports seriously. As a Yankee devoted to uplifting the freed people, he has long been a marked man in Memphis. He will not abandon his post, he decides, but will take precautions. He removes his most valued possessions from his house and distributes them among friends for safekeeping. If he is burned out tonight, he will not lose everything. What might happen to Lincoln Chapel, his church and school, is another matter.[80]

South Memphis has remained quiet since the schoolhouse fire. Around five o'clock, Captain Allyn, now back at the fort, sends orders to Smyth and Clifford to bring in their detachments. He wants the troops to get some sleep, for they must do guard duty tomorrow. He posts a few soldiers outside the fort with orders to prevent the men of the 3rd inside from leaving. He knows that many of those men have families in South Memphis and will try to go to them tonight if they can.[81]

Allyn thus obeys part of the order General Stoneman sent him early this morning, but he ignores the other part—to maintain a patrol of fifty men, night and day, in the area from Beale to South. With the night guard sent off as required to the navy yard and others of his men exhausted by their labors today, Allyn does not have fifty men fit for patrol duty.

At six o'clock, some members of the posse that Sheriff Winters led earlier today dutifully appear at his office as he instructed them to do when he dismissed them. He then recruits more men on the streets, bringing the total to nearly four dozen, and arms each one with a double-barreled shotgun. At eight o'clock he leads this posse down to South Street. It is very dark, for the sun set about six forty-five, the moon will not rise until nine twenty, and there are no streetlamps lit in this part of town tonight. It is also very quiet. There is hardly any-one on the streets of South Memphis, and no black people at all.[82]

North of South Memphis, however, there is increasing unrest. Around nine o'clock, at her home on Gayoso, Mrs. Samuel Cooper hears gun-shots. A crowd of white men has assembled close by and some are fir-ing pistols into the air. Cooper's four children are with her, but her husband is not home. She is frightened, for her husband, a Northerner like herself, is a friend of the freed people. He has addressed them in their churches, has rented rooms to them in a former army barracks that he bought from the government, and has worked closely with another Yankee immigrant, named Glasgow, who served in the Union army and now teaches in a school for blacks.[83]

Suspecting that the men gathered outside are after her husband, Cooper musters her courage and goes out to confront them. She sees that several are policemen. "What are you about[?]" she asks. "I have done nothing to you, nor have my children."[84]

An Irish policeman named Shurlin speaks for the crowd. He tells Cooper that they will not hurt her or the children, but her husband is another matter. They cannot tolerate a man who "gets up and talks to the colored people, and tells them that they are as good as white men." They will not allow a "damn abolitionist" to live here. If they get hold of him or his friend Glasgow they will kill them. They intend, further-more, to drive every black person out of Memphis.[85]

Cooper bravely stands her ground. "If you injure my husband," she says, "you injure me." And as for their threats against the blacks, "I do not know how you will live if you drive the colored people away, for one-half you get you get out of the colored people."[86]

Shurlin replies that whites got along just fine in this city before the freed slaves flocked to it, and will do the same after they are gone. And she had better move out of her house, he adds, because he and his friends intend to burn it down tomorrow night. Finally he and the others go off, assuring Cooper that they will be back tomorrow with more men.[87]

Near a fire station downtown, another crowd of whites has gathered. This is a large assembly, a hundred men or more. Walking together on the sidewalk nearby are Matthew C. Gallaway, coproprietor and editor-in-chief of the *Avalanche*, and M. W. Cluskey, one of his assistant editors. Recognizing Gallaway, the crowd gathers around him and begins cheering; several men try to hoist him on their shoulders, but he declines the honor.[88]

The cheers quickly turn to calls for action: "Let's go for the *Post*." Gallaway and Cluskey are appalled. "That won't do," they tell the men. They plead with them to let the Republican paper be.[89]

The crowd's excitement does not abate. A black man passes nearby, and three pistol shots ring out: some in the crowd have fired at him, but he escapes unharmed. The crowd grows larger. Cluskey suggests to Gallaway that they get out of there. Gallaway agrees, and the two hasten away.[90]

On Gayoso Street, not far from Mrs. Cooper's house, a group of twenty or so pistol-wielding white men approaches the home of a freed couple, Hannah and Solon Robinson. The Robinsons and a number of relatives and friends are inside. Among the whites are several policemen—one of them David Roach, whose lust for vengeance on black Memphians is still unsated.[91]

The men do not knock but simply break down the bolted door. Roach and some of the others crowd inside. Cursing the "God damned niggers" cowering before them, they search the dwelling, steal money hidden in a trunk, and assault Hannah and her son-in-law, knocking them down. Hannah fears that the men intend to kill them all, but eventually they leave without doing any more harm. As they go, Hannah hears Roach boast, "It is [the] white man's day now."[92]

From the Robinsons' home, Roach and his comrades make their way two blocks north to Monroe Street. They spot a black man and pounce. As they pummel him he breaks away and runs into a nearby saloon. He no doubt hopes to find refuge there, for it is the saloon of

Robert Church, one of the city's most prominent and prosperous freedmen. But Roach and the others follow him inside. There they pull out their pistols and start shooting.[93]

Twelve or fifteen bullets are fired, two of which hit Robert Church, one in the neck and one in the arm. The wounds are bad but not fatal. Church remains conscious as the whites put away their weapons and proceed to loot the place. It is a nicely furnished and well-stocked establishment, a billiard saloon that serves a white clientele. Some of the men ransacking it are, in fact, regular customers. The intruders help themselves to whiskey and cigars, then break into the cash drawer and take $290. They stay quite a while, drinking and smoking. When they leave, they pour what little whiskey remains onto the floor.[94]

Sheriff Winters and his posse march east on South Street to Desoto, where they turn left and head north. Winters has seen nothing this evening to suggest that trouble is brewing, or at least trouble serious enough to demand his attention, so he leads the posse back downtown. Here and there along the way he encounters groups of drunken white men. They do not seem particularly threatening, in Winters's estimation. He simply orders them to disperse and continues on his way.[95]

Around ten o'clock Reverend Tade and his wife settle into bed for the night. Suddenly a bright light illuminates the interior of their house through the back window. Tade gets up, goes to the window, and sees a building on fire not far away. It is a former army barracks at the corner of South and Hernando, now used as a freedmen's school.[96]

The flames are visible also from the parapet of Fort Pickering, a half mile west. Someone there eventually notices them and raises the alarm. When Allyn is informed, he is not altogether surprised; he has half expected more trouble tonight and would certainly have kept up a patrol if his men were not so exhausted. Now, he decides, he has no choice. He orders Smyth to rouse the troops, take command of all but a couple of dozen, and lead them to the scene of the fire. Besides fighting that fire, the soldiers are to try to prevent others from being set:

they are to scout around South Memphis, disperse all crowds, and arrest anyone caught in the act of arson.[97]

Smyth, assisted by Lieutenant Clifford, soon has the men ready. They leave the fort and see more fires in the direction they are marching.[98]

The sheriff and his posse make their way to the police station on Adams, arriving about eleven. Leaving the posse there, Winters goes to the *Memphis Commercial* office next door to give a report on what he has seen and done today.[99]

The clanging of a fire bell abruptly intrudes on the sheriff's visit. He rushes back to the station house. After some delay, he learns that a black schoolhouse at Hernando and Pontotoc is on fire. He gathers his men and leads them in that direction.[100]

As they reach Beale, a fire engine goes by. Winters is puzzled to see that it is going toward downtown and away from the reported location of the fire. But he makes no inquiries, and he and his men continue on their way.[101]

By the time they arrive at Hernando and Pontotoc, the schoolhouse is engulfed in flames. This fire was set about ten thirty, a half hour after the one that by now has leveled the schoolhouse at South and Hernando, a quarter mile to the south. There being no source of water suitable for a steam pump at either location, the fire engine that was summoned turned back.[102]

A sizeable crowd of white men is gathered around watching the fire as Winters and his men arrive, a crowd that includes some policemen and Recorder Creighton. The recorder and many of the others are drunk and jubilantly celebrating the fiery obliteration of this institution of black learning—and black worship, for it doubles as a meetinghouse known as Grace Church.[103]

The sheriff and his men stand around watching until midnight, by which time the schoolhouse is reduced to ash and embers. To the south, fires are clearly visible in the area of South Street. But Winters chooses not to go there; perhaps he and his men feel too exhausted to be of any use. He forms them up and leads them north.[104]

———

A mile to the northeast, on Washington Street near the intersection with Orleans, flames have erupted from yet another building, an imposing structure of brick and wood thirty feet tall. It is Collins Chapel, a black church founded before the war and affiliated with the Methodist Episcopal Church, South. Since the war its basement has been used as a school for freed people.[105]

This site, in the Eighth Ward near the city's eastern limit and nearly a mile from the heart of downtown, is far from any of the other scenes of violence of the past thirty-two hours. Water is available here, but the two engine companies that respond, horses at the gallop and steam whistles shrieking, arrive too late to be of any use. The building is destroyed.[106]

At the corner of Main and Vance fifteen or more Irishmen, all armed, are gathered beside a U.S. government–owned building used as a freedmen's school and church. Leading this gang is a county constable named William O'Hearn. He and two others stuff a mass of combustible material under one corner of the building and put a match to it. It catches fire, but the flames soon peter out.[107]

Just then a voice is heard, desperate and pleading. A white man who lives next door is begging the crowd not to torch the building for fear the flames will spread to his place. The Irishmen ignore him. The man hops over the fence separating the two lots and approaches them. O'Hearn tells one of his gang to "shoot the Goddamned son of a bitch if he interferes." The man hears this and retreats to his house.[108]

O'Hearn relights the fire. This time it does not fail. When one end of the building is burning well, the men go to the other end, smash a window, and throw in more combustibles along with a lit match. Then they break down a portion of a wall to further vent the fire. Soon the whole structure is burning vigorously.[109]

One of the men offers a benediction: "May the mon that sit that on fire niver be sick. God bless him." Others declare their intention to burn "every nigger building, every nigger church, and every God damn son of a bitch that [teaches] a nigger." There is talk, too, of visiting the same retribution on the *Memphis Post*. If they had the *Post*'s editor here in their hands, they say, they would throw him into the fire.[110]

In Fort Pickering, Allyn is not idle. Having sent Smyth and Clifford with most of the available regulars to deal with the fires in South Memphis, he takes direct command of the remaining twenty-five men and orders them to stand ready. He also orders that two cannons be prepared for action, horse-drawn field pieces known as Parrott guns that fire ten-pound shells. They can also fire canister, tin cylinders crammed with marble-size iron or lead pellets that scatter upon discharge, turning a cannon into a giant shotgun capable of cutting a wide, bloody swath through a crowd of human beings. Allyn orders the Parrott guns to be loaded with canister.[111]

Allyn intends to employ this little force of infantry and artillery as a mobile reserve, to be dispatched wherever needed in an emergency. Satisfied that it is ready, he posts himself on the parapet and looks out over the city to the east and north.[112]

To the east, along South and nearby streets, is a glimpse of hell. Many buildings are burning now, mostly freed peoples' houses and shanties. Bands of white men dart around, setting fires. Smyth and Clifford have found themselves overwhelmed. There is not sufficient water to extinguish the fires; all the troops can do is tear down fencing and drag away other inflammable material from around each burning building to keep the flames from spreading. Apprehending those who are setting the fires is almost impossible: whenever soldiers approach, the arsonists scurry away into the darkness beyond the yellow circles of light cast by the burning buildings—a Stygian darkness, for clouds now obscure the moon.[113]

Clifford grows exasperated with this game of hide-and-seek. He tells the fifteen or sixteen men under his direct command to ignore the order to arrest arsonists: any person setting a fire is to be shot on sight.[114]

Reverend Tade has been unable to sleep since he saw the burning schoolhouse from his rear window earlier tonight. At about one o'clock he notices light from a fire some distance in the opposite direction, to the north. Lincoln Chapel, his church and school, is in that general direction.[115]

Others nearby see this light, too. A young white man comes to Tade's door and asks if he has been to the chapel to check on it. No, replies Tade, and he will not go there now, saying that if it has been torched he can do nothing to save it and if it has not been torched by now it will not be. How he has arrived at this latter conclusion he does not explain. Perhaps it is an excuse to avoid confronting a mob at the chapel.[116]

Sheriff Winters has led his posse on a roundabout route from Hernando and Pontotoc and it is not until one o'clock that they reach his office. There Winters collects the shotguns and tells the men they can go home. They and he have nothing to show for all their marching around tonight. They have apprehended no rioters, have neither extinguished nor prevented any fires, have saved no black people from white assailants. They have, in fact, not laid eyes on a black person all night.[117]

By the time Winters stows the shotguns, locks up his office, and starts for home it is around two o'clock. His house is about a mile away in Pinch, the First Ward. On his way there he sees, above the rooftops to the north, the glare from a building on fire. He does not go to investigate, but continues on to his house.[118]

The burning building is the black Baptist church on Main Street near Overton, a brick structure just one block west of Winters's house and two or three blocks east of General Stoneman's headquarters. It is home to a congregation whose fellowship predates the war, and is in fact the oldest church building in the city. A large crowd of white people has collected at the scene, Creighton among them. They stand around watching the conflagration; none makes any attempt to put it out. The fire department has been alerted and eventually three steam engines arrive, but they are too late to do much good. The firemen manage to save a portion of the building, but everything inside is destroyed.[119]

On the parapet of Fort Pickering, nearly two miles away, Captain Allyn has spotted this fire. It is of particular concern to him because it seems to be close to General Stoneman's headquarters. He anticipates a call for help from the headquarters and prepares to dispatch his reserve squad of infantry and artillery. But no summons comes, and the squad stays in the fort.[120]

Black churches, schools, and homes are not the only victims of fire this night. A blacksmith shop owned by a freedman named Henry Alexander, not far from Collins Chapel, has gone up in flames; the three white men responsible sloshed kerosene around the shop's interior before lighting the match. Caldwell Hall, an elegant black-owned establishment that frequently hosts public meetings of the freed community, has nearly suffered the same fate. It stands near Third and Gayoso, just two blocks from the sheriff's office. A gang of white men, among them the ubiquitous David Roach, invaded the hall, smashing windows and chandeliers. They concluded their visitation by piling up the wooden seats, dousing them with lamp oil, and igniting the pyre. White men living nearby put out the fire before the building suffered serious damage.[121]

Two of the likeliest targets of white vengeance in the city are spared. The Freedmen's Bureau office, protected by the eleven-man guard provided by General Stoneman, is unmolested. The office of the *Memphis Post* also survives—miraculously, considering the repeated threats to obliterate it. At some point during the night two armed white men have approached the building, fired off a few shots at it, and fled. But no damage has been done, and no other attack materializes.[122]

Not one black school or church in the city survives the night. By two o'clock all are reduced to embers or otherwise wrecked, along with dozens of black dwellings.[123]

After two o'clock no new fires erupt except in the area centered on the intersections of Causey and Rayburn with South Street. There gangs of white men—prominent among them John Pendergrast and his father and brother Pat—continue to roam about with pistols and matches in hand, eluding the troops of Smyth and Clifford. These men intend to burn down every black dwelling they can. Some would prefer that the occupants not get out alive.[124]

On Rayburn a black woman and her twelve-year-old son huddle in terror inside their home as men surround it and set it afire. When she tries to escape out the door, one man—he is one of the Pendergrasts—fires a warning shot. She halts, drops to her knees, and begs him to let her and her boy get out. He orders her to go back inside, saying he will kill her if she does not.[125]

Another man speaks up. He is George McGinn, an Irishman who has a grocery a few blocks away, and he recognizes the woman as one he has had dealings with. "That is a very good woman," he says; "it is a pity to burn her up; let her come out." Pendergrast and the other men relent. The woman emerges from the building with her son.[126]

The boy is wearing a blue suit, a miniature U.S. Army uniform or something resembling one. As soon as the men see this, a cry goes up: "Put him back; put him back." Some of them shove the boy back through the doorway. "Go back, you damned son of a bitch," they say.[127]

Again the woman goes down on her knees. Let him out, she pleads; he is my only child. One of the men speaks up, perhaps McGinn: "Don't burn the boy; he isn't to blame for having blue clothes on." Again the others relent, and this time the woman and boy escape to safety.[128]

Inside his two-room frame house on the corner of South and Causey, black steamboat hand Andrew Minter hears banging on his front door. He is in bed and alone. His wife, Maggie, is not there tonight, nor is the woman who rooms with them; they have likely taken refuge in the fort. Well aware of what is going on in the streets around him, Minter does not answer the door. He stays in bed, lying very still.[129]

At the door are three or four white men. Getting no response, they try to break in but find the door securely barred. Two go around a corner of the house to the window of the room where Minter lies. He hears one say, "The damned son of a bitch is in there, I know." He recognizes the voice as that of John Callahan, an Irishman who owns a grocery on the opposite corner where Minter frequently shops.[130]

Callahan forces the window open—an easy task, for it is fastened only by a string—and peers inside. Minter sits up in bed. Callahan can see him by the light of burning buildings nearby. He raises a pistol, points it, and fires, narrowly missing Minter's head but hitting him in the left hand. Minter falls back onto the bed, feigning death.[131]

Callahan and his comrade hoist themselves through the window and into the room. "The damned son of a bitch," growls Callahan, "I know he has got money. He has always got money." He comes up to the bed, takes out a knife, and pokes Minter in the side with it. Minter remains motionless, eyes shut. Callahan concludes that the bullet has killed him or at least knocked him unconscious.[132]

Callahan knows that Minter has a money belt; he has seen him dip into it at the grocery. He looks around, finds the belt, and takes twenty-five dollars from it. But he is unsatisfied. "God damn him," he says, "I have got his money, but he has got some good clothes." He and the other man smash open Minter's trunk and rummage through it, taking four suits and some of Maggie's clothes. Then they leave.[133]

Minter stays in his house, aching from his wound but thankful to be alive. Soon, however, he again hears noises outside. Callahan has returned, with a larger gang and a new mission. "Now we will burn the damn son of a bitch up," Minter hears him say.[134]

The men set fire to the house, but they do not come inside. Minter slips into the adjoining room, which has a back door. He finds a quilt belonging to his roomer and drapes it over his head and shoulders like a shawl. Wearing this and his nightclothes, he hopes to pass for a woman and perhaps be spared if the men spot him.[135]

He unbolts the back door, opens it, and steps out. The ruse works. He is seen by some of the men, but they ignore him as he gets away.[136]

Reaching a point not far from his house where it is dark enough to provide some safety, he drops to the ground and huddles there. A black woman sees him and offers help. She throws some things over him, blankets or such, until all that is visible is an innocuous pile. There Minter stays as the mayhem continues all around.[137]

Jane Sneed and her husband, Albert, an invalid, are inside their house on South Street, not far from Minter's. Rachel Hatcher, Jane's fourteen-year-old daughter by a previous marriage and a star pupil of the school operated by Horatio Rankin until it was destroyed by fire twelve hours ago, is there, too. Rachel and her mother and stepfather have so far escaped harm. A little while ago some white men forced their way into the house to search for weapons, but left after finding none.[138]

Now, however, there is bad trouble. Next door is the house of Adam Lock, which was damaged by the fire that razed Rankin's school. Lock has already repaired the damage, but he still has many of his possessions bundled up in case he has to make another hurried exit. This precaution proves wise. John Callahan, having just set fire to Andrew Minter's place, now comes to Lock's. With him are George McGinn and a number of other men. They stack planks and other dry material against an outside wall and put a match to the pile.[139]

Lock comes out and throws a bucketful of water on the flames. Someone fires a shot at him, which misses. He runs around a corner of the house. Reentering by a different door, he begins carrying out his possessions. His daughter and son-in-law, who live with him, assist.[140]

Next door, Jane and Rachel see what is happening and decide to lend their neighbors a hand. But as they come out of their house they see armed white men nearby and hear a voice call out, "You had better go in or you will get shot." They retreat back inside.[141]

Within a few minutes, however, Rachel is ready to try again. "Let us go and help get the things out of Adam Lock's house," she tells her mother. Jane is not so bold: "We had better try and save ourselves," she says.[142]

But Rachel is determined. Tying a handkerchief around her nose and mouth to protect her from fumes, she goes next door alone and enters the burning building. When she emerges a few moments later, there is a fusillade of pistol fire. One bullet smashes into her mouth. She falls to the ground between Lock's house and her own.[143]

Lock and his daughter and son-in-law deposit the things they have saved about thirty yards away and stand there watching. They see McGinn set a second fire on a different part of their house. A white man comes up and tells them they had better get away from there "damn quick." They abandon their belongings and go off to a point a hundred yards away. From there they see their house swallowed by flames, and see white men pillaging the things they carried out.[144]

Jane Sneed has not witnessed the shooting of her daughter. When Rachel went to Lock's house, Jane went to help another neighbor who was reported to be asleep inside his burning house. Finding that he has gotten away safely, Jane returns home. Before she reaches the door she comes across Rachel's body, and sees that she is dead.[145]

Jane sees also that the flames from Lock's house are threatening her own. Frantically she runs to the door, which her husband locked after she left. She calls to him to let her in.[146]

No sooner is she inside than Callahan appears outside with a pistol in his hand. Jane knows him well, having traded often at his store. Callahan pushes the door open and says, "Who is in here?" Just Albert and I, Jane tells him. "Come out," he says.[147]

Another man is with Callahan, likewise armed. "Come out, God damn you," he tells the Sneeds. He points his pistol at them and declares his intention to shoot them. Callahan objects: "Let them alone; do you want to kill everybody?" "Yes," the man replies, and again tells the Sneeds, "God damn you, come out."[148]

At that moment some soldiers of the 16th appear, muskets in hand. They order the two men to leave the Sneeds alone and advise the Sneeds to go to the fort. As Callahan and his comrade retreat, Jane and Albert leave the house and head to the fort, taking nothing with them but the clothes they are wearing.[149]

The soldiers move on. Callahan returns to the Sneeds' house with McGinn and others. They loot it thoroughly and then set the place on fire.[150]

Rescuing the Sneeds is one of the last things that Smyth's and Clifford's troops accomplish this night. Around three o'clock, Captain Allyn decides they have done all he can ask of them and summons them back to the fort.[151]

Reverend Tade, still unable to sleep, is by now having second thoughts about his decision not to check on his beloved Lincoln Chapel. Mustering his courage, he gets dressed and sets out. A few minutes' walk brings him to Union Street. There he finds the chapel with its two attached schoolrooms burned to the ground.[152]

Rachel Hatcher remains where she has fallen between Adam Lock's house and her own. The bullet that entered her mouth penetrated her brain and exited from the back of her head, killing her instantly. Blood runs from the wound in a wide stream.[153]

As the two houses are devoured by fire, the narrow space between them becomes a furnace. The bullet-pierced handkerchief tied around Rachel's nose and mouth catches fire. Flame spreads from there to her clothes, which are soon burned off save for her stockings and shoes. Her face and most of the rest of her light brown skin are burned black.[154]

As dawn approaches, the mobs conclude their work, the fires die down, and South Memphis grows quiet. Beneath his sheltering pile, Andrew Minter nurses his wounded hand and waits until the sun comes up. Then he goes forth to see what the night has wrought.[155]

PART III

THE AFTERMATH

8

Recriminations and Investigations

[The riot] has put [the freed people] back further than they were when I began; . . . they will not heed my counsel; when they come to me they say, "You are the man we expected to protect us"; . . . they have had very little confidence in me or in the government since [the riot].

—Testimony of Benjamin Runkle

The riots and massacres of Memphis are only a specimen of what would take place throughout the entire south, should the government fail to afford adequate military protection.

—Excerpt from majority report of the Select Committee[1]

Not long after the sun came up on May 3, Reverend Tade returned to the ruins of Lincoln Chapel. His wife, Amanda, went with him. They found a crowd gathered there, consisting of students of the chapel's school and their parents, members of the congregation. Turning out like this was brave, for as far as anyone knew the rioting might erupt again at any moment. Most of the freed people and Yankee missionaries in Memphis were staying off the streets.[2]

Many of those assembled were in tears. Some came up and silently pressed Tade's hand. Others sought answers. "Oh they have burnt our meeting house," one woman said, "what shall we do?" Another asked, "Are the colored people to have no more schools in Memphis?"[3]

Tade picked through the wreckage to see what he could find. There was not much; those who set the fire had done their work well. He retrieved as keepsakes the mainspring of a clock, a piece of the school bell, a part of the melodeon, and a half-burned Bible. Before leaving he offered his flock words of comfort and hope: "Be of good courage—there are ashes enough here *to build two Lincoln Chapels.*" He assured them that the church would be rebuilt, and that the fellowship of the church would remain unbroken in the meantime. Come on Sunday as usual, he said, and we will meet in the lot across the street under the cottonwood trees.[4]

Later that morning a group of prominent white citizens, including *Appeal* editor J. H. McMahon, met downtown to discuss the rioting. They approved a resolution calling on Mayor Park and Sheriff Winters to form a sizeable posse to patrol the city in cooperation with the military for as long as rioting threatened, and another requesting McMahon and two others present to inform General Stoneman of the meeting. These resolutions, with an endorsement by the mayor, were printed up as a handbill and copies were posted around the city. The sheriff began enlisting men for the posse. But when McMahon and his two colleagues called on Stoneman, the general told them flatly that he would permit no more raising of posses, because he had been informed that those raised thus far had proved unreliable, even dangerous.[5]

That afternoon Stoneman formalized this decision in a letter addressed to the city and county officials. The letter revealed his ignorance of the behavior of the Memphis police over the past two days—or rather, revealed that he had chosen to ignore what Marshal Ryder told him Tuesday night, that the police were among the rioters. "It is forbidden," it read, "for any person, without authority from these headquarters, to assemble together any posse, armed or unarmed, white or colored. This does not include the police force of the city, and will not as long as they can be relied upon as preservers of the peace." Stoneman had the letter delivered to the mayor's office, only to learn that Park was too drunk to read and act on it. He then redirected it to one of the aldermen, who saw to it that the sheriff disbanded the posse he was organizing.[6]

The citizens' committee representatives were not the only callers Stoneman received that day. Several Northern missionaries appeared at his headquarters, frightened and pleading for military protection. They had heard rumors that the rioters would resume their work that night by murdering every meddling Yankee in the city, and they begged the general to post guards at the missionaries' homes. He refused, explaining that that would scatter and weaken his already insufficient force. However, he said, if the missionaries would take refuge in Fort Pickering they would be protected. Or, he added, they could leave the city altogether, in which case he would provide transportation.[7]

This latter recommendation was also made by Benjamin Runkle, the Freedmen's Bureau superintendent. He too had heard the rumors and was taking them seriously. He sent a message advising the missionaries to return to the North and stay there "until the present difficulty is over and quietude once more restored."[8]

Most of the missionaries hurriedly packed their trunks and left late that afternoon on the packet to Cairo, Illinois, bearing army travel vouchers. Runkle's wife was on that boat, too, as were a number of wives of officers of the 16th Infantry. Ewing and Amanda Tade did not go, nor did Horatio Rankin.[9]

That same afternoon Stoneman took direct control of maintaining order in the city. He commanded Captain Allyn to post an officer and fifty men at Court Square, in the heart of downtown; the officer was to report to Stoneman for further instructions. Allyn assigned Captain Smyth to this duty. After meeting with Stoneman, Smyth divided his men into patrol squads and sent them off around the city with orders to disperse all gatherings. Meanwhile, Stoneman called in reinforcements by telegraph—four companies of the Nashville garrison, which boarded a train and headed to Memphis.[10]

The general took one other step that day. Summoning Runkle to his headquarters, he told him that he intended to appoint a military commission to investigate the rioting and asked him if he would serve on it. Runkle said yes.[11]

Smyth's troops patrolled the city systematically from Thursday afternoon until dawn on Friday. This consistent and pervasive military presence on the streets—something that had not been in place during the previous two days—prevented any more mobs from forming. The city authorities helped, probably unintentionally, by not mustering the police to assist Smyth. There were scattered incidents of violence against freed people Thursday afternoon and evening, but by Friday morning it was clear that the rioting was at an end, having reached its climax in the burnings and killings of Wednesday night and the early hours of Thursday.[12]

Few blacks appeared in public on Thursday, and many corpses remained unburied. The county coroner, Francis Erickson, decided that day to do his prescribed duty although no one in authority had said a word to him about it. Conscripting seven white men downtown to serve as his jury, Erickson led them to South Memphis in search of bodies. He had trouble finding any; the black people he questioned were scared and suspicious. Eventually he coaxed enough information from some children and elderly women to locate eleven bodies. One was the charred corpse of Rachel Hatcher, lying between the ruins of her house and the one next door. Erickson's jury determined that she "came to her death . . . from a shot wound, inflicted by some person unknown."[13]

Later that day Erickson secured the services of an undertaker who saw to it that the eleven bodies were placed in paupers' coffins, loaded onto wagons, and buried in the freedmen's cemetery in the city's southern suburbs. These eleven were joined on Friday by two more that Erickson located. He knew there were others that had escaped his attention; how they were dealt with he did not know.[14]

Many blacks remained fearfully indoors even after Thursday. Some who ventured out did so only to seek safety in Fort Pickering or flee the city altogether. As late as Saturday there were several thousand in the fort. Stoneman offered transportation out of the city to any who wanted to go, as he had done for the missionaries, and many accepted the offer, heading up or down the river on steamboats. Stoneman's generosity was motivated by a practical as well as humanitarian impulse: he had long thought Memphis burdened by an excessive black population and now used this opportunity to do something about it.[15]

The freed people who remained in the city eventually returned to work and in other ways resumed the lives they had known before the riot—those, that is, who were able to. Fayette Dickerson, shot in the abdomen outside his house, died after a week of suffering. Some who survived their injuries were left crippled and unable to work. Among them were Allen Summers, who had been shot, stabbed, and beaten, and Austin Cotton, pistol-whipped by policemen.[16]

The emotional wounds inflicted on black Memphis by the rioters were in many cases as agonizing and slow to heal as the physical wounds. Harriet Armour, raped at gunpoint inside her shanty by two men, was described by a neighbor four weeks later as "a little deranged since then." Her neighbors sympathized, but she got no comfort from her husband, an ex-soldier who had taken refuge in the fort during the riot; returning home afterward and learning what had happened, he decided he wanted nothing more to do with her and deserted her. Those who lost loved ones in the riot also suffered emotional torment, their grief in many cases exacerbated by their inability to observe any last rites. Lavinia Godell never again saw the body of her husband, Jackson, after viewing it through the window of the jail; she could not even find out how it was finally disposed of or where it was laid to rest. Jane Sneed, Rachel Hatcher's mother, was a little more fortunate. Although she was not able to see to Rachel's burial, she did eventually locate her grave in the freedmen's cemetery. As she mourned her daughter's death, Sneed also had to find a new place to live and begin replacing lost possessions, as did the many other black Memphians whose homes had been destroyed.[17]

Stoneman, his force strengthened by the troops that arrived from Nashville on Friday, May 4, kept up the military patrols in the city for a time but withdrew them as soon as he was satisfied that more rioting was unlikely. He was not content to let the civil authorities resume business as if nothing had happened, however. He reserved the right to intervene again if necessary. Moreover, as he learned more about the riot he became convinced that the municipal officers, or many of them, were culpable, and he made up his mind to see that they atoned for their sins.[18]

On May 5 he wrote a letter to Mayor Park. It demanded answers to several questions: What steps are the civil authorities taking to punish the rioters? To compensate those whose property was destroyed? To ensure that citizens do not go around armed? To protect the rights of the freed people? The letter concluded with a warning: "[My] future action will be based upon your reply to this communication. . . . [I] assure you, and through you the people of Memphis, that if they cannot govern themselves as a law-abiding and Christian community, they will be governed."[19]

Stoneman enclosed a copy of this letter with one he wrote that day to his commanding officer, Major General George H. Thomas in Nashville. "I shall," he vowed to Thomas, "unless I am prohibited, make the city of Memphis pay the full value of all losses and expenses suffered or incurred [in the riot], either by individuals or the Government." This levy would not only secure financial restitution, he explained, but also "make the city of Memphis and through them, the people of the South, feel and realize that such disgraceful proceedings cannot and will not be tolerated by the United States Government."[20]

Stoneman also enclosed with the letter to Thomas a copy of his order of the same date appointing a commission to investigate the riot. This four-man body, to be headed by Runkle, was to call witnesses, gather facts about the causes and events of the riot, identify rioters and victims, and tally the property losses. By now Stoneman had a pretty good idea of what this investigation would reveal. As he told Thomas, the city's Rebel newspapers "had no little influence" in provoking the riot and among the rioters were "not a few prominent persons." He noted furthermore the role of the overwhelmingly Irish police force, describing it as "utterly unreliable" and "strongly tinctured with hatred to the 'damned naygur.'" But, he added, the great majority of whites in the city, including former Confederate soldiers, "not only had no hand in the business, but are violently opposed to any such disgraceful occurrences."[21]

Serving with Runkle on the commission would be Captain Allyn and Captain W. J. Colburn, an army quartermaster. Stoneman's choice for the fourth member no doubt surprised many Memphians. He was Marcus J. Wright, one of the city's most prominent Rebels. A thirty-four-year-old lawyer, Wright had lived in Memphis since 1850, except during the war, when he served in the Confederate army. He had risen to the rank of brigadier general and at one point had in his charge, as a prisoner of war, General Stoneman. After the war the latter repaid Wright's kind treatment by warmly endorsing his presidential pardon application, describing him as "a gentleman and a brave man." Wright was regarded in postwar Memphis as a Rebel of the politically moderate stripe. Stoneman wanted him on the investigative commission, as he told Thomas, to forestall any accusation "that the city or the people are on trial before an inquisition." Wright readily accepted the call.[22]

The commission convened on the morning of May 7 and began questioning witnesses. The next day, Stoneman received a reply from the mayor to his letter of the fifth. Long and lawyerly (it was composed, undoubtedly, in the city attorney's office), it addressed Stoneman's questions one by one, getting in some sly jabs at the Yankees and freed people even as it solemnly assured that justice would be done. The city and county authorities, said Park, would certainly do all they could to punish the rioters—including the black rioters—but of course their powers were limited by law; neither the mayor nor any other official could exercise the sort of despotic rule "upheld by military force, with which . . . the people of Memphis, have had a long time experience, even unto nausea." Regarding restitution for losses, the city would not "shirk any legal responsibility"; however, Park noted, he was informed that there was no such responsibility, for there was "no statute or law authorizing any such appropriation of money." As for the illegal carrying of weapons, it had never been condoned by the civil authorities; however, permits to carry arms for self-defense were granted on request to "good citizens . . . in that part of town infested with lawless negroes, and other bad characters." Furthermore, Stoneman need have no fear that the freed people would be abused: "the rights of the negro[es] are and will be religiously respected, and every allowance and provision made for their altered condition consistent with safety to our persons and property." The local civil authorities could, in fact, "better provide for [blacks] than can other law-makers: giving to them wholesome and healthful regulations, the result of a practical familiarity with [them] . . . free from the inoculation of a morbid, sickly sentimentalism." The letter could only have fueled Stoneman's determination to secure justice on the basis of his commission's findings.[23]

By this time the Freedmen's Bureau had an investigation of its own under way. Runkle had put it in motion on May 3, ordering his staff to start taking affidavits from witnesses. Like Stoneman, Runkle was determined to see that Memphis paid for its sins. He told his immediate superior, Brigadier General Clinton B. Fisk in Nashville, that he wanted to tax the city not only to cover property losses but also "to provide for every widow, orphan and cripple" the riot had left in its wake. Fisk dispatched an aide, Colonel Charles F. Johnson, to assist Runkle. When Johnson arrived on May 5, Runkle put the Bureau inquiry entirely into his hands and turned his own attention to the military commission. Six days later Captain T. W. Gilbreth arrived in the city from Bureau headquarters in Washington; he too had orders to investigate the riot. At Fisk's suggestion, Gilbreth and Johnson agreed to work together and produce a joint report.[24]

Fisk was in Memphis at that point, having come over from Nashville on May 9 to get a firsthand look at the riot's effects. A thirty-seven-year-old Michigander who did not drink or swear, he had been a businessman and active abolitionist before the war and a U.S. Army officer since 1862. He now served as an assistant commissioner of the Bureau, overseeing its operations in Tennessee and Kentucky. He was just as angry about the riot as Runkle and Stoneman and similarly determined to make Memphis pay. The day he arrived he declared that the black churches and schools would be rebuilt and that the city would be taxed to cover the costs. The work would begin with the construction of a large, four-classroom school in South Memphis. An advertisement in the *Argus* on May 10, placed by his order, announced the immediate hiring of one hundred black carpenters, masons, and laborers for this project; interested parties were directed to apply at the army quartermaster's office on Second Street. Fisk also sent telegrams urging the missionaries who had left the city to return.[25]

As the two federal investigations got under way, some of the rioters with the bloodiest hands lay low. John Pendergrast and his brother Pat went into hiding a few days after the riot. Others fled the city, among them fireman Michael Kenan, who had shot a white man to death in a saloon on May 2 for chatting with a black man. Rumor had it that some rioters hurriedly enlisted in the Fenian cause and were transported to the North as part of an armed force preparing to invade Canada.[26]

A number of these men were in fact being sought by the Freedmen's Bureau, for crimes attested to by witnesses who appeared before the Bureau investigators. Policeman David Roach, who did not hide or flee, was arrested by the Bureau on May 10. Held in the city jail, he walked out a few hours later after posting bond with the help of friends. Among the friends he called on was the eldest Pendergrast, known as the "old man." But when the old man appeared before Bureau officers on this errand, he himself was jailed—not for rioting, but for concealing the whereabouts of his sons John and Pat, both wanted by the Bureau. The old man swore he did not know where they were, and begged to be released on account of his poor health. He hired a lawyer, who brought a doctor to the jail to examine him. The doctor told the Bureau officials that the sixty-five-year-old man, feeble and suffering from diarrhea and a hernia, might not survive continued confinement. Unmoved, the officials threatened to keep him in jail until he told them what they wanted to know.[27]

Those who testimony revealed might be culpable in the rioting but who had not actually assaulted anybody were, for the time being, left undisturbed. Recorder John Creighton, who had exhorted white crowds to kill blacks, failed to show up for work on the morning of May 3 but reappeared soon after and resumed his duties. Stoneman did not intend to let such men off the hook but rather to wait until the army and Bureau investigators had finished gathering evidence of their guilt and then have them all arrested in one swoop; were the arrests made piecemeal, he thought, many of those accused would get away.[28]

Other Northerners in Memphis shared the outrage expressed by Stoneman, Runkle, and Fisk. John Eaton's *Post*, voice of the city's moderate Republicans, condemned the acts of the "lawless, unprincipled and worse than barbarian mob" and fiercely denied the Rebel papers' claims that blacks had started the trouble and that whites were the primary victims: "Has one white woman, one white child, been maltreated . . . ? Has a single dwelling of a white person been entered or molested? Has any unarmed white man been in any way injured by negroes?" The riot was the culmination of long-festering white resentment of black freedom, the *Post* argued. The police, who routinely brutalized freed people even before the riot, were particularly guilty. The Rebel newspapers had stoked the Negrophobic fury with their "utterly false and wicked" reports. What the city had experienced was nothing less than "a massacre of unarmed and unresisting" blacks. The U.S. government should force the civil authorities, who had failed in their duty to prevent the slaughter and destruction, to make restitution.[29]

The guilty must render not only unto Caesar, some Yankees insisted, but also unto God. On Sunday, May 6, the Reverend T. E. Bliss, pastor of a Northern white church in the city, sermonized on the riot. It was, in his view, evidence of "the desperate wickedness of the human heart" and "the awful power of prejudice and passion when unchecked by Christian principle." What had happened was terrible to behold and perhaps hard for a person of faith to make sense of, he told those in attendance, but be not dismayed, for "God reigns forever." Divine justice would be done. Bliss's text that morning was Jeremiah 5:29: "Shall I not visit for these things? saith the Lord: shall not my soul be avenged on such a nation as this?"[30]

Bliss specifically addressed the destruction of schools and churches. "God cannot be baffled," he reminded the congregation. "His great law of progress is irreversible." The rioters did not, and could not, "shut out the light of knowledge." Echoing Ewing Tade's words at the site of his ruined church three days earlier, Bliss proclaimed that "out of these very ashes shall spring up better school-houses and churches, with more secure foundations."[31]

Tade himself was already at work fulfilling this promise. On Saturday, May 5, he rented a building on Beale Street. Nearly a hundred of his congregants showed up there for services on Sunday morning; and the next day their children gathered there to resume school lessons, overseen by Amanda Tade. In the succeeding weeks three other teachers joined her, one of whom—Miss Warren—had taught at the Lincoln Chapel school before the riot and had fled the city on May 3. Ewing Tade proudly reported to his sponsor, the American Missionary Association, that only two days of school were missed due to the riot. "We feel strong," he wrote; "[God] is our strength—and He is our Shield."[32]

Other missionary exiles returned and resumed their work as Warren did. By the end of May, four freedmen's schools were operating in the city, with nine teachers and about eight hundred students. Others would be rebuilt before long. Horatio Rankin went north on a lecture tour to raise money to finance his. On May 30 the imposing new building constructed in South Memphis by Fisk's decree was dedicated in a ceremony at which Fisk and Runkle gave speeches. Forty by one hundred feet in size, erected with astonishing speed, and aptly named the Phoenix Educational Institute, it still needed plastering and painting and furnishings but would be ready when the new school year began in the fall.[33]

As Yankees, Irishmen, and freed people grappled with the consequences of the riot, so too did Southern whites. The city's Rebel newspapers editorialized on it passionately for many days after it ended. As the truth about the violence and the casualties became clear and undeniable, the newspapers dropped their insistence that blacks were the main perpetrators and whites the main victims. They continued to maintain, however, that blacks had provoked the riot—both in the immediate sense, by attacking the four policemen on the bayou bridge on the afternoon of May 1, and in the broader sense, by their intolerable misbehavior and outrageous demands since gaining freedom, egged on by their Yankee friends. "The negroes wantonly began the row," declared the *Argus* on May 4, "—without provocation shot down officers of the law while in the discharge of their duties—and so the storm began." The *Bulletin* took the broader view: "[The freedmen] are corrupted and misled by their wors[t] enemies, who approach under the guise of sincerest friendship. There are newspapers which pander to their passions, and civil rights bills which undo the work of Deity; make equal things created unequal. . . . Their woes are recited by diseased philanthropy, till, maddened by supposed wrong and real evil, incident to poverty, ignorance, and idleness, they are prepared for outrage and crime."[34]

The Rebel papers nevertheless deplored much of the violence, especially the destruction of churches and schools. "We deprecate from the bottom of our hearts the injury inflicted upon any innocent parties in the late terrible riot," said the *Avalanche*. Condemning the burnings as "a disgrace to all who participated," that paper printed the section of the Code of Tennessee dealing with arson and reminded its readers that "the law must be observed."[35]

Whatever the excesses of the rioters, however, several Rebel papers asserted that some good had come out of the riot, in the form of useful lessons for the freed people. "The negroes have been forced to swallow their own medicines," said the *Public Ledger*. "It has been a lesson, and they will now have an awe and respect for the law which they have at all times disregarded since their altered condition." The *Avalanche* stated that the riot had "satisfied all of one thing—that the Southern man will not be ruled by the negro. . . . The negroes now know, to their sorrow, that it is best not to arouse the fury of the white man. Such a thing as a 'riot' never occurred in Memphis till these negro troops came among us . . . and, from the lessons these brutes have lately received, we think it will be many a day before a riot will occur here again."[36]

Even as they applauded the moral benefits of the riot, however, the Rebel papers worried about its political consequences. "Our riots last week were a God-send to Radicalism everywhere," the *Public Ledger* commented. "It was sadly in want of something out of which to manufacture a new supply of capital. . . . In the face of all that can be said or proved to the contrary, Radicalism will have it that the riot had its origin in rebel dissatisfaction with the condition of things, and rebel disposition to murder the negroes." To counter such claims, the newspapers drew a line separating the former Confederate soldiers and other "respectable" whites from the rioters, whom the papers depicted as propertyless, immigrant rabble. "There were two classes of people that failed to participate in all this mobocracy," said the *Bulletin*. "Neither taxpayers, nor ex-soldiers . . . participated in these indefensible infractions of law and order." The municipal authorities—put into office, as the papers frequently reminded their readers, by the votes of the churlish underclass because the better sort of men were disenfranchised—were roundly criticized: "If the Mayor and Board of Aldermen properly appreciated their duties," the *Argus* remarked, "we would have had an efficient police; and if the police had been efficient, the late riots . . . would have been quelled in their incipiency." Two former Confederate soldiers wrote letters for publication in Eaton's *Post*, assuring its readers of the innocence of the men who had worn gray and the guilt of the unwashed—especially the Irish, and most especially the police.[37]

On May 22, Colonel Johnson and Captain Gilbreth concluded their investigation for the Freedmen's Bureau, having secured sworn affidavits from 210 witnesses, the great majority of them black. Lacking subpoena power, they had had to rely on voluntary testimony. Jane Sneed and Robert Church came forward to tell of their experiences and their losses, as did many other victims, but no policemen or other city or county officers appeared. Johnson and Gilbreth wrote a report based on this evidence, and Gilbreth sent it to the commissioner of the Bureau, Major General O. O. Howard in Washington.[38]

The report sketched the events of the riot and offered some judgments on it. "The remote cause," the two officers affirmed, was "a bitterness of feeling which has always existed between the low whites & blacks." Among the low whites were the police, who treated the freed people harshly and had "an especial hatred" of the black soldiers, "which was most cordially reciprocated." This racial antagonism, aggravated by the Rebel newspapers' "inflammatory" expressions of hostility to the freed people, had created an atmosphere in which "the slightest provocation [might] bring about an open rupture." The sparks that ignited the riot were the confrontations between policemen and black soldiers on Causey Street on the afternoon of April 30 and at the bayou bridge on South Street the next afternoon, in which both the whites and blacks bore culpability. What happened thereafter was essentially a series of horrific assaults on innocent and unresisting blacks by low whites, especially policemen, accompanied by threats against Northerners who sympathized with the freed people. Recorder Creighton urged on the rioters, while Mayor Park proved incompetent, or perhaps unwilling, to halt the violence. In the end, at least thirty blacks were dead and perhaps fifty wounded, while eleven black churches and schools and four or five dozen black dwellings lay in ashes. Two white men died as a result of the riot, but neither was killed by blacks.[39]

On May 23, the day after Gilbreth sent this report to his superior in Washington, Runkle sent one to his in Nashville. Based mostly on Johnson and Gilbreth's report, it cited also Runkle's personal experience in the riot. (It did not cite what Runkle had learned so far in the military commission investigation—he had been sworn to secrecy.) Runkle's judgments on the riot were similar to those of Johnson and Gilbreth, although he drew more attention to the guilt of the Rebel newspapers, the hostility to the Yankee friends of the freed people, and the utter worthlessness of the city government as a whole and the police department in particular. Moreover, he implied that Stoneman had not acted forcefully enough to suppress the riot in its early stages, a matter on which Johnson and Gilbreth did not comment.[40]

Runkle concluded his report with an anguished personal note: "I have endured the mortification of turning away the poor people who came to me for protection and whom I was sent here to protect. . . . I was powerless. . . . The Freedmen's Bureau in this City during the riot was a mockery. . . . This nation has set the black man free with the bayonet, then let the nation, if needs be, protect his life with the same weapon. . . . Better that there should be no Bureau, than that there should be one so weak that it can scarcely defend itself."[41]

Twelve days later, on June 4, the military commission ended its hearings, having interviewed 122 witnesses. The testimony of these men and women was recorded verbatim. The questioning was done behind closed doors, and the testimony kept confidential, so that witnesses could speak without fear of reprisal. Stoneman had vested in the commission the power to compel testimony, and it had summoned a number of people who had no doubt gladly avoided the Bureau inquiry, including Mayor Park, Sheriff Winters, Chief Garrett, and *Avalanche* editor Matthew Gallaway, and a number of others who were probably willing to testify but who had for whatever reason not gone before the Bureau, including Horatio Rankin, Ewing Tade, and Captain Allyn (himself a member of the commission). Among the thirty-three black witnesses besides Rankin were Jane Sneed and Lavinia Godell. The commission did not summon John Creighton or any of the other men revealed by testimony to be most deeply implicated in the rioting—perhaps for fear that doing so would provoke them to flee, or perhaps because it was assumed that if put on the stand they would simply invoke the constitutional right to avoid self-incrimination. (The commission was not trying anyone, of course, but it did require witnesses to swear an oath to tell the truth, violation of which could result in federal perjury charges; and the testimony it took could presumably be used in a criminal trial.)[42]

The commission did not write a report. Stoneman had originally instructed it simply to gather evidence. He later changed his mind, but the commission members begged off, noting that there would be other reports (the Bureau's and that of a congressional investigation getting under way); Runkle in particular objected to writing a commission report because he had to write one for Fisk. The commission did submit, however, along with the voluminous testimony, detailed lists of victims, perpetrators, crimes committed, and properties stolen or destroyed. Moreover, Stoneman himself summarized the evidence, as far as it had been developed, in a long report he telegraphed on May 12 to the general in chief of the army, Ulysses S. Grant, and another he sent by mail on May 19 to General Thomas. The report to Grant drew some general conclusions similar to those that Johnson and Gilbreth subsequently set forth. The report to Thomas reiterated Stoneman's intention to arrest the leading perpetrators and force the city authorities to make restitution once the investigation was complete. The testimony gathered by the commission provided a wealth of details about the riot not revealed by the Bureau investigation, but nothing to challenge the basic narrative of events constructed by Johnson and Gilbreth. The commission's figures on casualties and property losses were roughly similar to those of Johnson and Gilbreth, except that the commission put the number of slain freed people at forty-three.[43]

When the commission's work was done, Stoneman forwarded its records to Thomas in Nashville, who reviewed them and sent them on to Grant in Washington, along with an endorsement in which he asked the same questions of Grant that Stoneman had raised in his May 19 report: How exactly can the city be taxed to compensate the riot's victims? If Stoneman arrests and holds rioters and they secure writs of habeas corpus, how should he respond? Assuming that the rioters are not arraigned in a local court, can they be tried by a U.S. district court or army tribunal? Grant replied on July 6. He had by then examined the commission records and was preparing to send them up the chain of command to Secretary of War Edwin Stanton for his review and recommendations, and for answers to Thomas's questions. For now, Grant told Thomas, have Stoneman compile a list of the names and addresses of the principal rioters still in the city "so that if orders are telegraphed to him to make arrests he can do so at once."[44]

Federal action of some sort would be essential if rioters were to be punished and financial restitution made, for the Memphis civil authorities were intransigent. This became increasingly apparent as the weeks went by. Mayor Park's position that the city and county governments were not legally authorized to expend funds to compensate riot victims was, in fact, unimpeachable. (Barbour Lewis, a Yankee lawyer and Republican activist in the city, researched the matter hopefully but in the end had to concede the mayor's point.) Moreover, few if any city officers, from the mayor down to the policemen on the beat, had any interest in arresting rioters, and none did so; nor did any city or county officer issue warrants authorizing the sheriff to make arrests.[45]

Nor was any rioter taken before a grand jury. This would have been primarily the responsibility of William Wallace, the state attorney general for Memphis and its suburbs. Wallace was a Southern Unionist, a Republican, and an appointee of Radical governor Brownlow, and thus might have been expected to go after rioters willingly. Moreover, the district criminal court judge was a Yankee and a Brownlow appointee, so Wallace could have had no fear of an unfriendly presence on the bench if he took a case against a rioter to court.[46]

Wallace's failure to pursue indictments against rioters might have been connected to his own role in the riot as the leader of two armed posses on May 2, about which questions could be raised. More probably, however, he simply recognized the futility of trying to get a jury to cooperate. Jurymen were by law selected from the ranks of those eligible to vote, and these voters—predominantly Irish, the same men who had put Park's administration into office—were, to say the least, generally sympathetic to the rioters and unsympathetic to the rioters' victims. And even if Wallace somehow managed to get indictments from a grand jury, he would then have to reckon with a criminal court jury likewise composed of enfranchised local men. This same stubborn fact would frustrate any riot victim who tried to sue a rioter for damages in the circuit court.[47]

The virtual impossibility of getting a judgment against a rioter in a local court was widely acknowledged in Memphis, as was the absolute impossibility of securing voluntary restitution from the city fathers. Stoneman, Runkle, Fisk, and Thomas came to understand these realities as well as anybody else, and therefore invested their hope for justice in federal action. Runkle and his staff gave up trying to apprehend rioters, for they would just have to turn them over to the criminal court (the Bureau court was abolished not long after the riot). Old man Pendergrast was soon released from jail, and the charges against David Roach were apparently dropped. With the heat off, some of the rioters who had gone underground reappeared. John Pendergrast was back at work in his grocery by the end of May. Pat Pendergrast also surfaced by then, although, as one of his neighbors remarked, "he dodges back and forth."[48]

At this point, four weeks after the riot, federal intervention was appearing more and more likely. Telegraph wires had spread reports of the riot across the country with lightning speed even before it was over, and the public had responded with fascination, horror, and anger. On May 2, the *Chicago Tribune*, *Cleveland Daily Herald*, and *Jackson* (Mississippi) *Standard* published accounts of the riot's outbreak the day before. The *New York Herald, New York Times, Philadelphia Inquirer,* and *Milwaukee Daily Sentinel* picked up the story on May 3. Quickly thereafter many other papers, from Georgia to California and from Maine to Utah Territory, followed suit. Some of these accounts were copied from the Memphis papers; others were based on dispatches from correspondents on the scene. A good number of papers published updated reports, lengthy and detailed, for several days running. *Harper's Weekly* printed on its front page two large and dramatic, albeit fanciful, engraved illustrations of the killing and burning.[49]

Newspaper commentary followed hard on the heels of the reports, many of which were inaccurate. Like the Rebel papers in Memphis, Democratic papers north and south brandished the riot as evidence of the foolishness of the Emancipation Proclamation and the Civil Rights Act. Republican papers around the nation drew predictably different conclusions. Many argued that President Johnson bore the ultimate blame for the riot. "Such are some of the fruits of the lenient treatment of rebels by our magnanimous Government," said the *Cincinnati Gazette*; "such is the result of reconstruction on the basis of 'my policy' . . . [which has given the Rebels] back their power to crush and destroy the poor black man." The *Chicago Tribune* stated that "the Memphis riots exhibit to the gaze of Congress and the country, the marvellous progress the Johnson policy of reconstruction has made in West Tennessee."[50]

The riot did indeed attract the gaze of Congress. On May 10, during a House debate on the proposed Fourteenth Amendment to the Constitution (which embodied Republican demands regarding reconstruction), Radical member Thaddeus Stevens of Pennsylvania responded with characteristic acerbity to the calls by some of his colleagues to restore the South to the Union without further delay: "Let not these friends of secession sing to me their siren song of peace and good will until they can stop my ears to the screams and groans of the dying victims at Memphis."[51]

Four days later Stevens introduced the resolution to create a House committee to investigate the riot, which was approved; the committee was designated the Select Committee on the Memphis Riots. The speaker chose Elihu Washburne to chair it. A New Englander by birth, a Puritan by heritage, an Illinoisan by adoption, and a lawyer by profession, the forty-nine-year-old Washburne held himself to rigid standards of morality, justice, and economy and thought the government should do likewise. He distinguished himself from many of his congressional colleagues by opposing pork-barrel spending and abstaining from smoking, card-playing, and whiskey-drinking. An ardent enemy of slavery, he had moved from the Whig to the Republican Party when the latter was founded in 1854. He was a close friend of Abraham Lincoln until the president's death; and he was a devoted supporter of his fellow Galena, Illinois, resident Ulysses S. Grant, and had done much to advance Grant's career and rank during the war. He was regarded as a moderate Republican, not a Radical.[52]

Serving with Washburne on the Select Committee would be Republican John M. Broomall of Pennsylvania and Democrat George S. Shanklin of Kentucky (a Southern state that had not seceded). The committee members were directed to proceed to Memphis with a stenographer and a sergeant at arms, gather evidence, and submit a report to the House. They were armed with authority to subpoena witnesses, examine them under oath, and secure relevant documents.[53]

The committee convened in a room of the Gayoso House on May 22, the day of its arrival in Memphis. Between then and their adjournment on June 6, the three members questioned 164 witnesses and examined numerous documents, including back issues of the Memphis newspapers and rosters of city employees that noted the ethnicity of each man. Some of the witnesses were among those questioned by the Freedmen's Bureau and military commission investigators; but most were not, including Stoneman, Runkle, prominent Rebel Marcus Wright, rape victim Harriet Armour, and beating victim Austin Cotton. The committee summoned no rioters for questioning, probably for the same reason as the military commission.[54]

The committee's witnesses, many of whom testified at great length, provided much new information about the riot. The committee's proceedings, however, were from start to finish highly politicized. Chairman Washburne ruled with a strong hand, took first crack at nearly all the witnesses, and made no secret about where his sympathies lay and who he thought was culpable. At one point, questioning a Conservative witness who spoke respectfully of the former Confederates, Washburne reminded him sharply that those were "the men who have involved this country in this terrible war, costing three hundred thousand [Union] lives, and three billions of dollars, and that has clothed the whole country in mourning." When the same witness claimed that the city's whites treated the freed people quite well on the whole, Washburne exploded: "Who was it that burned the colored schoolhouses and churches of Memphis . . . ? Who was it that set fire to the houses, and attempted to burn up the inmates? Who was it that robbed the colored people? Who was it that ravished the women? Who was it that shot down women and children in cold blood?" Meanwhile, Southern Democrat Shanklin did everything in his power to elicit from the witnesses evidence of black misbehavior before the riot, black guilt in triggering the riot, and black mayhem during the riot.[55]

Their hearings concluded, the committeemen returned to Washington to prepare their report. What emerged, however, was not one report but two, for Washburne denied Shanklin any say in writing the committee report and Shanklin therefore wrote one of his own. The two reports were submitted to the House in late July and subsequently published by the Government Printing Office in a thick, indexed volume that included the testimony of the committee's witnesses and the testimony of the Freedmen's Bureau and military commission witnesses who had not appeared before the committee. The House ordered that one thousand copies of this volume be printed and distributed. No thought was given, apparently, to the possibility of reprisals against witnesses, all of whom were identified by full name and in many cases by address.[56]

The committee report—that is, Washburne and Broomall's report—was thirty-six pages long. It detailed the course of the riot, drawing special attention to the most heinous acts, such as the murder and burning of Rachel Hatcher, and to the guiltiest rioters, including John Creighton, the Pendergrasts, John Callahan, and David Roach. It strongly condemned Mayor Park for his drunken fecklessness and gently criticized General Stoneman for failing to act forcefully in the riot's early stages. The basic cause of the riot, Washburne and Broomall stated, was the intense hatred of the freed people by the city's whites, especially the Irish—a hatred stoked by the Rebel newspapers. These papers had, in the months leading up to the riot, not only "appeal[ed] to the lowest and basest prejudices against the colored population" but also expressed "bitter hostility to the [U.S.] government . . . [and to]

northern people residing in Memphis." Those whom Washburne and Broomall absolved of any guilt included Sheriff Winters and Chief Garrett, depicted as well-intentioned but ineffective, and the Northern missionaries and Freedmen's Bureau officers, who had long been subjected to "false and malicious" allegations that their teachings stirred the freed people to violence. What had occurred in Memphis was "an organized and bloody massacre of the colored people," the final tally of which was forty-six blacks dead, seventy-five injured, five raped, and a hundred robbed, along with four black churches, twelve schools, and ninety-one dwellings destroyed. Of the dead, at least fourteen were former federal soldiers and three were women or girls.[57]

Noting indignantly the municipal officials' refusal to secure justice since the riot, Washburne and Broomall recommended that the army "arrest, try, and punish" the rioters and tax the city to pay for property losses. They also offered a judgment that went to the heart of the great political issues of the day. What the events in Memphis demonstrated, they said, was that the Southerners who had rebelled against the U.S. government in 1861 were just as disloyal now, wholly unreconciled to Union victory and black freedom despite their avowals to the contrary. If federal troops were withdrawn from the South and full control of the region was returned to Rebel hands, the blacks and loyal whites there would be in great danger. The Memphis riot was "a specimen of what would take place throughout the entire south, should the government fail to afford adequate military protection."[58]

Shanklin's eight-page minority report made no excuses for the rioters; they had committed "acts that would disgrace the most ferocious savage, and cause civilization and religion to blush and mourn over the depravity of mankind." He wanted it understood, however, that in the shootout at the bayou bridge that sparked the rioting "the colored soldiers were the aggressors and commenced the fight with the officers of the law in the discharge of their official duty, and that they were [thus] guilty of a very high offence." Shanklin insisted, too, that the riotous mobs were "exclusively composed of the police, firemen, rowdy and rabble population . . . the greater part of whom are voters in the city of Memphis, under the franchise law of the State of Tennessee." The "more intelligent and better portion" of white Tennesseans were "kind, liberal, and just" to the freed people. That these respectable whites were mostly disenfranchised was "a prominent cause of the sad and cruel tragedy of Memphis," for it put the municipal government in the wrong hands.[59]

Shanklin's report, like that of his two colleagues, addressed the central questions before the nation, but he reached a contrary conclusion: "The most certain and quickest practicable mode to guard against a repetition of the Memphis tragedy would be to restore political rights to all from whom they have been taken . . . or at least to those who have received the Executive pardon. Were this policy adopted, we might hope to see harmony and prosperity restored to a distracted country; the military removed to the frontier and coast; and, above all, the Freedmen's Bureau, the manufacturer of paupers and vagabonds, the fruitful source of strife, vice, and crime, dispensed with."[60]

As the House Select Committee members labored over their reports, the executive branch of government also grappled with the riot. On July 7, Grant forwarded the records of the military commission to Stanton. Grant's accompanying letter briefly summarized the commission's findings, recommended that the army arrest and hold the rioters until the Memphis civil authorities agreed to prosecute them, urged that the U.S. government force the city to pay restitution, and requested answers to General Thomas's questions about how exactly to proceed in these last two matters. Stanton promptly sent all the material to the White House. President Johnson turned it over to Attorney General James Speed for review and recommendations.[61]

Speed responded on July 13 in a letter of two paragraphs. While acknowledging that the assaults on "helpless and unresisting colored citizens" and the city's failure to do justice were reprehensible, he found no legal basis for army intervention now:

This conduct . . . constitutes no offence against the laws and dignity of the United States of America. Under our frame of government, the States are charged with the duty of protecting citizens from outrage, by public prosecutions, and the citizens themselves have the right to appear in the appropriate courts, State or national, for the redress of any private wrongs that they may have sustained. The military stationed at Memphis performed their duty in aiding to suppress the mob violence. Having done that, they have and can have nothing to do with the redress of private grievances, or prosecutions for public wrongs. The Courts, State and national, are open in Tennessee, and there is no war. Under the State laws, as well as United States laws, the injured party may appeal to the courts for redress.[62]

Speed confined his opinion to Grant's question of military intervention, but he clearly implied that the executive branch as a whole had no business getting involved in the aftermath of the Memphis riot. President Johnson made no recorded comment on Speed's letter; but, doctrinaire state-rights Democrat that he was, he doubtless concurred wholeheartedly with the attorney general. Speed, his duty done, sent the military commission records back to the White House, where the president instructed a secretary to return them to Stanton for filing.[63]

By this time, moreover, the local momentum in favor of federal intervention was waning. Before June ended, Benjamin Runkle received orders to report to Charleston, South Carolina, for a new assignment. In mid-August, Clinton Fisk resigned from the Bureau, was mustered out of the army, and moved north to pursue a different career. The men who succeeded Runkle and Fisk had not been intimately connected with the riot and showed no interest in further federal involvement. In early September, George Stoneman was reassigned and left Memphis. No one succeeded to his position there; the headquarters was eliminated in a reorganization of Thomas's command.[64]

Thomas again raised the issue of military intervention in mid-August, telegraphing Grant to inform him that the most recently convened grand jury in Memphis had failed to indict any rioters, and asking if the army should go forward with arrests. Grant referred this message to Stanton with a recommendation in favor of arrests. Stanton sent it on to the White House. There was no response, and the executive branch took no subsequent action regarding the riot—not the White House, not the attorney general's office, not the army, not the Freedmen's Bureau, not any other agency under presidential authority.[65]

Black Memphians expressed disappointment, even bitterness, over the U.S. government's failure to protect them during the riot and to secure justice after it. Questioned by the Select Committee on June 5, Runkle said that the freed people were no longer willing to "heed my

counsel; . . . when they come to me they say, 'You are the man we expected to protect us'; . . . they have had very little confidence in me or
in the government since [the riot]." Indeed, he thought, the government's apparent impotence had soured their whole outlook on the
future, dashing the hope fostered by the passage of the Civil Rights
Act only two months earlier: "They have lost all confidence . . . in
everything."[66]

Runkle was partly right and partly wrong. That black Memphians
were disillusioned with the federal government was undoubtedly true,
and hardly surprising. But that they had lost hope for a better tomorrow was demonstrably untrue. In the weeks following the riot, there
were plenty of signs that their quest to reap the full harvest of freedom
was undeterred. If they could no longer rely on the U.S. government,
they could still rely on themselves.

One indication was an incident on May 22 that began down on the
levee. The black stevedores who hung out there awaiting the arrival of
steamboats decided that day to strike for higher wages. According to
some reports they were incited by a white steamboat hand of Radical
sympathies. Even if this was so, they quickly made the protest their
own. Securing a flag and a drum and constructing a banner that proclaimed "2.50 per day or fifty cents per hour," they proceeded to march
around the levee in double file, fifty or a hundred strong, with flag flying, drum beating, and banner hoisted. They went from one anchored
steamer to the next, encouraging—with some success—black boat
hands to join them. Eventually they marched up the bluff and into the
city, recruiting as they went.[67]

This was a breathtakingly bold protest, coming as it did less than
three weeks after the riot and undertaken in the presence of any number of white stevedores, hackmen, policemen, and others hostile to
blacks. It could easily have sparked a violent response, perhaps even
another riot. This possibility occurred to the army authorities, who
grew concerned enough to intervene. As the strikers and their sym-
pathizers, by now two hundred strong, headed from downtown back to
the levee, a detachment of the 16th Infantry appeared and took them
all into custody. None were prosecuted, apparently; the army simply
wanted to head off trouble, and no doubt quickly released those
arrested. They returned to work for their usual wage, and thus the
strike failed to achieve its declared purpose. But it had dramatically

demonstrated that black Memphis had not been cowed into abject submission by the riot and had not abandoned hope for the future.[68]

More evidence soon followed. In late May, the Memphis Sons of Ham, a black fraternal organization, announced plans for a big picnic on June 6 to celebrate the fourth anniversary of the city's capture by federal forces. They were warned against it: "We think the darkeys had better subside," the *Bulletin* remarked. "Their demonstration can do no good, and mischievous consequences may result." But the festivities were held as announced, in a grove beside the Memphis and Charleston Railroad track; the featured speaker was Clinton Fisk. A few weeks later, the Sons of Ham and other black organizations in the city celebrated the Fourth of July with picnics, speeches, and a parade.[69]

Some of the speeches at the black gatherings on Independence Day were explicitly political, and there followed further signs that black Memphis's quest for equality was undeterred. On July 19, freedmen gathered in Caldwell Hall—a black-owned venue damaged in the riot but since repaired—in anticipation of the second Tennessee State Colored Men's Convention, to be held in Nashville in August. The attendees at Caldwell Hall elected thirteen men to go as delegates to Nashville and formally instructed them to take a stand there for full legal equality for blacks and for black male suffrage.[70]

In seeking these privileges—or rights, as they saw them—the freedmen set their sights not on the federal government but on the state government. Their approach was by no means quixotic, for in recent months Governor Brownlow and the Radical-dominated Tennessee legislature had shown themselves willing, if not exactly eager, to expand black equality. Earlier in the year they had enacted a law, which took effect on May 25, allowing blacks to testify in the state's courts. This was a great stride forward for equal justice in Tennessee. It was not, however, an unmixed blessing for the freed people of Memphis, for it eliminated the legal justification for the Freedmen's Bureau court, at least as the Bureau interpreted it. Fisk promptly ordered the Bureau court to cease operation; it held its last session on June 2. Thereafter, black Memphians charged with major crimes went before the district criminal court—and before a white jury, for the legislature did not change the law restricting jury service to enfranchised men. Moreover, blacks charged with lesser offenses now went before the recorder's court—the domain of John C. Creighton.[71]

Creighton undoubtedly relished his new power over alleged black criminals, but he did not wield it for long. On July 1 the recorder's office was abolished as part of a sweeping reform of the Memphis police department decreed by the state legislature. The Metropolitan Police Act, under consideration for several months and passed on May 14, did away with the existing department and replaced it with one controlled not by the city government but by three state-appointed commissioners. The act also mandated stricter qualifications for policemen, gave the commissioners the exclusive power to hire and fire them, and replaced the recorder's court with a police court presided over by the commissioners. Brownlow's three appointees, confirmed on May 22, were all professional men of Memphis and loyal Republicans, one a former Union army officer.[72]

The first of July, when the act took effect, was a Sunday. At eight thirty that morning the city police force disbanded and the newly recruited metropolitan police, sporting official uniforms, were sworn into office. The next day, the new police court convened in the former recorder's courtroom. Later in the summer the metropolitan police arrested Mayor Park for getting into a fistfight with an alderman at a supper honoring city firemen; convicted in the police court of drunkenness and disorderly conduct, Park was fined eleven dollars.[73]

As the weeks passed, the debris of the Memphis riot—the charred remains of shanties and schools and churches—was cleared away. Soon no physical evidence of the three days of violence could be seen except for the scars on some of the victims who had survived and the graves of those who had not. But the riot remained a vivid, disturbing presence in the consciousness of very many people, not just in Memphis but all across America.

On July 30, in New Orleans, hundreds of Southern white men went on a rampage in reaction to a political gathering of Radical whites and blacks. Although this riot lasted only a few hours and involved no burnings, no rapes, and little robbery, it shocked the nation no less than the Memphis riot, for the death toll—several dozen black men, along with a number of white Radicals—was just as sickening. "Memphis and New Orleans" quickly became a rallying cry in the momentous battle over the nation's reconstruction.[74]

One who took up the cry was a post office functionary in Washington named Isaac Arnold. He had held his job since shortly after the assassination of Abraham Lincoln, whom he revered. Over time his hope that Andrew Johnson would carry on in the spirit of Lincoln was dashed, and by the fall of 1866 he had concluded that he could no longer in good conscience remain a part of Johnson's administration. On September 29, he wrote the president an impassioned letter of resignation: "To the loyal black man, and the loyal white man of the South, Mr. Lincoln promised protection and security. . . . How can you, Mr. President occupy the Executive Mansion as the successor of Lincoln, how could you visit his grave with the bloody outrages of Memphis and New Orleans unpunished? . . . Believing [that] you are today exerting your vast power in the interests of traitors, and that your policy should be over thrown at the ballot box, that the Republic based on liberty and justice may live, I retire from office that I may more freely and effectively aid in that overthrow."[75]

Among the great quantity of mail delivered to the White House this letter was hardly important; it may have been simply filed away by a secretary without being shown to the president. But whether he read the letter or not, Johnson was very aware of the surging anger and disgust at his reconstruction program that it epitomized. As 1866 gave way to 1867, the "screams and groans of the dying victims at Memphis" that Congressman Stevens had professed to hear continued to echo across America, and they would not be ignored.

9

The Riot in History and Memory

The 1866 Memphis riot was one of the earliest—and would remain one of the bloodiest—battles in a vast counterrevolution carried out by white men in the South who were determined to deny full freedom and equality to the former slaves among them. This counterrevolution provoked the U.S. government to take extraordinary measures to protect the freed people, measures that launched one of the most remarkable periods in the South's history, which historians call the era of Radical reconstruction. Ironically, however, the Memphis riot, having assisted at the birth of Radical reconstruction, also had a hand in its death.

In the congressional elections of 1866, Northern Republican candidates and the Republican press invoked the riot (along with other incidents of white violence in the South since the war ended) to condemn President Johnson's policies of letting the ex-Confederates restore their state governments on their own and deal with the freed people as they saw fit. This line of attack worked: in the elections, the party substantially reinforced its majorities in the House and Senate.[1]

In early March 1867 Congress passed, over the president's veto, an act with which it seized control of reconstruction and struck down Johnson's program. This act and its subsequent amendments abolished (with one exception) the resurrected Southern state governments recognized by Johnson, imposed temporary federal military rule on those ten states, and decreed a strict procedure they would have to follow to restore their governments and be readmitted to the Union. The key provisos were that they must adopt new state constitutions that granted black men the right to vote and must ratify the Fourteenth Amendment. The Memphis riot again figured prominently in

the deliberations that produced this legislation; the act's preamble asserted that in the former Rebel states there was no "adequate protection
for life or property."[2]

All ten states were readmitted within three years, and in the ensuing period of Radical reconstruction—which varied in duration from
state to state, but was wholly ended by 1877—Republican-dominated
state governments, elected by the votes of freedmen and white "scalawags" and "carpetbaggers," pursued a vision of biracial democracy,
legal equality for the freed people, public education for the children of
both races, and economic development (while not infrequently engag-
ing in fraud and graft).[3]

But the interpretation of the Memphis riot endorsed by the authors
and proponents of the congressional reconstruction act, based mostly
on the federal investigations, was not the only one that influenced
public opinion. The Conservative interpretation of the riot depicted it
as an understandable, if excessive, reaction to the insufferable provo-
cations of the freed slaves—who were unrestrained by law or morality
and whipped into a frenzy by meddling Yankees—and extolled its sal-
utary lessons for blacks. Here, in other words, was further evidence
that emancipation had been a grievous mistake, that the freed people
were dangerously out of control, and that violence in the service of
white supremacy was justified and indeed necessary. These beliefs fueled the clandestine, guerrilla-style terrorism of organizations such as
the Ku Klux Klan and later the paramilitary onslaughts of the White
League, the Red Shirts, and the like, which challenged the Republican state regimes in the South.[4]

Pressured by Northerners who had grown disgusted with the
seeming inability of the freedmen and their scalawag and carpetbagger friends to maintain order in the Southern states and govern
them honestly, the federal government eventually stopped intervening
to protect the Republican governments, standing aside as the last of
them fell. The Rebel "redeemers" promptly undid nearly all the progressive accomplishments of the Republican regimes (while generally
perpetuating the fraud and graft) and gradually relegated blacks to the
bottom tier of a new racial caste system that endured into the second
half of the twentieth century. Thus did the Memphis riot, having helped
usher in the extraordinary experiment of Radical reconstruction, also

help obliterate it and pave the way for its successor, the New South era of black disenfranchisement and Jim Crow segregation.[5]

There is another irony in all of this. The Memphis riot, which played so prominent a role in persuading Northerners to reject Johnsonian reconstruction and embrace Congress's alternative, occurred in the only former Rebel state not at the time dominated politically by ex-Confederates. Tennessee was in fact exempted from the congressional reconstruction act because it was under Republican control and had (in July 1866) ratified the Fourteenth Amendment, had immediately thereafter been readmitted to the Union by congressional resolution, and had (in February 1867) enfranchised its black male inhabitants (thereby becoming the first Southern state to do so). Moreover, the main perpetrators of the Memphis riot were not ex-Confederates, but Irish immigrants who had not served the Rebel cause. The Northerners who waved the bloody shirt of the Memphis riot did not always mention these facts. Those who did often insisted that the city's Rebel press had incited the Irish to riot.[6]

The riot in fact resists any easy characterization, Republican, Conservative, or otherwise. As much as it told contemporaries about the state of their nation, and as much as it tells us today about the Civil War era and the origins of the Jim Crow South, the riot was a highly distinctive event, and Memphis in 1866 was a highly distinctive city. Paradoxically, the extraordinary sources that the riot left in its wake are the kind of thing historians who study the nineteenth century long for, yet they simultaneously vex the historian, whose job it is to analyze, synthesize, and contextualize, to make order out of chaos. Another way of putting this is to say that the Memphis riot raises challenging questions about the history historians write. Perhaps this is why the riot has not been extensively written about before now.

For instance, while the riot was very much a part of the broad phenomenon of white reactionary violence in the reconstruction South, it differed in significant ways from the other instances of that violence. It was a spontaneous, unorganized event in a city, which set it apart from the planned, well-organized, and predominantly rural mayhem of the Klan, the White League, and similar groups. It differed from that mayhem, too, in that its perpetrators were, for the most part, not ex-Confederates. This same fact set the riot in Memphis apart from those in New Orleans and other Southern cities during reconstruction.[7]

Moreover, the Southern white counterrevolution of the reconstruction era is not the only historical context within which the Memphis riot can be meaningfully situated. It can also be seen as a late manifestation of the mobbing of blacks by whites during the insurrection panics that intermittently seized the antebellum South and reared up again in December 1865. It can be seen, too, as an instance of the periodic mob violence inflicted on blacks by working-class whites in urban America (mostly in the North) in the mid-nineteenth century—notably the horrific New York City riot of 1863. Nor would it be unreasonable to cite the riot as an early instance of the racial lynching that appeared in the postemancipation South and rose to a gruesome intensity in the early years of the twentieth century. In this sense, the Memphis riot illustrates the power of racism and mob psychology to turn ordinary human beings into vicious, conscienceless killers. All of these interpretations are useful and valid, but when the riot is placed too confidently in any one of them, it begins to stick out.[8]

The origin and nature of the riot further set it apart from ostensibly similar events. For one thing, it bears repeating that the rioters were almost all Irish-American. This fact was attested to by witness after witness in the official investigations—blacks, Southern whites, and Yankees alike (few Irish were questioned). This testimony is persuasive for two reasons besides its sheer volume. First, the great majority of Irish immigrants in that era were readily distinguishable by their manners and accents and in many cases by their dress. Second, while the Southern white witnesses might have had reason to exaggerate the guilt of the Irish, in order to absolve their own class, the blacks had much less reason and the Yankees none: if native-born white Southerners (who were also readily distinguishable to contemporary observers) had made up a significant portion of the riotous mobs, the freed people and Yankees would certainly have said so.[9]

Yet here the historian runs into another obstacle: the Irish rioters were a very small segment of Memphis's Irish male population. Exactly how small it is impossible to say, for the number of rioters can only be guessed at. The mobs described by reliable witnesses seem to have numbered in no case more than a few dozen men, but of course there were many different mobs at work in various parts of the city over the three days of rioting. Considering that some individuals accompanied more than one mob, a very generous estimate of the total number of rioters would be two or three hundred—including policemen and citizens who professed to be acting officially. This is a small portion indeed of the Irish male inhabitants of the city and suburbs, who (children included) probably numbered at least three thousand. Simply blaming the Irish for the riot is thus unfair, and can seem to involve the person doing the blaming in a racial calculus similar to that of the city's elite Rebels of the time.

Though the actions of the rioters are unpardonable, the Irish in Memphis had, as they saw it, good reasons for disliking blacks. They too struggled to survive and be accepted in America, and saw blacks as rivals in that twofold quest. The revolutionary events between mid-1862 and early 1866 saw enslaved Memphians emancipated and thousands of other newly free blacks flock to the city to escape the plantations. These freed people crowded into neighborhoods throughout the city, established communal institutions, competed with the Irish for jobs, took up arms as Union soldiers, and sometimes got drunk and rowdy and committed crimes. Having thus gained and asserted freedom, they insisted that that freedom must be more than nominal, and they were aided and defended by Northerners.

Irish resentment of blacks, in other words, had more proximate causes than the national political situation, which may explain why the role of the city's Rebel press in provoking the Irish to violence was overstated by Republicans. The newspapers were certainly racist (and anti-Yankee), fiercely so in some cases, and they often denounced the character and behavior of the freed people so viciously as to utterly dehumanize them. They also repeatedly declared that the city would be better off without the blacks, or at least most of them. But whether the Irish paid much attention to any of this is questionable. As the voice of the Rebel elite, the papers were generally condescending and often downright disparaging toward the Irish and could not have appealed much to those Irish who were inclined (and able) to read. And, in any event, the Irish needed no prodding by others to be roused to destructive fury against the freed people. Even had there been no Rebel press in Memphis in 1865–66, there would very likely still have been a riot.[10]

It was the city's Southern-born whites, much more than the Irish, who took the rhetoric of the Rebel press to heart. But then what is the historian supposed to make of the fact that they did not join the Irish rioters, at least not in significant numbers? There are a few possible answers. In many cases paternalist ties bound white Southerners and former slaves; such ties were almost wholly absent in black-Irish relations. But the Rebels were certainly capable of murderous assaults on the freed people. This was made clear beginning in 1868, when west Tennessee became the scene of extensive Ku Klux Klan violence. That violence seems, however, to have been provoked mostly by the political activism of the recently enfranchised freedmen. It may be that in 1866, with the ex-slaves still unenfranchised, west Tennessee Rebels did not yet feel sufficiently aggrieved to wreak bloody, large-scale vengeance on blacks. Or it may be that once the Memphis riot was under way, the city's Rebels, deeming it an Irish affair and generally contemptuous of the Irish, chose to stay out of it.[11]

Yet to say that Rebels played little role in the riot, and that Rebel newspapers were not to blame for inciting it, is not to say that Republicans were altogether mistaken or deceitful in using the riot as evidence for their cause. Numerous witnesses swore to hearing rioters damn emancipation, damn the Yankees who aided and protected the freed people, and declare their intention to kill or burn out as many blacks as they could and scare the rest out of the city, along with their Yankee friends. That these expressions of the rioters' sentiments and aims were uttered by presumably loyal Irish immigrants rather than unrepentant Rebels may have diminished their relevance to the argument for the congressional reconstruction act; but they were nevertheless good evidence for the broader argument that Southern blacks' freedom and rights and indeed lives were threatened and that they, along with the Northerners who stood by them, needed federal protection. (The Conservative claim that the riot demonstrated the need to reenfranchise Tennessee's "respectable" whites, so they could regain control of the city from the Irish and thus protect the ex-slaves, is unpersuasive. A Rebel-controlled city government would not likely have proved a better steward of the freed people's safety and interests than the Irish-controlled government. The New Orleans municipal government, it should be noted, was under Rebel control at the time of the riot in that city.)[12]

Further complicating things is the fact that, while Irishmen were the main perpetrators of the riot, the incident that ignited it—the clash between the four Irish policemen and the raucous crowd of black ex-soldiers on South Street on the afternoon of May 1—cannot be blamed on the Irish. The policemen did exceed their authority in try-ing to disperse the revelers, who were congregated just outside the city limit; the policemen knew this, but nevertheless obeyed Recorder Creighton's command. The black men were within their rights to ig-nore the order to disperse. However, when the policemen, recognizing the futility of their mission, broke off the encounter and retreated up the street toward the bayou bridge, the matter should have ended there. The blacks were wrong to follow and harass them, and wrong to fire their pistols into the air. The policemen cannot be blamed for as-suming they were being shot at and returning fire. It goes without say-ing that the misconduct of the ex-soldiers in this incident in no way justified the savage mob assaults on South Memphis that ensued, but the tidy story about blacks' victimization at the hands of whites does not entirely hold up.[13]

One of the few aspects of the riot that can be known with preci-sion is the number of whites who died in it, for the Rebel press gave it much attention. (The Select Committee's total of forty-six blacks killed, while probably not exactly correct for various reasons, is likely near the mark.) To the Select Committee's total of two whites—policeman John Stevens, who died of the wound accidentally self-inflicted in the initial shootout at the bayou bridge, and fireman Henry Dunn, shot a short while later by John Pendergrast, who mistook him for a black—should be added a third: Benjamin Dennis, gunned down in a saloon on May 2 by a fireman for talking with a freedman. That none of these three white victims died at the hands of a black person is worth reiterating.[14]

This book constitutes a thorough overhaul of the modern historical record on the riot, meager as it is, and will, I hope, help revive the memory of the riot, which is dim. From the late nineteenth century to the mid-twentieth, works of history (popular and scholarly alike) that discussed the riot portrayed it much like the Rebel and North-ern Democratic press had portrayed it in 1866. This understanding derived from the judgment on Radical reconstruction embraced by most of the American public in the postreconstruction decades. During that time, white Americans North and South generally agreed that Radical reconstruction had been a colossal mistake—a mistake based on the "fallacy" that blacks were capable of exercising freedom responsibly and thus deserving of legal and political equality—and that its overthrow, followed by the suppression of black rights in the South, was necessary and beneficial. A handful of black historians, along with a few aged white Republicans who had not abandoned their reconstruction-era racial idealism, challenged this broad consensus but were almost wholly ignored.[15]

Typical of the way the riot was portrayed in the postreconstruction decades was a history of Memphis published in 1888 that described the black soldiers in the months leading up to the riot as "very impudent and self-assertive. Gangs of them had assaulted white women as well as men." Black misbehavior in the city, the author went on to say, was encouraged by the Freedmen's Bureau, "a pet scheme of the extreme radicals in Congress, [and] a law unto itself, . . . so managed as to minister to the vanity of the negro and the humiliation of the white people." The soldiers engaged "in self-indulgences and orgies in low places near the fort, obtruding themselves in an overbearing manner" on the poor whites in the vicinity, who eventually got fed up and reacted violently. Another history of the city, published in 1939, informed readers that black Memphians in 1866 were "scarcely two centuries removed from the African jungle" and constituted "an undigested body in the city's craw," living in "idleness and crime."[16]

History books and essays are not, of course, the only repositories of historical memory. Stories of the past are also handed down orally and in private memoirs; retold in vernacular and highbrow fiction, art, and music; and narrated in public exhibitions, ceremonies, and monuments. But anyone seeking evidence that the Memphis riot was remembered in any of these ways from the late nineteenth to the mid-twentieth centuries will likely come up empty-handed (with the single exception of a brief passage in a manuscript memoir written in 1916 by a ninety-two-year-old white Memphian). If the memory of the riot was preserved during those decades outside of historians' writings, there is precious little evidence of it even in Memphis, not to mention the South or the nation as a whole.[17]

This should perhaps not surprise us. Southern blacks in that era faced new waves of terrorism—lynchings (including some in Memphis) and urban race riots—that may have made the Memphis riot of 1866 seem but a distant precursor to present horrors, a faded sepia image forgotten among the fresh portraits rendered in blood-red. Moreover, while white Americans of that era frequently retold stories of the counterrevolutionary violence of reconstruction, these stories—embodied most notably in films and novels such as *Birth of a Nation* and *Gone With the Wind*—were almost all celebrations of the "valiant knights" of the Ku Klux Klan, those robed and hooded paragons of the Old South who rode their steeds through the countryside meting out due punishment to their black and white Radical oppressors. In this vision of the past there was no place for the Irish thugs of Memphis.

Beginning in the 1950s there came a sea change in white racial attitudes in America, generated especially by the civil rights movement. A new consensus on Radical reconstruction eventually emerged among historians (professional historians, at least), depicting it as a worthy endeavor whose ultimate collapse should not be applauded but deplored. In this telling, the ex-slaves' quest for equality was a noble undertaking and the whites who opposed it were on the wrong side of history. Those writing from this revisionist standpoint who have discussed the Memphis riot see the city's freed people not as villains but as victims.[18]

Modern historians of the reconstruction era all acknowledge the riot's significance and several have investigated aspects of it in depth. But the public memory of the riot is still almost wholly confined to historiography. The riot is today no more a part of the typical American's consciousness of the past than it was a century ago. Granted, a Google search for "Memphis riot 1866" yields hundreds of thousands of hits, including a Wikipedia article and a short piece on the Tennessee state library's website (under the rubric "Disasters in Tennessee"). But the vast majority of Americans these days, if asked about "the Memphis riot," would likely either confess their ignorance or mention the events of April 1968, following the assassination of Martin Luther King.[19]

Even in Memphis the riot is generally absent from public memory. During the first half of the 1960s, Memphis, like the rest of the country, was awash in centennial commemorations of the Civil War; but when May 1966 came around, the public silence was deafening. Today a visitor to the city can see a statue of Confederate hero Nathan Bedford Forrest, a monument honoring victims of the devastating yellow fever epidemic of 1878, and a civil rights museum (at the site where King was shot). But there is no memorial marking the events of May 1–3, 1866. Perhaps the sesquicentennial in 2016 will provide an opportunity to rectify this lapse of memory, to acknowledge publicly the "screams and groans of the dying victims at Memphis," and to allow their ghosts at last to rest.[20]

NOTES

ABBREVIATIONS

Appeal   *Memphis Daily Appeal*
Argus   *Memphis Daily Argus*
Avalanche   *Memphis Daily Avalanche*
Bulletin   *Memphis Daily Bulletin*
Commercial   *Memphis Daily Commercial*
LROAG   Letters Received by the Office of the Adjutant General (Main Series), 1861–1870, M619, National Archives and Records Administration, Washington, DC
Post   *Memphis Daily Post*
Public Ledger   *Memphis Public Ledger*
RACST   Records of the Assistant Commissioner for the State of Tennessee, Bureau of Refugees, Freedmen, and Abandoned Lands, 1865–1869, RG 105, M999, National Archives and Records Administration, Washington, DC
RSC   *Report of the Select Committee on the Memphis Riots and Massacres* (Washington, DC: Government Printing Office, 1866). Also published, with same pagination, as United States Congress, *Memphis Riots and Massacres*, House Rpts., 39th Cong., 1st Sess. (1866), No. 101, Serial 1274.
SRTFO   Selected Records of the Tennessee Field Office of the Bureau of Refugees, Freedmen, and Abandoned Lands, 1865–1872, RG 105, T142, National Archives and Records Administration, Washington, DC

PROLOGUE

1. John Smith to Elihu Washburne, 8 December 1865, and W. H. Morgan to Elihu Washburne, 11 May 1866, Elihu Washburne Papers, Library of

Congress, Washington, DC; Elihu Washburne to Thaddeus Stevens, 24 May 1866, Thaddeus Stevens Papers, Library of Congress, Washington, DC; United States Congress, *Riot at Memphis*, House Exec. Docs., 39th Cong., 1st Sess. (1866), No. 122, Serial 1263, pp. 1–3; "Report of an investigation . . . ," enclosed in T. W. Gilbreth to O. O. Howard, 22 May 1866, Affidavits Relating to Outrages, March 1866–August 1868, reel 34, RACST.

2. Gaillard Hunt, *Israel, Elihu, and Cadwallader Washburn* [sic]: *A Chapter in American Biography* (New York: Macmillan, 1925), 235–38; Eric Foner, *Reconstruction: America's Unfinished Revolution, 1863–1877* (New York: Harper & Row, 1988), 216–47.

3. Howard Carroll, *Twelve Americans: Their Lives and Times* (New York: Harper & Brothers, 1883), 414; Foner, *Reconstruction*, 176–216, 239–62.

4. *Post*, 23 May 1866; *Memphis City Directory, 1866* (Memphis: Bingham, Williams, 1866), 276; *Memphis and Its Environs, 1860* (Memphis: Monsarrat, Dupree, 1860).

5. *Public Ledger*, 20, 21, 23 March, 12 April, 22, 23, 24 May 1866; *Commercial*, 4 April, 24 May 1866; *Appeal*, 4 January, 8 March 1866; Walter J. Fraser Jr. and Pat C. Clark, eds., "The Letters of William Beverly Randolph Hackley: Treasury Agent in West Tennessee, 1863–1866," *West Tennessee Historical Society Papers* 25 (1971): 106; Peter Eltinge to father, 14 March 1866, Eltinge-Lord Families Papers, Perkins Library, Duke University.

6. *Memphis and Its Environs*; *RSC*, 210; J. T. Trowbridge, *The South: A Tour of Its Battlefields and Ruined Cities, a Journey through the Desolated States, and Talks with the People* (Hartford, CT: L. Stebbins, 1866), 333; John Preston Young, *Standard History of Memphis, Tennessee, from a Study of the Original Sources* (Knoxville: H. W. Crew, 1912), 108, 137; Joseph H. Parks, "Memphis under Military Rule, 1862–1865," *East Tennessee Historical Society's Publications* 14 (1942): 35, 54; J. E. Hilary Skinner, *After the Storm; or, Jonathan and His Neighbours in 1865–6*, 2 vols. (London: Richard Bentley, 1866), 2:8, 22; *The Statistics of the Population of the United States . . . (June 1, 1870) . . .* (Washington, DC: Government Printing Office, 1872), 268; *Public Ledger*, 19 March 1866.

7. *RSC*, 45–46, 50–60.

8. *RSC*, 62–71, 78–79.

9. Elihu Washburne to Thaddeus Stevens, 24 May 1866, Stevens Papers.

1. YANKEE MEMPHIS

1. *RSC*, 276, 278, 279.

2. William Wilder to Thaddeus Stevens, 22 April 1866, Stevens Papers; Frederick H. Dyer, *A Compendium of the War of the Rebellion*, 3 vols. (New York: Thomas Yoseloff, 1959), 3:1024–25.

3. *Avalanche*, 3 April 1866.

4. *RSC*, 57, 239; Charles L. Lufkin, "The Northern Exodus from Memphis during the Secession Crisis," *West Tennessee Historical Society Papers* 42 (1988): 6–29.

5. *Memphis City Directory*, 276; *Appeal*, 17 November 1865; *RSC*, 202, 205, 211, 216, 217, 223, 237, 250.

6. James E. Sefton, *The United States Army and Reconstruction, 1865–1877* (Baton Rouge: Louisiana State University Press, 1967), 5–76.

7. Ezra J. Warner, *Generals in Blue: Lives of the Union Commanders* (Baton Rouge: Louisiana State University Press, 1964), 459–60; John Smith to William Whipple, 9 January 1866, folder 6, box 12, reel 3, Adjutant General's Office (Tennessee) Records, 1796–1900, RG 21, Tennessee State Library and Archives, Nashville; Steven Hahn, Steven F. Miller, Susan E. O'Donovan, John C. Rodrigue, and Leslie S. Rowland, eds., *Land and Labor: 1865* (Chapel Hill: University of North Carolina Press, 2008), 99–100.

8. John Smith to William Whipple, 21 December 1865, 9 January 1866, folder 6, box 12, reel 3, Adjutant General's Office (Tennessee) Records; John Smith to Elihu Washburne, 8 December 1865, Washburne Papers.

9. Hahn, *Land and Labor*, 888–89; *Appeal*, 30 January 1866; *RSC*, 156, 238; John Smith to Mr. Bullock and Mr. Stahl, 20 December 1865, folder 6, box 12, reel 3, Adjutant General's Office (Tennessee) Records.

10. Mark Mayo Boatner III, *The Civil War Dictionary* (New York: David McKay, 1959), 801; Sefton, *United States Army and Reconstruction*, 16–17; *RSC*, 50, 265; *Post*, 15, 19 January 1866.

11. Sefton, *United States Army and Reconstruction*, 16–17, 21; Benjamin Runkle to Clinton Fisk, 7 May 1866, Registered Letters Received, vol. 2, reel 11, RACST; *Appeal*, 27 February 1866; *RSC*, 50, 56, 58–59, 164, 265–66, 269–70; Marcus Wright file, Case Files of Applications from Former Confederates for Presidential Pardons ("Amnesty Papers"), 1865–1867—Tennessee Applications, M1003, National Archives and Records Administration, Washington, DC.

12. *RSC*, 358.

13. Collection guide, Arthur W. Allyn Letters, Connecticut Historical Society, Hartford, CT; Dyer, *Compendium*, 3:1714–15; *The War of the Rebellion: A Compilation of the Official Records of the Union and Confederate Armies*, 70 vols. in 128 (Washington, DC: Government Printing Office, 1880–1901), Series One, 12(1):401–402.

14. Arthur Allyn to father, 3 March, 16 April 1865, Allyn Letters.

15. Special Order 60, 10 April 1866, Special Orders Issued, April 1866–March 1869, Post of Memphis, E-811, Part 4, Records of the U.S. Army Continental Commands, 1821–1920, RG 393, National Archives and Records Administration, Washington, DC; Arthur Allyn to W. L. Porter, 15 April 1866, Letters Sent, April 1866–March 1869, Post of Memphis, E-808, Part 4, ibid.; A. W. Allyn testimony, Proceedings of a Military Commission, 412T1866, reel 520, LROAG; *RSC*, 358.

16. General Order 1, 16 April 1866, Special Orders Issued, April 1866–March 1869, Post of Memphis, E-811, Part 4, Records of the U.S. Army Continental Commands; *Post*, 27 April 1866; *RSC*, 358.

17. Joe M. Richardson, *Christian Reconstruction: The American Missionary Association and Southern Blacks, 1861–1890* (Athens: University of Georgia Press, 1986), passim; Alrutheus Ambush Taylor, *The Negro in Tennessee, 1865–1880* (Washington, DC: Associated Publishers, 1941), 168–72, 205–207; Ernest W. Hooper, "Memphis, Tennessee: Federal Occupation and Reconstruction, 1862–1870" (PhD diss., University of North Carolina, 1957), 157, 162; E. O. Tade to M. E. Strieby, 28 August 1865, H8969, American Missionary Association Papers, Tennessee Manuscripts, Amistad Collection, Tulane University; "Consolidated Monthly Report of the Freedmen Schools of the Sub Dist of Memphis Tenn," 26 November 1865, Monthly Reports from District Superintendents, reel 7, Records of the Superintendent of Education for the State of Tennessee, Bureau of Refugees, Freedmen, and Abandoned Lands, 1865–1870, RG 105, M1000, National Archives and Records Administration, Washington, DC.

18. *RSC*, 20, 259–63; *Christian Advocate*, 15 March 1866; *Post*, 19 January, 13 March 1866; *Extracts from Documents in the Office of the General Superintendent of Refugees and Freedmen, Headquarters, Memphis, Tennessee, March, 1865* (Memphis: Freedmen Press, 1865), 11–15.

19. C. Stuart McGehee, "E. O. Tade, Freedmen's Education, and the Failure of Reconstruction in Tennessee," *Tennessee Historical Quarterly* 43 (1984): 376–78; *RSC*, 88, 91, 92, 93; Ewing Tade to corresponding secretary, 1 August 1865, H8965–67, and E. O. Tade to M. E. Strieby, 28 August 1865, H8969, American Missionary Association Papers.

20. Ewing Tade to corresponding secretary, 1 August 1865, H8965–67; E. O. Tade to M. E. Strieby, 30 October 1865, H8986; E. O. Tade to Mr. Whipple and Mr. Strieby, 16 January 1866, H9023AA-C; E. O. Tade to M. E. Strieby, 6 February 1866, H9041–46; J. P. Bardwell to George Whipple, 21 February 1866, H9063; E. O. Tade to M. E. Strieby, 23 March 1866, H9078–79; E. O. Tade to Samuel Hunt, 26 April 1866, H9096–99; and Monthly Report, Lincoln School, April 1866, H9108, American Missionary Association Papers; *RSC*, 93.

21. *RSC*, 92, 93, 94; A. L. Rankin to M. E. Strieby, 20 July 1865, H8961; Ewing Tade to corresponding secretary, 1 August 1865, H8965–67; T. E. Bliss to Dear Brethren, 23 August 1865, H8968; T. E. Bliss to Dear Brethren, 3 March 1866, H9074; E. O. Tade to M. E. Strieby, 23 March 1866, H9078–79; and E. O. Tade to M. E. Strieby, 25 April 1866, H9094–95, American Missionary Association Papers; John Cimprich, *Slavery's End in Tennessee, 1861–1865* (University: University of Alabama Press, 1985), 61–62.

22. E. O. Tade to Mr. Whipple and Mr. Strieby, 16 January 1866, H9023AA-C; E. O. Tade to M. E. Strieby, 6 February 1866, H9041–46; E. O. Tade to M. E. Strieby, 23 March 1866, H9078–79; and E. O. Tade to M. E.

Strieby, 25 April 1866, H9094–95, American Missionary Association Papers.

23. *RSC*, 57, 71–73, 74, 76–77, 84–85, 104, 108, 118, 121, 164, 190, 229, 283–85, 286–87, 288–93, 307; Kenneth M. Stampp, *The Era of Reconstruction, 1865–1877* (New York: Vintage Books, 1965), 158–59.

24. Trowbridge, *The South*, 333–35; Joseph H. Parks, "A Confederate Trade Center under Federal Occupation: Memphis, 1862–1865," *Journal of Southern History* 7 (1941): 289–314; Gerald M. Capers Jr., *Biography of a River Town: Memphis: Its Heroic Age* (Chapel Hill: University of North Carolina Press, 1939), 162–63, 183–85; Hooper, "Memphis, Tennessee," 255; Parks, "Memphis under Military Rule," 35; Jack D. L. Holmes, "The Underlying Causes of the Memphis Race Riot of 1866," *Tennessee Historical Quarterly* 17 (1958): 204; Peter Eltinge to sister, 18 March 1866, Eltinge-Lord Families Papers.

25. "Collection Overview," Eltinge-Lord Families Papers; Dyer, *Compendium*, 3:1463.

26. "Collection Overview," Peter Eltinge to father, 14 March, 11 April 1866, and Peter Eltinge to sister, 2 May 1866, Eltinge-Lord Families Papers.

27. "Collection Overview" and Peter Eltinge to father, 14 March, 11, 17 April 1866, ibid.

28. "Collection Overview," Peter Eltinge to father, 11, 17 April 1866, and Peter Eltinge to sister, 20 April, 2, 10 May 1866, ibid.

29. William S. McFeely, *Yankee Stepfather: General O. O. Howard and the Freedmen* (New Haven, CT: Yale University Press, 1968), passim; Taylor, *Negro in Tennessee*, 12–15; Hooper, "Memphis, Tennessee," 143–44.

30. Hooper, "Memphis, Tennessee," 142–43; Kevin R. Hardwick, "'Your Old Father Abe Lincoln Is Dead and Damned': Black Soldiers and the Memphis Race Riot of 1866," *Journal of Social History* 27 (1993): 114–16; Dernoral Davis, "Hope versus Reality: The Emancipation Era Labor Struggle of Memphis Area Freedmen," in *Race, Class, and Community in Southern Labor History*, ed. Gary M. Fink and Merl E. Reed (Tuscaloosa: University of Alabama Press, 1994), 105–106.

31. Davis Tillson to W. T. Clarke, 10 July 1865, vol. 133, Letters Sent by the Memphis District, Office of the Superintendent, reel 17, SRTFO; entries passim, vols. 169, 170, 171, 172, Complaint Books of the Freedmen's Court in the Memphis District, reel 24, ibid.; Hooper, "Memphis, Tennessee," 144–46; *Argus*, 15 April 1866; *New York Independent*, 7 September 1865.

32. Davis Tillson to W. T. Clarke, 21 July 1865, and superintendent (Dudley) to W. T. Clarke, 13 September 1865, vol. 133, Letters Sent by the Memphis District, Office of the Superintendent, reel 17, SRTFO; A. T. Reeve to Clinton Fisk, 27 December 1865, Registered Letters Received, vol. 1, reel 8, RACST; Hahn, *Land and Labor*, 266, 272–73.

33. *Avalanche*, 5 May 1866; *Columbus* (GA) *Daily Sun*, 21 February 1866; Benjamin Runkle to Clinton Fisk, 4 April 1866, Narrative Reports of

Operations and Conditions, February–September 1866, reel 17, RACST; superintendent to W. T. Clarke, 28 October 1865, Benjamin Runkle to W. L. Porter, 9 April 1866, and W. W. Walsh to Thomas Leonard, 18 April 1866, vol. 134, Letters Sent by the Memphis District, Office of the Superintendent, reel 17, SRTFO; H. Swartzwelder to J. H. Grove, 25 September 1865, vol. 159, Letters Sent by the Memphis District, Office of the Chief Medical Officer, reel 21, ibid.; "To the Benevolent and Philanthropic Friends of Freedmen," H8980, American Missionary Association Papers; *Appeal*, 17 November 1865.

34. *Post*, 1 March 1866; *RSC*, 274, 280; Boatner, *Civil War Dictionary*, 713; Ross A. Webb, "'The Past Is Never Dead. It's Not Even Past': Benjamin P. Runkle and the Freedmen's Bureau in Kentucky, 1866–70," *Register of the Kentucky Historical Society* 84 (1986): 350–51.

35. *RSC*, 274; Benjamin Runkle to J. E. Jacobs, 1 March 1866 and 30 April 1866, Registered Letters Received, vol. 2, reel 11, RACST; Benjamin Runkle to J. B. Wilson, 20 March 1866, vol. 134, Letters Sent by the Memphis District, Office of the Superintendent, reel 17, SRTFO; *Appeal*, 21 November 1865.

36. Benjamin Runkle to Clinton Fisk, 4 April 1866, Narrative Reports of Operations and Conditions, February–September 1866, reel 17, RACST; Benjamin Runkle to J. E. Jacobs, 3 April 1866, Registered Letters Received, vol. 2, reel 11, ibid.; *RSC*, 276, 279; *Appeal*, 10 April 1866; *Post*, 26, 29 April 1866.

37. Benjamin Runkle to Clinton Fisk, 26 April 1866, and A. T. Reeve to Clinton Fisk, 3 January 1866, vol. 134, Letters Sent by the Memphis District, Office of the Superintendent, reel 17, SRTFO; A. T. Reeve to Clinton Fisk, 21 December 1865, Registered Letters Received, vol. 1, reel 8, RACST; Hahn, *Land and Labor*, 273; *RSC*, 276; *Post*, 12, 13, 25 April 1866; *Appeal*, 10 April 1866.

38. Benjamin Runkle to Clinton Fisk, 4 April 1866, Narrative Reports of Operations and Conditions, February–September 1866, reel 17, RACST; Benjamin Runkle to Clinton Fisk, 23 May 1866, Reports of Outrages, Riots, and Murders, 1866–1868, reel 34, ibid.; *RSC*, 274, 276, 277, 278.

39. Benjamin Runkle to Clinton Fisk, 5 May 1866, vol. 134, Letters Sent by the Memphis District, Office of the Superintendent, reel 17, SRTFO; *Post*, 26, 29 April 1866.

40. *RSC*, 57, 59, 85, 213, 279; *Avalanche*, 12 April 1866.

41. *Appeal*, 28 December 1865; *Post*, 16, 17, 23 March, 26 April 1866; *Avalanche*, 12, 26 April 1866; Hooper, "Memphis, Tennessee," 201.

42. *Avalanche*, 12 April 1866; John Eaton, *Grant, Lincoln, and the Freedmen: Reminiscences of the Civil War with Special Reference to the Work for the Contrabands and Freedmen of the Mississippi Valley* (New York: Longmans, Green, 1907), x, xii–xiii, xv–xvii; Boatner, *Civil War Dictionary*, 259; Frank B. Williams, "John Eaton, Jr., Editor, Politician, and School Administrator,

1865–1870," *Tennessee Historical Quarterly* 10 (1951): 291–93; Cimprich, *Slavery's End in Tennessee*, 63–64.

43. Eaton, *Grant, Lincoln, and the Freedmen*, xvii, 248; *Post*, 14 March 1866; John Eaton to J. H. Tomeny, 9 November 1865, John H. Eaton Jr. Papers, 1865–1881, Special Collections, University of Tennessee, Knoxville; Hooper, "Memphis, Tennessee," 250–51; Alice Eaton Diary, 1865–1908, entry for 20 November 1865, Special Collections Library, Duke University.

44. *Post*, 15 January 1866.

45. Ibid.; *RSC*, 94, 308; Williams, "John Eaton," 293; LeRoy P. Graf, Ralph W. Haskins, and Paul H. Bergeron, eds., *The Papers of Andrew Johnson*, 16 vols. (Knoxville: University of Tennessee Press, 1967–2000), 10:401; Alice Eaton Diary, 6 November 1865, 29 June 1866.

46. *RSC*, 240, 241; *Post*, 18 January, 16, 21 February, 13, 15 March 1866.

47. *Post*, 13, 18, 19, 29 April 1866.

48. *Post*, 2 February, 9, 11, 23 March 1866.

49. *RSC*, 90; John Leftwich to Elihu Washburne, 15 May 1866, Washburne Papers; Shelby County, TN, district 14, p. 51 (W. Wallace), Ninth Census, 1870, Manuscript Returns of Inhabitants, National Archives and Records Administration, Washington, DC; Graf, Haskins, and Bergeron, *Papers of Andrew Johnson*, 10:401.

50. *RSC*, 94–95, 212–15, 241; *Appeal*, 28 December 1865; *Avalanche*, 12 April 1866.

51. *RSC*, 145–46, 214, 215, 219, 238–39, 254, 255, 262, 271–72, 278–79; *Chicago Tribune*, 13 May 1866; *Avalanche*, 14 April 1866.

52. *RSC*, 284, 285, 287, 299.

2. REBEL MEMPHIS

1. *RSC*, 244, 285–86.

2. Trowbridge, *The South*, 332.

3. *RSC*, 274–75, 278.

4. *RSC*, 286, 298.

5. W. Raymond Cooper, "Four Fateful Years—Memphis, 1858–1861," *West Tennessee Historical Society Papers* 11 (1957): 63–75; Douglas Wayne Cupples, "Memphis Confederates: The Civil War and Its Aftermath" (PhD diss., University of Memphis, 1995), 57, 62–63; Young, *Standard History of Memphis*, 118–19, 120, 337–39; Lufkin, "Northern Exodus," 6–29; Hooper, "Memphis, Tennessee," 188.

6. Hooper, "Memphis, Tennessee," chaps. 1–7; Parks, "Memphis under Military Rule," 31–58; Parks, "Confederate Trade Center," 289–314; Cupples, "Memphis Confederates," 92–93, 128–29, 137.

7. Whitelaw Reid, *After the War: A Southern Tour, May 1, 1865, to May 1, 1866* (Cincinnati: Moore, Wilstach, & Baldwin, 1866), 426; Cupples,

"Memphis Confederates," 154–56; *RSC*, 139, 297, 300, 304; Parks, "Memphis under Military Rule," 34–35; Lufkin, "Northern Exodus," 8.

8. Paul H. Bergeron, *Andrew Johnson's Civil War and Reconstruction* (Knoxville: University of Tennessee Press, 2011), chap. 3; Foner, *Reconstruction*, 181–84; Kathleen Rosa Zebley, "Rebel Salvation: The Story of Confederate Pardons" (PhD diss., University of Tennessee, 1998), passim.

9. Bergeron, *Andrew Johnson's Civil War and Reconstruction*, chaps. 1 and 2; Foner, *Reconstruction*, 176–81, 183–84; Zebley, "Rebel Salvation," passim; William Avery file, Case Files of Applications; Shelby County, TN, district 5, p. 98 (W. T. Avery), Eighth Census, 1860, Manuscript Returns of Free Inhabitants, National Archives and Records Administration, Washington, DC; Shelby County, TN, district 5, p. 1 (W. T. Avery), Eighth Census, 1860, Manuscript Returns of Slaves, National Archives and Records Administration, Washington, DC.

10. Foner, *Reconstruction*, 176–227; Bergeron, *Andrew Johnson's Civil War and Reconstruction*, chap. 3; William Avery file, Case Files of Applications.

11. Foner, *Reconstruction*, 224–27; Bergeron, *Andrew Johnson's Civil War and Reconstruction*, chap. 3.

12. Foner, *Reconstruction*, 189–90; *RSC*, 91, 146, 268, 270.

13. Hooper, "Memphis, Tennessee," 256–57.

14. Stephen V. Ash, *When the Yankees Came: Conflict and Chaos in the Occupied South, 1861–1865* (Chapel Hill: University of North Carolina Press, 1995), 2–7, 24–25.

15. *RSC*, 133, 138, 286, 293, 295, 298, 299; *Appeal*, 1 May 1866.

16. *RSC*, 132, 133, 286, 295, 297, 304–305; *Post*, 8 May 1866.

17. *Memphis City Directory*, 281; *Long's Memphis Directory . . . 1865–'66* (Memphis: Blelock, 1865), 14; *RSC*, 299–301, 303–304; Shelby County, TN, Memphis, Ward 4, p. 50 (J. H. McMahon), Ward 5, p. 65 (M. C. Gallaway), and Ward 8, p. 138 (Lewis J. Dupree), Eighth Census Returns of Free Inhabitants; Marius Carriere, "An Irresponsible Press: Memphis Newspapers and the 1866 Riot," *Tennessee Historical Quarterly* 60 (2001): 5; Thomas Harrison Baker, *The Memphis "Commercial Appeal": The History of a Southern Newspaper* (Baton Rouge: Louisiana State University Press, 1971), 75, 95; M. C. Gallaway file, Case Files of Applications; Shelby County, TN, Memphis, Ward 8, p. 17 (Lewis J. Dupree), Eighth Census Manuscript Returns of Slaves.

18. *RSC*, 59, 85, 86, 91, 307–308, 328; Graf, Haskins, and Bergeron, *Papers of Andrew Johnson*, 6:326n, 10:401; Benjamin Runkle to Clinton Fisk, 23 May 1866, Reports of Outrages, Riots, and Murders, 1866–1868, reel 34, RACST.

19. John David Smith, *An Old Creed for the New South: Proslavery Ideology and Historiography, 1865–1918* (Westport, CT: Greenwood Press, 1985), chap. 1; *Appeal*, 26 November 1865, 12 April 1866; *Public Ledger*, 6 March 1866.

20. Hahn, *Land and Labor*, 833–34; *Argus*, 22 February 1866. For an illuminating discussion of gender distinctions in the white view of blacks, see

Hannah Rosen, *Terror in the Heart of Freedom: Citizenship, Sexual Violence, and the Meaning of Race in the Postemancipation South* (Chapel Hill: University of North Carolina Press, 2009), 55–60.

21. James L. Roark, *Masters without Slaves: Southern Planters in the Civil War and Reconstruction* (New York: Norton, 1977), 123–24, 153–54; *RSC*, 268; *Appeal*, 26 November 1865.

22. Roark, *Masters without Slaves*, 165–68, 168–69; *Appeal*, 26 November 1865, 2, 18 February 1866; *Avalanche*, 4, 16, 28 January 1866.

23. United States Congress, *Report of the Joint Committee on Reconstruction*, House Reports, 39th Cong., 1st Sess. (1866), No. 30, Serial 1273, pp. 107–108; Dan T. Carter, *When the War Was Over: The Failure of Self-Reconstruction in the South, 1865–1867* (Baton Rouge: Louisiana State University Press, 1985), 187, 217–26.

24. Carter, *When the War Was Over*, 183–84; *RSC*, 134, 138, 140, 285–86, 293–94, 296–97, 298, 304; *Appeal*, 18, 30 November 1865, 4 January, 16 February, 18, 20 March, 12 April 1866; *Public Ledger*, 6 March 1866.

25. *Argus*, 3, 7, 18, 22 February, 29 March 1866; *Avalanche*, 7, 10, 11, 14 January, 3, 9, 22 February, 17, 21 April 1866; John Smith to Elihu Washburne, 8 December 1865, Washburne Papers; Rosen, *Terror in the Heart of Freedom*, 44–49; George C. Rable, *But There Was No Peace: The Role of Violence in the Politics of Reconstruction* (Athens: University of Georgia Press, 1984), 37.

26. Carter, *When the War Was Over*, 191–202; Steven Hahn, "'Extravagant Expectations' of Freedom: Rumour, Political Struggle, and the Christmas Insurrection Scare of 1865 in the American South," *Past and Present* 157 (1997): 122–58; Bobby L. Lovett, "Memphis Riots: White Reaction to Blacks in Memphis, May 1865–July 1866," *Tennessee Historical Quarterly* 38 (1979):16; A. T. Reeve to Clinton Fisk, 23 December 1865, Unregistered Telegrams Received, reel 15, RACST; A. T. Reeve to Clinton Fisk, 21 and 27 December 1865, Registered Letters Received, vol. 1, reel 8, ibid.; Hahn, *Land and Labor*, 883–84, 886–87, 889; *Appeal*, 27 January 1866; Stephen V. Ash, *A Year in the South: Four Lives in 1865* (New York: Palgrave Macmillan, 2002), 225–27.

27. *RSC*, 91, 276; Benjamin Runkle to Clinton Fisk, 23 May 1866, Reports of Outrages, Riots, and Murders, 1866–1868, reel 34, RACST; *Avalanche*, 7 January 1866; *Bulletin*, 4 February 1866; *Argus*, 22, 23 February 1866; *Little Rock* (AR) *Daily Gazette*, 23 April 1866 (quoting *Public Ledger*); Rosen, *Terror in the Heart of Freedom*, 40–42.

28. *Little Rock* (AR) *Daily Gazette*, 23 April 1866 (quoting *Public Ledger*); *Appeal*, 24 April 1866.

29. *RSC*, 278–79, 298; Graf, Haskins, and Bergeron, *Papers of Andrew Johnson*, 10:226; Benjamin Runkle to Clinton Fisk, 4 April 1866, Narrative Reports of Operations and Conditions, February–September 1866, reel 17, RACST; Paul David Phillips, "White Reaction to the Freedmen's Bureau in

Tennessee," *Tennessee Historical Quarterly* 25 (1966): 50–62; *Appeal*, 3, 20 March 1866; Holmes, "Underlying Causes of the Memphis Race Riot," 210–13 (quoting *Avalanche*).

30. Benjamin Runkle to Clinton Fisk, 23 May 1866, Reports of Outrages, Riots, and Murders, 1866–1868, reel 34, RACST; *RSC*, 91, 261, 301; Holmes, "Underlying Causes of the Memphis Race Riot," 213 (quoting *Appeal*); Hooper, "Memphis, Tennessee," 161.

31. *Appeal*, 2 January 1866; *Avalanche*, 1 April 1866.

32. *RSC*, 57, 59, 73, 85, 91, 146, 213, 238, 276, 281, 285, 304.

33. *Appeal*, 9 January, 10, 17 April 1866.

34. Ibid., 28 December 1865, 16 February 1866; *Post*, 20 February, 11 March 1865; *Avalanche*, 27 February, 15, 25, 30 March, 1, 6 April 1866.

35. *RSC*, 57, 291; *Avalanche*, 15, 25, 30 March, 1, 6 April 1866.

36. *Avalanche*, 3 April 1866; Holmes, "Underlying Causes of the Memphis Race Riot," 201–202; *RSC*, 73, 84, 145, 146, 219, 238, 255, 262, 272, 278–79, 285, 294, 301; Elizabeth Avery Meriwether, *Recollections of 92 Years, 1824–1916* (Nashville: Tennessee Historical Commission, 1958), 181.

37. *RSC*, 264–65, 278.

38. *RSC*, 268–69; *Appeal*, 28 April 1866; Gaines Foster, *Ghosts of the Confederacy: Defeat, the Lost Cause, and the Emergence of the New South, 1865–1913* (New York: Oxford University Press, 1987), chaps. 1–3; Thomas L. Connelly and Barbara L. Bellows, *God and General Longstreet: The Lost Cause and the Southern Mind* (Baton Rouge: Louisiana State University Press, 1982), chap. 1.

39. *RSC*, 58–59, 244, 265, 278; *Post*, 13, 31 March 1866; *Argus*, 31 March, 19 April 1866.

40. Cupples, "Memphis Confederates," 160–65; *Bulletin*, 13, 15 January 1866; *Avalanche*, 4, 11 January, 21, 23 March, 11, 25 April 1866; *Appeal*, 23, 24 December 1865.

41. *Avalanche*, 16 January, 25 April, 1 May 1866; *Appeal*, 27 April 1866; Patricia M. La Pointe, "The Disrupted Years: Memphis City Hospitals, 1860–1867," *West Tennessee Historical Society Papers* 37 (1983): 10–11; Caroline E. Janney, *Burying the Dead but Not the Past: Ladies' Memorial Associations and the Lost Cause* (Chapel Hill: University of North Carolina Press, 2008), chaps. 1 and 2; William A. Blair, *Cities of the Dead: Contesting the Memory of the Civil War in the South, 1865–1914* (Chapel Hill: University of North Carolina Press, 2004), 77–87.

42. Shelby County, TN, Memphis, Ward 5, p. 65, Eighth Census Returns of Free Inhabitants; Shelby County, TN, Memphis, Ward 4, p. 25, Ninth Census Returns of Inhabitants; *Appeal*, 14 April, 1 May 1866; *Avalanche*, 16 January, 21, 23 March, 11, 25 April, 1 May 1866.

43. Janney, *Burying the Dead*, chap. 2; Blair, *Cities of the Dead*, chap. 3; David W. Blight, *Race and Reunion: The Civil War in American Memory*

(Cambridge, MA: Belknap Press of Harvard University, 2001), 64–65, 77–78; *Appeal*, 14, 27, 28 April 1866; *Avalanche*, 11, 25, 27 April 1866.
44. *Avalanche*, 25, 27 April 1866; *Appeal*, 27 April, 1 May 1866.

3. IRISH MEMPHIS

1. *RSC*, 178, 276, 299.
2. *Appeal*, 18 March 1866; *Long's Memphis Directory*, 19; *Avalanche*, 17, 18 March 1865.
3. *Avalanche*, 18 March 1866; *Appeal*, 18 March 1866.
4. David T. Gleeson, *The Irish in the South, 1815–1877* (Chapel Hill: University of North Carolina Press, 2001), 35.
5. Ibid., 1–9, 94–95, 99–100, and passim; Margaret Lynch-Brennan, *The Irish Bridget: Irish Immigrant Women in Domestic Service in America, 1840–1930* (Syracuse, NY: Syracuse University Press, 2009), 22–27, 40–42.
6. Gleeson, *Irish in the South*, 1–9, 138–39, 141, 173, and passim.
7. Ibid., 6–8, 94–95; Joe Brady, "The Irish Community in Antebellum Memphis," *West Tennessee Historical Society Papers* 40 (1986): 24–44; Darrell B. Uselton, "Irish Immigration and Settlement in Memphis, Tennessee, 1820s–1860s," *West Tennessee Historical Society Papers* 50 (1996): 115–26; A. T. Reeve to Clinton Fisk, 21 December 1865, Registered Letters Received, vol. 1, reel 8, RACST; *RSC*, 178, 242, 300.
8. Robert C. Rauchle, "The Political Life of the Germans in Memphis, 1848–1880," *Tennessee Historical Quarterly* 27 (1968): 165–75; Kathleen C. Berkeley, *"Like a Plague of Locusts": From an Antebellum Town to a New South City, Memphis, Tennessee, 1850–1880* (New York: Garland, 1991), 16, 20–23, 32–37, 139–43; Robert C. Rauchle, "Biographical Sketches of Prominent Germans in Memphis, Tennessee, in the Nineteenth Century," *West Tennessee Historical Society Papers* 22 (1968): 73–85; Rabbi James A. Wax, "The Jews of Memphis, 1860–1865," *West Tennessee Historical Society Papers* 3 (1949): 39–89; *Long's Memphis Directory*, 14, 16, 18; *Memphis City Directory*, 279, 282–83; *Appeal*, 23 December 1865, 18 February 1866; *Avalanche*, 28 March, 7 April 1866; *Statistics of the Population*, 268, 389.
9. Berkeley, *"Like a Plague of Locusts,"* 33–37, 64, 138; Brady, "Irish Community in Antebellum Memphis," 31–32; Mary Grady testimony, Proceedings of a Military Commission, 412T1866, reel 520, LROAG; *RSC*, 99, 114, 163, 167, 187–88; Shelby County, TN, Memphis, Ward 1, p. 40/20 (John Callahan), Ward 10, p. 1/461 (John Pendergrast), Ninth Census Returns of Inhabitants; Altina Waller, "Community, Class and Race in the Memphis Riot of 1866," *Journal of Social History* 18 (1984): 240; *Memphis City Directory*, 95; *Long's Memphis Directory*, 125.

10. Berkeley, *"Like a Plague of Locusts,"* 33–37, 64, 138; *Appeal,* 27 March 1866; Shelby County, TN, Memphis, Ward 10, p. 10/465 (Michael Pendergrast), Ninth Census Returns of Inhabitants; *RSC,* 365–71; Shelby County, TN, Memphis, Ward 3, p. 10 (Eugene McGeveney [*sic*]), Eighth Census Returns of Free Inhabitants; Brady, "Irish Community in Antebellum Memphis," 25–26, 41; Uselton, "Irish Immigration and Settlement," 123.

11. Berkeley, *"Like a Plague of Locusts,"* 32–37, 64, 138; Lynch-Brennan, *Irish Bridget,* 42–47; Uselton, "Irish Immigration and Settlement," 123. For occupations of Irishwomen, see Shelby County, TN, Memphis, passim, Ninth Census Returns of Inhabitants.

12. *Public Ledger,* 19 March 1866; Uselton, "Irish Immigration and Settlement," 120–21; Berkeley, *"Like a Plague of Locusts,"* 30–33; Brady, "Irish Community in Antebellum Memphis," 29; *Post,* 25 April 1866; Waller, "Community, Class and Race," 235. For the living arrangements of single and married Irish, see Shelby County, TN, Memphis, passim, Ninth Census Returns of Inhabitants.

13. Lynch-Brennan, *Irish Bridget,* 41–42; Berkeley, *"Like a Plague of Locusts,"* 18; *Appeal,* 2 January 1866; *Memphis Daily Tribune,* 4 February 1866; *Public Ledger,* 5, 9, 17 March, 28 May 1866; *Commercial,* 4 March 1866.

14. Michael Kaplan, "New York City Tavern Violence and the Creation of a Working-Class Male Identity," *Journal of the Early Republic* 15 (1995): 591–617; Peter Way, "Evil Humors and Ardent Spirits: The Rough Culture of Canal Construction Laborers," *Journal of American History* 79 (1993): 1397–1428; *Public Ledger,* 22, 28, 29 March, 23 April, 30 May 1866; *Post,* 29 March 1866; *RSC,* 300.

15. *Public Ledger,* 15, 22 March, 10, 30 May 1866; *RSC,* 82, 300; *New York Times,* 21 May 1866.

16. Foner, *Reconstruction,* 477–79; *Appeal,* 27, 30 March, 10 April 1866; *Avalanche,* 27, 30 March, 10 April 1866.

17. Brady, "Irish Community in Antebellum Memphis," 37.

18. Uselton, "Irish Immigration and Settlement," 124–25; Brady, "Irish Community in Antebellum Memphis," 32–37; Berkeley, *"Like a Plague of Locusts,"* 14–15; *Memphis City Directory,* 279.

19. Perry County, OH, Reading Township, p. 60, Eighth Census Returns of Free Inhabitants; *Memphis City Directory,* 279; Berkeley, *"Like a Plague of Locusts,"* 139; *Avalanche,* 11 February 1866; Gleeson, *Irish in the South,* 91–93.

20. Christian G. Samito, *Becoming American under Fire: Irish Americans, African Americans, and the Politics of Citizenship during the Civil War* (Ithaca, NY: Cornell University Press, 2009), 120–25, 180, 183–85; Mitchell Snay, *Fenians, Freedmen, and Southern Whites: Race and Nationality in the Era of Reconstruction* (Baton Rouge: Louisiana State University Press, 2007), 50–51, 54–57, 150–53; Gleeson, *Irish in the South,* 71.

21. Gleeson, *Irish in the South*, 69–71; *Appeal*, 9 December 1865, 18 March 1866; *Post*, 19 April 1866; *Memphis City Directory*, 271; *Avalanche*, 18 February, 18 March 1866; *Memphis Daily Tribune*, 3 February 1866.

22. Samito, *Becoming American under Fire*, 180–85; *Post*, 7 March, 19, 26 April 1866; *Avalanche*, 27 March, 18, 19, 20, 26 April 1866; *Argus*, 14 April 1866; *Appeal*, 19 April 1866.

23. Samito, *Becoming American under Fire*, 43–44, 120–22, 125, 132–33, 172–79; Snay, *Fenians, Freedmen, and Southern Whites*, 150–53; *Argus*, 23 February 1866; Chancery Court Naturalization Records, 1865–1866, passim, reel 77, Shelby County Miscellaneous City/County Records, Tennessee State Library and Archives, Nashville.

24. Gleeson, *Irish in the South*, 107–108, 121, 127; Samito, *Becoming American under Fire*, 25; Snay, *Fenians, Freedmen, and Southern Whites*, 52–54; Brady, "Irish Community in Antebellum Memphis," 43–44; Matthew Frye Jacobson, *Whiteness of a Different Color: European Immigrants and the Alchemy of Race* (Cambridge, MA: Harvard University Press, 1998), 13–14, 42–55; David R. Roediger, *The Wages of Whiteness: Race and the Making of the American Working Class* (London: Verso, 1991), 13–14, 133–56; Noel Ignatiev, *How the Irish Became White* (New York: Routledge, 1995), passim.

25. Holmes, "Underlying Causes of the Memphis Race Riot," 198–99; Hooper, "Memphis, Tennessee," 191–92; *RSC*, 132, 137–39, 242, 284, 286, 310–11, 365, 366.

26. *Digest of the Charters and Ordinances of the City of Memphis, from 1826 to 1867* . . . (Memphis: Bulletin Publishing, 1867), 183–217; *Long's Memphis Directory*, 14–15, 270; *Memphis City Directory*, 270–72, 275–76; *Avalanche*, 21 March, 6, 10 April 1866.

27. *Avalanche*, 18 April 1866.

28. John Mark Long, "Memphis Mayors, 1827–1866: A Collective Study," *West Tennessee Historical Society Papers* 52 (1998): 118; Shelby County, TN, Memphis, Ward 8, p. 122, Eighth Census Returns of Free Inhabitants.

29. *RSC*, 137, 210, 310–11, 365; *Argus*, 12 August 1866.

30. Gleeson, *Irish in the South*, 176; Berkeley, *"Like a Plague of Locusts,"* 222–23; *RSC*, 137, 310–11, 365.

31. *Argus*, 12 August 1866; *RSC*, 137, 210, 310–11.

32. *RSC*, 335, 370; *Digest of the Charters and Ordinances of the City*, 185–86, 189.

33. *RSC*, 335, 370–71; *Memphis City Directory*, 271; *Appeal*, 16 February 1866.

34. *Commercial*, 15 April 1866; *Avalanche*, 15 April 1866; *Argus*, 22 February 1866.

35. *Argus*, 22 February 1866; *Memphis City Directory*, 271; Shelby County, TN, Memphis, Ward 7, p. 79 (Benjamin Garrett), Eighth Census Returns of Free Inhabitants; *RSC*, 297, 366–69.

36. Waller, "Community, Class and Race," 241; Brance Hull testimony, Proceedings of a Military Commission, 412T1866, reel 520, LROAG; *RSC*,

63, 72, 115, 122, 165, 193, 221, 326, 327, 353; Payroll of City Day Police, 1 June 1866, and Payroll of City Night Police, 1 June 1866, reel 435, Shelby County Miscellaneous City/County Records.

37. *RSC*, 367; Shelby County, TN, Memphis, Ward 6, p. 137, Eighth Census Returns of Free Inhabitants; Shelby County, TN, Memphis, Ward 6, p. 39/204, Ninth Census Returns of Inhabitants; *Memphis City Directory*, 169; *Commercial*, 18 April 1866.

38. Benjamin Runkle to Clinton Fisk, 23 May 1866, Reports of Outrages, Riots, and Murders, 1866–1868, reel 34, RACST; *RSC*, 210, 326–27, 370.

39. *RSC*, 164, 165, 326–27; *Post*, 29 March 1866; Payroll of City Day Police, 1 June 1866, and Payroll of City Night Police, 1 June 1866, reel 435, Shelby County Miscellaneous City/County Records; *Appeal*, 14 December 1865.

40. Hooper, "Memphis, Tennessee," 220–21; Rable, *But There Was No Peace*, 35–36; *Post*, 29 March 1866; *Memphis Southern Loyalist*, 28 October 1865; *RSC*, 60, 164, 165, 276, 326, 327; *Appeal*, 1 May 1866; Robert H. White, ed., *Messages of the Governors of Tennessee, 1857–1869* (Nashville: Tennessee Historical Commission, 1959), 504.

41. *RSC*, 198, 311; *Memphis City Directory*, 103, 271; *Avalanche*, 10 April 1866; Shelby County, TN, Memphis, Ward 1, p. 80, Eighth Census Returns of Free Inhabitants.

42. *Memphis City Directory*, 103; Shelby County, TN, Memphis, Ward 1, p. 80, Eighth Census Returns of Free Inhabitants; *RSC*, 198, 253, 254, 256, 291, 311; Hooper, "Memphis, Tennessee," 192.

43. *RSC*, 198, 210, 253, 254, 255, 366; Shelby County, TN, Memphis, Ward 1, p. 117 (L. R. Richards, city register), Eighth Census Returns of Free Inhabitants.

44. *Post*, 6 March 1866; Shelby County, TN, Memphis, Ward 1, p. 54, Eighth Census Returns of Free Inhabitants; *Memphis City Directory*, 194, 275; Ralph A. Wooster, *Politicians, Planters, and Plain Folk: Courthouse and Statehouse in the Upper South, 1850–1860* (Knoxville: University of Tennessee Press, 1975), 99; *RSC*, 80; *Avalanche*, 23 February 1866.

45. "Municipal Record," *Long's Memphis Directory*; Wooster, *Politicians, Planters, and Plain Folk*, 106.

46. Lovett, "Memphis Riots," 18; *RSC*, 132, 140, 286, 287, 293–94, 296–97, 304, 307.

47. Gleeson, *Irish in the South*, 127, 173; *RSC*, 90, 115, 117, 132, 135, 255, 276, 286, 293–94, 296–97, 304.

48. *Avalanche*, 3, 22 February 1866; *Argus*, 3 February 1866; James Cannon Mitcher [*sic*] testimony, Proceedings of a Military Commission, 412T1866, reel 520, LROAG; *Appeal*, 22 February, 3 March 1866.

49. *RSC*, 100, 117, 163, 167, 172; W. H. Morgan et al. to William Brownlow, 22 December 1865, Governor William G. Brownlow Papers, 1865–1869, Tennessee State Library and Archives, Nashville; Waller, "Community, Class and Race," 238.

50. *RSC*, 87, 114–15, 178, 203, 218, 219, 262, 276–77, 287, 289.
51. Hahn, *Land and Labor*, 888; *RSC*, 87, 90, 145, 166, 178, 213, 331.
52. *RSC*, 213.

4. BLACK MEMPHIS

1. *RSC*, 124, 166, 199.
2. *Memphis Southern Loyalist*, 28 October 1865.
3. *Chicago Tribune*, 13 May 1866; Trowbridge, *The South*, 333–35; *Post*, 23 May 1866; *Memphis Southern Loyalist*, 28 October 1865; Skinner, *After the Storm*, 2:5–6, 16.
4. Armstead Robinson, "Plans Dat Comed from God: Institution Building and the Emergence of Black Leadership in Reconstruction Memphis," in *Toward a New South? Studies in Post–Civil War Southern Communities*, ed. Orville V. Burton and Robert C. McMath Jr. (Westport, CT: Greenwood Press, 1982), 84; Record 37, Registers of Signatures of Depositors in Branches of the Freedman's Savings and Trust Company, 1865–1874, Memphis Branch, RG 101, M816, National Archives and Records Administration, Washington, DC; *RSC*, 96, 100, 233–34, 318; Taylor, *Negro in Tennessee*, 154, 155.
5. Rable, *But There Was No Peace*, 34; Rosen, *Terror in the Heart of Freedom*, 264n28; Lovett, "Memphis Riots," 9–10.
6. Records 192, 278, Registers of Signatures of Depositors, Memphis Branch.
7. Records 37, 280, 289, 397, 568, ibid.; *RSC*, 62. General studies of emancipation in Tennessee and elsewhere during and immediately after the war include Cimprich, *Slavery's End in Tennessee*; Leon F. Litwack, *Been in the Storm So Long: The Aftermath of Slavery* (New York: Alfred A. Knopf, 1979), chaps. 1–4; and Ash, *When the Yankees Came*, chap. 5.
8. Record 190, Registers of Signatures of Depositors, Memphis Branch; Dyer, *Compendium*, 3:1722, 1725–26.
9. Ash, *When the Yankees Came*, 153–56, 160–62; Cimprich, *Slavery's End in Tennessee*, 46–59; Rosen, *Terror in the Heart of Freedom*, 29–30; Lovett, "Memphis Riots," 9; Richardson, *Christian Reconstruction*, 27; Hardwick, "'Your Old Father Abe Lincoln,'" 109–28; Litwack, *Been in the Storm*, 311, 313; T. E. Bliss to Dear Brethren, 23 August 1865, H8968, American Missionary Association Papers.
10. Hahn, *Land and Labor*, 587–88, 934–36; Litwack, *Been in the Storm*, 399–403; Davis, "Hope versus Reality," 106–12; Ira Berlin et al., eds., *The Wartime Genesis of Free Labor: The Lower South* (Cambridge: Cambridge University Press, 1990), 819–20; *Post*, 12 April 1866.
11. Hahn, *Land and Labor*, 586–88; Davis, "Hope versus Reality," 112–18; Hardwick, "'Your Old Father Abe Lincoln,'" 113–14; Benjamin Runkle to J. E. Jacobs, 3 April 1866, Registered Letters Received, vol. 2, reel 11, RACST.

12. *Post*, 12 April 1866; Hardwick, "'Your Old Father Abe Lincoln,'" 112, 113–14, 116; Hahn, *Land and Labor*, 266, 272, 841; Benjamin Runkle to Clinton Fisk, 4 April 1866, Narrative Reports of Operations and Conditions, February–September 1866, reel 17, RACST; Skinner, *After the Storm*, 2:15–16, 22; United States Congress, *Report of Commissioners of Freedmen's Bureau*, House Exec. Docs., 39th Cong., 1st Sess. (1866), No. 70, Serial 1256, p. 46.

13. Skinner, *After the Storm*, 2:7; P. D. Beecher to Benjamin Runkle, 18 May 1866, Unregistered Letters Received, reel 15, RACST; T. E. Bliss to Mr. Whipple and Mr. Strieby, 28 December 1865, H9008, and E. O. Tade to M. E. Strieby, 23 March 1866, H9078–79, American Missionary Association Papers; A. T. Reeve to Clinton Fisk, 3 January 1866, vol. 134, Letters Sent by the Memphis District, Office of the Superintendent, reel 17, SRTFO; *Appeal*, 9 November 1865; *Bulletin*, 4 February 1866; *RSC*, 97–98.

14. Undated insert (probably ca. 18 August 1865) regarding black population of Memphis, vol. 133, Letters Sent by the Memphis District, Office of the Superintendent, reel 17, SRTFO; *RSC*, 171–72, 233–34, 319 (where the name is given as Meadows rather than Minter); Lovett, "Memphis Riots," 12–13; Robinson, "Plans Dat Comed from God," 84–85.

15. Hooper, "Memphis, Tennessee," 154; Taylor, *Negro in Tennessee*, 162; Record 1, Registers of Signatures of Depositors, Memphis Branch; *RSC*, 62–63, 340, 352.

16. H. Swartzwelder to J. H. Grove, 25 September 1865, vol. 159, Letters Sent by the Memphis District, Office of the Chief Medical Officer, reel 21, SRTFO; superintendent to W. T. Clarke, 28 October 1865, and Benjamin Runkle to W. L. Porter, 9 April 1866, vol. 134, Letters Sent by the Memphis District, Office of the Superintendent, reel 17, ibid.; Robinson, "Plans Dat Comed from God," 80–81; Benjamin Runkle to Clinton Fisk, 4 April 1866, Narrative Reports of Operations and Conditions, February–September 1866, reel 17, RACST; report for April 1866, Reports of Numbers of Persons Issued Rations, Clothing, and Medicines, November 1865–October 1868, reel 19, ibid.; *Post*, 19 January 1866; *Extracts from Documents*, 11–15; *Appeal*, 27 February, 18 March 1866; *Bulletin*, 15 January 1866.

17. Undated insert (probably ca. 18 August 1865) regarding black population of Memphis, vol. 133, Letters Sent by the Memphis District, Office of the Superintendent, reel 17, SRTFO; superintendent to J. E. Jacobs, 16 February 1866, vol. 134, ibid.; H. Swartzwelder to J. H. Grove, 25 September 1865, vol. 159, Letters Sent by the Memphis District, Office of the Chief Medical Officer, reel 21, ibid.; Special Order 3, 2 February 1866, vol. 167, Special Orders Issued by the Provost Marshal for Freedmen in the Memphis District, reel 23, ibid.; 1865 Memphis census, passim (indicating numerous single black people living in white households), reel 7, Shelby

County Miscellaneous City/County Records; P. D. Beecher to Benjamin Runkle, 18 May 1866, Unregistered Letters Received, reel 15, RACST; Hardwick, "'Your Old Father Abe Lincoln,'" 113; *Appeal*, 20 December 1865, 19 April 1866; Cimprich, *Slavery's End in Tennessee*, 46–47; *RSC*, 187–88.

18. Lovett, "Memphis Riots," 9–10; Cimprich, *Slavery's End in Tennessee*, 46–47, 57–58; *Appeal*, 20 December 1865, 24, 28 January, 28 February, 17, 19 April 1866; *RSC*, 155; Benjamin Runkle to Clinton Fisk, 4 April 1866, Narrative Reports of Operations and Conditions, February–September 1866, reel 17, RACST; superintendent to J. E. Jacobs, 16 February 1866, vol. 134, Letters Sent by the Memphis District, Office of the Superintendent, reel 17, SRTFO; *Avalanche*, 9 February 1866; *Post*, 25 April 1866.

19. Records 2, 10, 12, 278, 297, Registers of Signatures of Depositors, Memphis Branch; Herbert G. Gutman, *The Black Family in Slavery and Freedom, 1750–1925* (New York: Pantheon Books, 1976), chaps. 7–9; Cimprich, *Slavery's End in Tennessee*, 73–75. I have estimated the proportion of children in the black population from statistics in Hahn, *Land and Labor*, 267, with allowance for the black federal troops in the city, who were not included in Hahn's tally.

20. Record 170, Registers of Signatures of Depositors, Memphis Branch.

21. *RSC*, 139–40, 189, 193–94, 200, 227; *Appeal*, 19 April 1866; *Commercial*, 18 April 1866; *Post*, 18 April 1866; *Avalanche*, 18 April 1866; Record 66, Registers of Signatures of Depositors, Memphis Branch.

22. Andrew L. Slap, "The Loyal Deserters: African American Soldiers and Community in Civil War Memphis," in *Weirding the War: Stories from the Civil War's Ragged Edge*, ed. Stephen Berry (Athens: University of Georgia Press, 2011), 234–48; Hardwick, "'Your Old Father Abe Lincoln,'" 110–11; Barrington Walker, "'This Is the White Man's Day': The Irish, White Racial Identity, and the Memphis Riots," *Left History* 5 (1997): 34–35; Dyer, *Compendium*, 3:1642, 1721; United States Congress, *Riot at Memphis*, 1; John Smith to William Whipple, 21 December 1865, folder 6, box 12, reel 3, Adjutant General's Office (Tennessee) Records; *RSC*, 144, 203, 204, 207–208, 217, 218; Cimprich, *Slavery's End in Tennessee*, 73–74, 89.

23. Henry Hunt file, 3rd U.S. Colored Heavy Artillery, Compiled Military Service Records, National Archives and Records Administration, Washington, DC; Record 231, Registers of Signatures of Depositors, Memphis Branch; *RSC*, 352; Henry Hunt affidavit, Affidavits Relating to Outrages, March 1866–August 1868, reel 34, RACST.

24. Hardwick, "'Your Old Father Abe Lincoln,'" 112–13; Holmes, "Underlying Causes of the Memphis Race Riot," 216; Hooper, "Memphis, Tennessee," 175–76; I. G. Kappner to Lorenzo Thomas, 16 January 1866, Regimental Letterbook, 3rd U.S. Colored Heavy Artillery, Records of the Adjutant General's Office (U.S.), 1780s–1917, RG 94, National Archives and Records Administration, Washington, DC. On the experience of black Union troops

in the Civil War, see Joseph T. Glatthaar, *Forged in Battle: The Civil War Alliance of Black Soldiers and White Officers* (New York: Free Press, 1990). A number of soldiers from other black regiments in Memphis whose terms of enlistment had not expired when their regiment mustered out were transferred to the 3rd USCHA; see Slap, "Loyal Deserters," 240–41, 246n. This accounts for the extraordinarily large size of the 3rd: heavy artillery regiments normally numbered no more than about twelve hundred men.

25. I. G. Kappner to W. W. Cameron, 13 December 1865, Regimental Letterbook, 3rd U.S. Colored Heavy Artillery, Records of the Adjutant General's Office (U.S.); John Smith to William Whipple, 21 December 1865, folder 6, box 12, reel 3, Adjutant General's Office (Tennessee) Records.

26. Arthur Allyn to W. L. Porter, 15 April 1866, Letters Sent, April 1866–March 1869, Post of Memphis, E-808, Part 4, Records of the U.S. Army Continental Commands; J. A. Copeland to J. A. Alwood, 11 April 1866, and I. G. Kappner to A. L. Hough, 25 April 1866, Regimental Letterbook, 3rd U.S. Colored Heavy Artillery, Records of the Adjutant General's Office (U.S.); General Order 16, 10 April 1866, and General Order 18, 17 April 1866, Regimental Order Book, ibid.; *Post*, 19, 29 April 1866; *RSC*, 144, 203, 205, 207–208, 211, 223; Henry Hunt affidavit, Affidavits Relating to Outrages, March 1866–August 1868, reel 34, RACST.

27. Litwack, *Been in the Storm*, 450–71.

28. David M. Tucker, *Black Pastors and Leaders: Memphis, 1819–1972* (Memphis: Memphis State University Press, 1975), 3, 4–5; *RSC*, 318, 321, 323–24.

29. Tucker, *Black Pastors and Leaders*, 7–9; Records 7, 34, 40, Registers of Signatures of Depositors, Memphis Branch; T. O. Fuller, *The History of the Negro Baptists of Tennessee* (Memphis: Haskins Printing, 1936), 53, 73–74; *Post*, 6 March 1866; *Extracts from Documents*, 13; Rosen, *Terror in the Heart of Freedom*, 32, 52.

30. Ewing Tade to corresponding secretary, 1 August 1865, H8965–67, E. O. Tade to M. E. Strieby, 30 October 1865, H8986, T. E. Bliss to Mr. Whipple and Mr. Strieby, 28 December 1865, H9008, T. E. Bliss et al. to Mr. Whipple and Mr. Frisbie, 3 January 1866, H9014, E. O. Tade to Mr. Whipple and Mr. Strieby, 16 January 1866, H9023AA-C, E. O. Tade to M. E. Strieby, 6 February 1866, H9041–46, E. O. Tade to M. E. Strieby, 23 March 1866, H9078–79, E. O. Tade to M. E. Strieby, 25 April 1866, H9094–95, American Missionary Association Papers; Tucker, *Black Pastors and Leaders*, 6; *RSC*, 92.

31. Hooper, "Memphis, Tennessee," 157–60; *RSC*, 259, 260, 261, 263; Skinner, *After the Storm*, 2:9–10.

32. *RSC*, 236, 260, 313; Shelby County, TN, Memphis, Ward 7, p. 119, Ninth Census Returns of Inhabitants; Tucker, *Black Pastors and Leaders*, 7; Records 1, 167, Registers of Signatures of Depositors, Memphis Branch; Hahn, *Land and Labor*, 275–76.

33. Litwack, *Been in the Storm*, 472–501; *Post*, 13 March 1866; *RSC*, 98–100, 105, 162, 232, 235–36, 260, 277; Record 127, Registers of Signatures of Depositors, Memphis Branch; Joe M. Richardson, ed., "The Memphis Race Riot and Its Aftermath: Report by a Northern Missionary," *Tennessee Historical Quarterly* 24 (1965): 66, 66n.

34. *RSC*, 160, 233, 260; affidavits, passim, Affidavits Relating to Outrages, March 1866–August 1868, reel 34, RACST (the vast majority of black affiants, including Robert Church, signed by mark); Records 164, 176, 189, 207, 217, 237, 278, 746, Registers of Signatures of Depositors, Memphis Branch; Joseph Lee file, 3rd U.S. Colored Heavy Artillery, Compiled Military Service Records; *Post*, 15 January, 12 April 1866; Hahn, *Land and Labor*, 275–76; Hooper, "Memphis, Tennessee," 154; Shelby County, TN, Memphis, Ward 7, p. 43 (William Foster), Eighth Census Returns of Free Inhabitants; Shelby County, TN, Memphis, Ward 10, p. 84 (Anthony Motley), Ward 7, p. 227 (C. C. Dickinson), Ward 7, p. 37 (William Foster), Ward 5, p. 19 (Warner Madison), Ward 1, p. 17 (Reuben Alexander), Ward 9, p. 8 (Robert Trezevant), Ward 7, p. 64 (Green Williams), Ward 7, p. 119 (Joseph Clouston), Ninth Census Returns of Inhabitants.

35. Hardwick, "'Your Old Father Abe Lincoln,'" 117; Rosen, *Terror in the Heart of Freedom*, 33–34; Hooper, "Memphis, Tennessee," 171; Tucker, *Black Pastors and Leaders*, 25–26; *Appeal*, 2 January 1866; *Post*, 15 January, 12 April 1866; Benjamin Runkle to Clinton Fisk, 26 April 1866, vol. 134, Letters Sent by the Memphis District, Office of the Superintendent, reel 17, SRTFO; Hahn, *Land and Labor*, 273–74, 275–76. A notable exception to the rule of black leaders' poverty was barber and real estate investor Joseph Clouston, a free man before the war, who in 1860 was worth over $20,000; see Hooper, "Memphis, Tennessee," 154.

36. On gender divisions and the role of women in postwar black Memphis, see Rosen, *Terror in the Heart of Freedom*, 49–55.

37. Graf, Haskins, and Bergeron, *Papers of Andrew Johnson*, 10:226; *Avalanche*, 17 April 1866.

38. Superintendent to W. T. Clark, 13 September 1865, vol. 133, Letters Sent by the Memphis District, Office of the Superintendent, reel 17, SRTFO; entries passim, vols. 169, 170, 171, 172, Complaint Books of the Freedmen's Court in the Memphis District, reel 24, ibid.; *Appeal*, 11, 29 November 1865, 28 April 1866; Benjamin Runkle to Clinton Fisk, 4 April 1866, Narrative Reports of Operations and Conditions, February–September 1866, reel 17, RACST; *Argus*, 29 March 1866; *Post*, 24 March 1866.

39. *Public Ledger*, 15 March, 23 April, 14 May 1866; Mary Grady and A. W. Allyn testimonies, Proceedings of a Military Commission, 412T1866, reel 520, LROAG; *RSC*, 166, 245, 248, 329, 330, 358; *Argus*, 23 February 1866; Skinner, *After the Storm*, 2:6; *Appeal*, 28 February 1866; *Avalanche*, 28 January 1866.

40. RSC, 238; Post, 3 May 1866; Hahn, Land and Labor, 275–76; Appeal, 27 February 1866; United States Congress, Riot at Memphis, 1. The regiment had a much greater rate of desertion than the average black regiment in the Civil War. Some 572 men deserted over the life of the regiment, one-fourth of them in the first three months of 1866. See Slap, "Loyal Deserters," 234–48.

41. L. Methudy to J. A. Copeland, 13 January 1866, Regimental Letterbook, 3rd U.S. Colored Heavy Artillery, Records of the Adjutant General's Office (U.S.); Post, 13 April 1866; Henry Hunt file, 3rd U.S. Colored Heavy Artillery, Compiled Military Service Records; Hahn, Land and Labor, 888–89; RSC, 127–28, 130, 138–39, 147, 164, 184–85, 207–208, 217–218, 225, 245, 248, 358; John Smith to W. L. Porter, 20 January 1866, folder 6, box 12, reel 3, Adjutant General's Office (Tennessee) Records.

42. I. G. Kappner to J. B. Johnston, 25 February 1866, and captain of Company C to J. A. Copeland, 8 February 1866, Regimental Letterbook, 3rd U.S. Colored Heavy Artillery, Records of the Adjutant General's Office (U.S.); RSC, 144–45, 203; Avalanche, 23 February, 9 May 1866; Appeal, 26 January, 4 February, 7 March 1866; Hahn, Land and Labor, 888–89; John Smith to William Whipple, 21 December 1865, folder 6, box 12, reel 3, Adjutant General's Office (Tennessee) Records.

43. Taylor, Negro in Tennessee, 1–9, 15–20; RSC, 102; Benjamin Runkle to W. L. Porter, 9 April 1866, vol. 134, Letters Sent by the Memphis District, Office of the Superintendent, reel 17, SRTFO. The Tennessee legislature passed a law in January 1866 allowing black testimony, but it did not take effect until late May. The Freedmen's Bureau court continued until that time to adjudicate all criminal and civil matters involving freed people in Memphis.

44. Post, 25 January, 25 May 1866; Avalanche, 31 January 1866; unnamed captain to J. B. Wilson, 14 April 1866, vol. 134, Letters Sent by the Memphis District, Office of the Superintendent, reel 17, SRTFO.

45. Waller, "Community, Class and Race," 234–38; Rosen, Terror in the Heart of Freedom, 35–36; Post, 25 April 1866.

46. John Cimprich, Fort Pillow, a Civil War Massacre, and Public Memory (Baton Rouge: Louisiana State University Press, 2005), 108 and passim; Cimprich, Slavery's End in Tennessee, 95; Special Order 15, 1 March 1866, Company I Letterbook, 3rd U.S. Colored Heavy Artillery, Records of the Adjutant General's Office (U.S.); Company C reports, April 1866, Morning Reports, ibid.; Jerry Roberts file, 3rd U.S. Colored Heavy Artillery, Compiled Military Service Records; Record 562, Registers of Signatures of Depositors, Memphis Branch.

47. RSC, 288; Skinner, After the Storm, 2:13–15.

48. RSC, 287, 297, 303, 305, 306.

49. RSC, 96, 198, 226, 306; Hahn, Land and Labor, 884; Post, 12 April 1866; New York Independent, 7 September 1865.

50. Litwack, *Been in the Storm*, 455; *Post*, 1 February, 26, 29 April 1866; Hardwick, "'Your Old Father Abe Lincoln,'" 114–16; Hahn, *Land and Labor*, 269–79; *RSC*, 280; Shelby County, TN, Memphis, Ward 10, p. 85 (Anthony Motley), Ninth Census Returns of Inhabitants.

51. Walker, "'This Is the White Man's Day,'" 48–49; Holmes, "Underlying Causes of the Memphis Race Riot," 205; *RSC*, 127–28, 145, 147, 166, 178, 199, 306; Hardwick, "'Your Old Father Abe Lincoln,'" 117–19; Benjamin Runkle to Clinton Fisk, 23 May 1866, Reports of Outrages, Riots, and Murders, 1866–1868, reel 34, RACST; *Argus*, 18 February 1866; *Appeal*, 22 February, 3 March 1866; *Post*, 22, 24 February 1866; *Avalanche*, 22 February 1866.

52. *RSC*, 145, 367; *Appeal*, 20 April 1866.

53. *RSC*, 156–57, 169–70.

54. *RSC*, 101–102, 199.

55. Charles Nelson file, 3rd U.S. Colored Heavy Artillery, Compiled Military Service Records.

56. Judy Bussell LeForge, "State Colored Conventions of Tennessee, 1865–1866," *Tennessee Historical Quarterly* 65 (2006): 236–37.

57. *Post*, 12 April 1866.

58. *Avalanche*, 15, 17 April 1866; Lovett, "Memphis Riots," 12.

5. AN INCIDENT ON THE BAYOU BRIDGE

1. *Argus*, 1 May 1866; *Commercial*, 1 May 1866; *Post*, 1 May 1866; *Public Ledger* 30 April 1866; *Avalanche*, 1 May 1866.

2. *RSC*, 63–64, 67–68, 118.

3. *RSC*, 64, 67, 68; Rachel Dills [*sic*] testimony, Proceedings of a Military Commission, 412T1866, reel 520, LROAG; Mrs. S. E. Dilts affidavit, Affidavits Relating to Outrages, March 1866–August 1868, reel 34, RACST.

4. *RSC*, 64, 67–68, 118; Mrs. Samuel Dills [*sic*] and Rachel Dills [*sic*] testimonies, Proceedings of a Military Commission, 412T1866, reel 520, LROAG; Mrs. S. E. Dilts affidavit, Affidavits Relating to Outrages, March 1866–August 1868, reel 34, RACST.

5. *RSC*, 67–68, 118.

6. *RSC*, 245, 358; A. W. Allyn testimony, Proceedings of a Military Commission, 412T1866, reel 520, LROAG.

7. *RSC*, 245, 358; Mary Grady and A. W. Allyn testimonies, Proceedings of a Military Commission, 412T1866, reel 520, LROAG.

8. *RSC*, 64; *Argus*, 2 May 1866; *Public Ledger*, 1 May 1866; data for Memphis, 30 April 1866, United States Naval Observatory, "Complete Sun and Moon Data for One Day: U.S. Cities and Towns," accessed 12 July 2009, www.usno.navy.mil/USNO/astronomical-applications/data-services/rs-one -day-US.

9. *RSC*, 68–69; Mrs. Samuel Dills [*sic*] and Rachel Dills [*sic*] testimonies, Proceedings of a Military Commission, 412T1866, reel 520, LROAG.

10. Data for Memphis, 1 May 1866, United States Naval Observatory, "Complete Sun and Moon Data"; Patzy Tolliver affidavit, Affidavits Relating to Outrages, March 1866–August 1868, reel 34, RACST.

11. S. J. Quinby testimony, Proceedings of a Military Commission, 412T1866, reel 520, LROAG; *RSC*, 104, 105, 115, 182, 320; *Argus*, 2 May 1866; *Commercial*, 2 May 1866; *Avalanche*, 2 May 1866.

12. S. J. Quinby testimony, Proceedings of a Military Commission, 412T1866, reel 520, LROAG; *RSC*, 104, 105, 106, 115, 182, 315, 332, 346; *Post*, 3 May 1866.

13. S. J. Quinby and John Battie testimonies, Proceedings of a Military Commission, 412T1866, reel 520, LROAG; *RSC*, 104, 115, 116, 173, 320, 332, 346, 367–68; *Washington Daily National Intelligencer*, 7 May 1866; Patzy Tolliver affidavit, Affidavits Relating to Outrages, March 1866–August 1868, reel 34, RACST; *Post*, 3 May 1866.

14. *RSC*, 115, 116, 182, 321.

15. *RSC*, 182, 321.

16. *RSC*, 116, 182, 332, 346.

17. *RSC*, 182, 321, 367; Charles Nelson file, 3rd U.S. Colored Heavy Artillery, Compiled Military Service Records.

18. S. J. Quinby testimony, Proceedings of a Military Commission, 412T1866, reel 520, LROAG; R. McGowen affidavit, Affidavits Relating to Outrages, March 1866–August 1868, reel 34, RACST; *RSC*, 127, 182.

19. S. J. Quinby testimony, Proceedings of a Military Commission, 412T1866, reel 520, LROAG; *RSC*, 104, 106, 232, 315, 316, 320, 321, 324, 346; S. J. Quinby affidavit, Affidavits Relating to Outrages, March 1866–August 1868, reel 34, RACST.

20. S. J. Quinby testimony, Proceedings of a Military Commission, 412T1866, reel 520, LROAG; *RSC*, 104, 106, 116, 183, 232, 315, 324, 346.

21. *RSC*, 124, 182, 315–16, 320, 332; R. W. Creighton affidavit, Affidavits Relating to Outrages, March 1866–August 1868, reel 34, RACST.

22. S. J. Quinby and John Battie testimonies, Proceedings of a Military Commission, 412T1866, reel 520, LROAG; *RSC*, 104, 106, 116, 127, 182, 184, 232, 320, 332; *Post*, 3 May 1866; S. J. Quinby affidavit, Affidavits Relating to Outrages, March 1866–August 1868, reel 34, RACST.

23. S. J. Quinby, John Battie, and R. W. Creighton testimonies, Proceedings of a Military Commission, 412T1866, reel 520, LROAG; 5 May 1866 entry, Register of Deaths, 1848–1884, reel 35, Shelby County Miscellaneous City/County Records; *Washington Daily National Intelligencer*, 7 May 1866; *RSC*, 104, 106, 116, 124, 126, 133–34, 184, 320, 321, 332; R. W. Creighton affidavit, Affidavits Relating to Outrages, March 1866–August 1868, reel 34, RACST.

24. *RSC*, 106, 127, 182, 320.

25. RSC, 104, 106, 116, 184, 232, 316, 320, 321, 332; *Washington Daily National Intelligencer*, 7 May 1866; S. J. Quinby testimony, Proceedings of a Military Commission, 412T1866, reel 520, LROAG; S. J. Quinby affidavit, Affidavits Relating to Outrages, March 1866–August 1868, reel 34, RACST.

26. S. J. Quinby and James Finn testimonies, Proceedings of a Military Commission, 412T1866, reel 520, LROAG; S. J. Quinby affidavit, Affidavits Relating to Outrages, March 1866–August 1868, reel 34, RACST; RSC, 104, 106, 182, 184, 332; *Washington Daily National Intelligencer*, 7 May 1866.

27. RSC, 118.

28. S. J. Quinby affidavit, Affidavits Relating to Outrages, March 1866–August 1868, reel 34, RACST; RSC, 104, 106.

29. *Washington Daily National Intelligencer*, 7 May 1866; RSC, 127, 182, 319; "Report of an investigation . . . ," enclosed in T. W. Gilbreth to O. O. Howard, 22 May 1866, Affidavits Relating to Outrages, March 1866–August 1868, reel 34, RACST.

30. RSC, 80, 173.

31. RSC, 80, 81, 326, 332; P. M. Winters testimony, Proceedings of a Military Commission, 412T1866, reel 520, LROAG; *Columbus (GA) Daily Enquirer*, 8 May 1866; *Washington Daily National Intelligencer*, 7 May 1866; *Appeal*, 2 May 1866; *Argus*, 2 May 1866.

32. RSC, 80, 81, 326; *Argus*, 2 May 1866; P. M. Winters testimony, Proceedings of a Military Commission, 412T1866, reel 520, LROAG; *Columbus (GA) Daily Enquirer*, 8 May 1866.

33. RSC, 115, 169, 275; John Battie testimony, Proceedings of a Military Commission, 412T1866, reel 520, LROAG; *Argus*, 2 May 1866.

34. RSC, 115, 169, 236, 275, 314; John Battie testimony, Proceedings of a Military Commission, 412T1866, reel 520, LROAG.

35. RSC, 125–27, 131.

36. RSC, 71, 115, 154, 314, 326–27; *Argus*, 2 May 1866; C. M. Cooley, Mrs. Samuel Dills [*sic*], and John Battie testimonies, Proceedings of a Military Commission, 412T1866, reel 520, LROAG; J. N. Sharpe affidavit, Affidavits Relating to Outrages, March 1866–August 1868, reel 34, RACST.

37. John Battie and Henry Taylor testimonies, Proceedings of a Military Commission, 412T1866, reel 520, LROAG; RSC, 128–29.

38. John Battie testimony, Proceedings of a Military Commission, 412T1866, reel 520, LROAG; Alex McQuatters affidavit, Affidavits Relating to Outrages, March 1866–August 1868, reel 34, RACST; 2 May 1866 entry, Register of Deaths, 1848–1884, reel 35, Shelby County Miscellaneous City/County Records; *Memphis City Directory*, 109; *Columbus (GA) Daily Enquirer*, 8 May 1866; RSC, 165, 370; *Long's Memphis Directory*, 15.

39. RSC, 65, 154, 327.

40. Mrs. Samuel Dills [*sic*] testimony, Proceedings of a Military Commission, 412T1866, reel 520, LROAG; RSC, 68, 118.

41. *RSC*, 64, 68, 118.
42. *RSC*, 106, 115, 116, 118, 128, 129, 189, 313, 317, 343–44; Alex McQuatters and J. N. Sharpe affidavits, Affidavits Relating to Outrages, March 1866–August 1868, reel 34, RACST.
43. *RSC*, 115, 116, 118, 154, 184, 313; John Battie testimony, Proceedings of a Military Commission, 412T1866, reel 520, LROAG.

6. "YOU HAVE KILLED HIM ONCE, WHAT DO YOU WANT
TO KILL HIM AGAIN FOR?"

1. P. M. Winters testimony, Proceedings of a Military Commission, 412T1866, reel 520, LROAG; *Columbus* (GA) *Daily Enquirer*, 8 May 1866; *RSC*, 50, 80.
2. P. M. Winters testimony, Proceedings of a Military Commission, 412T1866, reel 520, LROAG; *Columbus* (GA) *Daily Enquirer*, 8 May 1866; *RSC*, 50, 52, 80, 81.
3. *RSC*, 50, 52, 81; P. M. Winters testimony, Proceedings of a Military Commission, 412T1866, reel 520, LROAG; *Columbus* (GA) *Daily Enquirer*, 8 May 1866.
4. *RSC*, 128–29, 317.
5. James Cannon Mitcher [sic] testimony, Proceedings of a Military Commission, 412T1866, reel 520, LROAG; *RSC*, 317, 343–44; Alex McQuatters affidavit, Affidavits Relating to Outrages, March 1866–August 1868, reel 34, RACST.
6. *Long's Memphis Directory*, 125; James Cannon Mitcher [sic] testimony, Proceedings of a Military Commission, 412T1866, reel 520, LROAG; James Cannon Mitchell and Alex McQuatters affidavits, Affidavits Relating to Outrages, March 1866–August 1868, reel 34, RACST; *RSC*, 308, 317, 343–44.
7. *RSC*, 308, 317, 343–44; James Cannon Mitchell and Alex McQuatters affidavits, Affidavits Relating to Outrages, March 1866–August 1868, reel 34, RACST; James Cannon Mitcher [sic] testimony, Proceedings of a Military Commission, 412T1866, reel 520, LROAG.
8. *RSC*, 310; Joe Lynch testimony, Proceedings of a Military Commission, 412T1866, reel 520, LROAG.
9. *RSC*, 160, 163, 309, 343; James Cannon Mitchell affidavit, Affidavits Relating to Outrages, March 1866–August 1868, reel 34, RACST; James Cannon Mitcher [sic] testimony, Proceedings of a Military Commission, 412T1866, reel 520, LROAG; Lewis Robinson file, 3rd U.S. Colored Heavy Artillery, Compiled Military Service Records; *Washington Daily National Intelligencer*, 7 May 1866.
10. *RSC*, 163, 343; *Washington Daily National Intelligencer*, 7 May 1866.
11. *RSC*, 308–309; James Cannon Mitchell affidavit, Affidavits Relating to Outrages, March 1866–August 1868, reel 34, RACST.

12. *RSC*, 343.
13. *RSC*, 162–63, 309.
14. *RSC*, 129, 160, 161, 309, 317, 321, 343–44; *Washington Daily National Intelligencer*, 7 May 1866; "Abstract of persons killed, wounded, and maltreated" and John Battie testimony, Proceedings of a Military Commission, 412T1866, reel 520, LROAG; Alex McQuatters affidavit, Affidavits Relating to Outrages, March 1866–August 1868, reel 34, RACST.
15. *RSC*, 308, 317; *Washington Daily National Intelligencer*, 7 May 1866.
16. John Battie testimony, Proceedings of a Military Commission, 412T1866, reel 520, LROAG; J. N. Sharpe affidavit, Affidavits Relating to Outrages, March 1866–August 1868, reel 34, RACST; *RSC*, 115, 116, 119, 120, 126, 129, 154, 235, 313, 321, 331.
17. *RSC*, 115, 116, 126, 129, 184, 211, 235–36, 257, 258, 313.
18. *RSC*, 182–83; Toney [sic] Cherry file, 3rd U.S. Colored Heavy Artillery, Compiled Military Service Records.
19. *RSC*, 182–83, 211, 318; Isaac Richardson file, 3rd U.S. Colored Heavy Artillery, Compiled Military Service Records.
20. Allen Summers testimony, Proceedings of a Military Commission, 412T1866, reel 520, LROAG; *RSC*, 171, 321; Allen Summers file, 3rd U.S. Colored Heavy Artillery, Compiled Military Service Records.
21. *RSC*, 148, 154, 155, 171, 321; Allen Summers testimony, Proceedings of a Military Commission, 412T1866, reel 520, LROAG; Allen Simmons [sic] affidavit, Affidavits Relating to Outrages, March 1866–August 1868, reel 34, RACST.
22. *RSC*, 154, 155, 171; Allen Summers testimony, Proceedings of a Military Commission, 412T1866, reel 520, LROAG.
23. *RSC*, 119–20.
24. *RSC*, 120.
25. *RSC*, 64–65.
26. *RSC*, 65.
27. *RSC*, 88–89.
28. *RSC*, 160, 179, 190, 314, 317, 324, 325; J. A. Swain testimony, Proceedings of a Military Commission, 412T1866, reel 520, LROAG; Albert Butcher affidavit, Affidavits Relating to Outrages, March 1866–August 1868, reel 34, RACST.
29. *RSC*, 199, 332, 341.
30. *RSC*, 337, 341.
31. *RSC*, 179.
32. *RSC*, 179, 203, 206; Silas Garrett affidavit, Affidavits Relating to Outrages, March 1866–August 1868, reel 34, RACST.
33. *RSC*, 203, 205–206; Silas Garrett affidavit, Affidavits Relating to Outrages, March 1866–August 1868, reel 34, RACST.
34. *RSC*, 205–206, 217; Silas Garrett affidavit, Affidavits Relating to Outrages, March 1866–August 1868, reel 34, RACST.

35. *RSC*, 7, 104, 205–206, 211–12, 216–17, 252, 318; S. J. Quinby testimony, Proceedings of a Military Commission, 412T1866, reel 520, LROAG; S. J. Quinby affidavit, Affidavits Relating to Outrages, March 1866–August 1868, reel 34, RACST; *Argus*, 2 May 1866.

36. *RSC*, 124; R. W. Creighton affidavit, Affidavits Relating to Outrages, March 1866–August 1868, reel 34, RACST.

37. *RSC*, 124; R. W. Creighton testimony, Proceedings of a Military Commission, 412T1866, reel 520, LROAG; R. W. Creighton affidavit, Affidavits Relating to Outrages, March 1866–August 1868, reel 34, RACST.

38. *RSC*, 124–25, 368; *Avalanche*, 2 May 1866; R. W. Creighton testimony, Proceedings of a Military Commission, 412T1866, reel 520, LROAG; R. W. Creighton affidavit, Affidavits Relating to Outrages, March 1866–August 1868, reel 34, RACST.

39. *RSC*, 80, 81, 83, 253; *Columbus* (GA) *Daily Enquirer*, 8 May 1866.

40. *RSC*, 52, 80–83, 190–91, 253, 356; *Columbus* (GA) *Daily Enquirer*, 8 May 1866.

41. *RSC*, 80, 81, 133, 356; *Avalanche*, 2 May 1866.

42. *RSC*, 7, 68–69, 106, 144, 216–17, 252, 327; *Argus*, 2 May 1866; *Washington Daily National Intelligencer*, 7 May 1866.

43. *RSC*, 10, 144, 148, 330; P. D. Beecher testimony, Proceedings of a Military Commission, 412T1866, reel 520, LROAG.

44. Ewing Tade testimony, Proceedings of a Military Commission, 412T1866, reel 520, LROAG; Richardson, "Memphis Race Riot," 65; *RSC*, 88–89.

45. *RSC*, 89; Ewing Tade testimony, Proceedings of a Military Commission, 412T1866, reel 520, LROAG; Richardson, "Memphis Race Riot," 65.

46. *RSC*, 83, 356; George Todd and P. M. Winters testimonies (including testimony of Todd when recalled), Proceedings of a Military Commission, 412T1866, reel 520, LROAG; George Todd affidavit, Affidavits Relating to Outrages, March 1866–August 1868, reel 34, RACST.

47. *RSC*, 256, 356; George Todd testimony (including testimony when recalled), Proceedings of a Military Commission, 412T1866, reel 520, LROAG; George Todd affidavit, Affidavits Relating to Outrages, March 1866–August 1868, reel 34, RACST.

48. *RSC*, 256; George Todd affidavit, Affidavits Relating to Outrages, March 1866–August 1868, reel 34, RACST.

49. *Appeal*, 2 May 1866; *Argus*, 2 May 1866; *Avalanche*, 2 May 1866; *Macon* (GA) *Weekly Telegraph*, 7 May 1866; *RSC*, 52, 253.

50. *Argus*, 2 May 1866; *Avalanche*, 2 May 1866; *Appeal*, 2 May 1866.

51. *Appeal*, 2 May 1866; *Argus*, 2 May 1866; *Avalanche*, 2 May 1866.

52. *RSC*, 100, 100–101, 190, 252; Till Hunt testimony, Proceedings of a Military Commission, 412T1866, reel 520, LROAG.

53. *RSC*, 72, 100.

54. *RSC*, 72, 100, 101.

55. *RSC*, 72, 100, 101–102; C. M. Cooley testimony, Proceedings of a Military Commission, 412T1866, reel 520, LROAG.

56. *RSC*, 72, 100.

57. *RSC*, 72, 100, 101.

58. *RSC*, 71–72, 73, 77, 78, 86, 89; *Washington Daily National Intelligencer*, 7 May 1866.

59. *RSC*, 72–73, 165, 322; Lavinda Gooding [*sic*] and C. M. Cooley testimonies, Proceedings of a Military Commission, 412T1866, reel 520, LROAG.

60. *RSC*, 72, 165, 322; C. M. Cooley and Joe Lynch testimonies, Proceedings of a Military Commission, 412T1866, reel 520, LROAG.

61. *RSC*, 72, 165, 322; Joe Lynch testimony, Proceedings of a Military Commission, 412T1866, reel 520, LROAG.

62. *RSC*, 78, 89, 100, 198; *Washington Daily National Intelligencer*, 7 May 1866.

63. *RSC*, 77.

64. *RSC*, 77, 78; Lavinda Gooding [*sic*] testimony, Proceedings of a Military Commission, 412T1866, reel 520, LROAG.

65. *RSC*, 78.

66. *RSC*, 77–78, 89.

67. *RSC*, 223, 245, 250, 358; Walter Clifford testimony, Proceedings of a Military Commission, 412T1866, reel 520, LROAG.

68. *RSC*, 148, 223, 245, 250, 324, 358.

69. *RSC*, 148, 225, 226, 245, 250, 324, 358.

70. *RSC*, 206, 208, 223, 225.

71. *RSC*, 206, 208, 217, 218, 223, 225.

72. Walter Clifford testimony, Proceedings of a Military Commission, 412T1866, reel 520, LROAG; *RSC*, 250.

73. Walter Clifford testimony, Proceedings of a Military Commission, 412T1866, reel 520, LROAG.

74. *RSC*, 80, 81, 324, 356; P. M. Winters testimony, Proceedings of a Military Commission, 412T1866, reel 520, LROAG.

75. *RSC*, 80, 81–82.

76. *RSC*, 78, 89; Ewing Tade testimony, Proceedings of a Military Commission, 412T1866, reel 520, LROAG; Richardson, "Memphis Race Riot," 65–66.

77. *RSC*, 78, 87, 89.

78. *RSC*, 7, 8, 104, 106, 208; W. H. Peirce testimony, Proceedings of a Military Commission, 412T1866, reel 520, LROAG.

79. *RSC*, 74, 106, 236, 252, 327; *Argus*, 2 May 1866; Channing Richards testimony, Proceedings of a Military Commission, 412T1866, reel 520, LROAG; *Post*, 2 May 1866; *Avalanche*, 2 May 1866.

80. *RSC*, 80; P. M. Winters and Walter Clifford testimonies, Proceedings of a Military Commission, 412T1866, reel 520, LROAG.

81. *RSC*, 80; P. M. Winters and Walter Clifford testimonies, Proceedings of a Military Commission, 412T1866, reel 520, LROAG.
82. *RSC*, 72, 80; P. M. Winters and Walter Clifford testimonies, Proceedings of a Military Commission, 412T1866, reel 520, LROAG; *Washington Daily National Intelligencer*, 7 May 1866.
83. *RSC*, 82, 322, 323; *Macon (GA) Weekly Telegraph*, 7 May 1866; *Post*, 2 May 1866; data for Memphis, 1 May 1866, United States Naval Observatory, "Complete Sun and Moon Data."
84. *Argus*, 2 May 1866; *Macon (GA) Weekly Telegraph*, 7 May 1866; *Post*, 2 May 1866; *RSC*, 84, 317, 319, 343; Shedrick Smith affidavit, Affidavits Relating to Outrages, March 1866–August 1868, reel 34, RACST; P. M. Winters and Henry Jackson testimonies, Proceedings of a Military Commission, 412T1866, reel 520, LROAG.
85. *RSC*, 253, 255; Shelby County, TN, Memphis, Ward 8, p. 147, Eighth Census Returns of Free Inhabitants; Shelby County, TN, Memphis, Ward 6, p. 74, Ninth Census Returns of Inhabitants.
86. *RSC*, 252.
87. *RSC*, 252–53; *Long's Memphis Directory*, 14; *Public Ledger*, 2 May 1866.
88. *RSC*, 253.
89. Ibid.
90. Ibid.
91. Ibid.
92. *RSC*, 80, 82, 83, 106, 322; P. M. Winters and Walter Clifford testimonies, Proceedings of a Military Commission, 412T1866, reel 520, LROAG.
93. *RSC*, 322.
94. Ibid.
95. *RSC*, 50.
96. Ibid.; *Appeal*, 2 May 1866.
97. *RSC*, 50; *Appeal*, 2 May 1866.
98. *RSC*, 246, 359, 360.
99. *Post*, 2, 3 May 1866; *Macon (GA) Weekly Telegraph*, 7 May 1866; *Avalanche*, 3 May 1866; *New York Times*, 12 May 1866; *Argus*, 2 May 1866; *Public Ledger*, 2 May 1866; *RSC*, 90, 106; Walter Clifford testimony, Proceedings of a Military Commission, 412T1866, reel 520, LROAG.
100. *RSC*, 245–46, 250, 324, 358–59; Walter Clifford testimony, Proceedings of a Military Commission, 412T1866, reel 520, LROAG.
101. *RSC*, 7, 80, 82, 106, 126, 127, 161, 190, 327; Walter Clifford testimony, Proceedings of a Military Commission, 412T1866, reel 520, LROAG.
102. *RSC*, 7, 8, 104, 106, 190, 327; data for Memphis, 1, 2 May 1866, United States Naval Observatory, "Complete Sun and Moon Data"; *Argus*, 2 May 1866.
103. *RSC*, 7, 104, 106, 190–91, 327.
104. *RSC*, 7, 104–105, 106.
105. *RSC*, 160–61, 162; Rosen, *Terror in the Heart of Freedom*, 68.

106. *RSC*, 161.
107. Ibid.; Rosen, *Terror in the Heart of Freedom*, 72, 78.
108. *RSC*, 161.
109. *RSC*, 104–106, 107, 114, 153, 155, 220, 222, 342–43; J. N. Sharpe affidavit, Affidavits Relating to Outrages, March 1866–August 1868, reel 34, RACST.
110. *RSC*, 18, 152–53, 179–80, 222. This man was identified by some witnesses as Shade (or Shedd) Long.
111. Walter Clifford testimony, Proceedings of a Military Commission, 412T1866, reel 520, LROAG; *RSC*, 324.
112. Walter Clifford testimony, Proceedings of a Military Commission, 412T1866, reel 520, LROAG.
113. *RSC*, 153, 327.
114. Data for Memphis, 2 May 1866, United States Naval Observatory, "Complete Sun and Moon Data"; *Public Ledger*, 2 May 1866; *Post*, 3 May 1866; *New York Independent*, 31 May 1866.
115. *RSC*, 109, 151, 167, 170, 202, 222, 237, 252; Walter Clifford testimony, Proceedings of a Military Commission, 412T1866, reel 520, LROAG; *Post*, 3 May 1866; *New York Independent*, 31 May 1866; Silas Garrett affidavit, Affidavits Relating to Outrages, March 1866–August 1868, reel 34, RACST; *Argus*, 3 May 1866.

7. FIRE

1. *RSC*, 78.
2. Ibid.
3. *Avalanche*, 3 May 1866; *RSC*, 105, 107, 167, 183, 191, 231, 232, 246.
4. *RSC*, 167.
5. Ibid.
6. Ibid.
7. Ibid.
8. *RSC*, 105, 107, 191, 236, 313.
9. *RSC*, 78, 198; 2 May 1866 entry, vol. 171, Complaint Books of the Freedmen's Court in the Memphis District, reel 24, SRTFO; *Argus*, 3 May 1866; *Post*, 3 May 1866.
10. *RSC*, 78, 198, 366; *Appeal*, 23 December 1865; *Avalanche*, 5 May 1866.
11. *RSC*, 78, 198; Lavinda Gooding [*sic*] testimony, Proceedings of a Military Commission, 412T1866, reel 520, LROAG.
12. *RSC*, 78.
13. *RSC*, 78, 275; Benjamin Runkle to Clinton Fisk, 23 May 1866, Reports of Outrages, Riots, and Murders, 1866–1868, reel 34, RACST.
14. *RSC*, 275.
15. Ibid.; Benjamin Runkle to Clinton Fisk, 23 May 1866, Reports of Outrages, Riots, and Murders, 1866–1868, reel 34, RACST.

16. *RSC*, 51, 275, 360–61; Benjamin Runkle to Clinton Fisk, 23 May 1866, Reports of Outrages, Riots, and Murders, 1866–1868, reel 34, RACST; *Post*, 3 May 1866.

17. *RSC*, 275; Benjamin Runkle to Clinton Fisk, 23 May 1866, Reports of Outrages, Riots, and Murders, 1866–1868, reel 34, RACST.

18. *RSC*, 275, 361; Benjamin Runkle to Clinton Fisk, 23 May 1866, Reports of Outrages, Riots, and Murders, 1866–1868, reel 34, RACST.

19. *Post*, 2 May 1866; *Argus*, 2 May 1866; *Avalanche*, 2 May 1866.

20. *RSC*, 80, 90, 105, 107, 170, 188, 202, 314, 322; *Post*, 3 May 1866; Silas Garrett and S. J. Quinby affidavits, Affidavits Relating to Outrages, March 1866–August 1868, reel 34, RACST; *Public Ledger*, 2 May 1866; *New Orleans Times*, 6 May 1866; *New York Times*, 12 May 1866; *Avalanche*, 3 May 1866; *Columbus* (GA) *Daily Enquirer*, 8 May 1866; P. M. Winters testimony, Proceedings of a Military Commission, 412T1866, reel 520, LROAG.

21. *New Orleans Times*, 6 May 1866; *Public Ledger*, 2 May 1866; *Appeal*, 3 May 1866; *RSC*, 80, 227, 314; *Memphis City Directory*, 275, 276; P. M. Winters testimony, Proceedings of a Military Commission, 412T1866, reel 520, LROAG.

22. *RSC*, 246, 359; A. W. Allyn testimony, Proceedings of a Military Commission, 412T1866, reel 520, LROAG.

23. *RSC*, 66, 246, 359; A. W. Allyn and Rachel Dills [sic] testimonies, Proceedings of a Military Commission, 412T1866, reel 520, LROAG.

24. A. W. Allyn testimony, Proceedings of a Military Commission, 412T1866, reel 520, LROAG; *RSC*, 246, 359.

25. *RSC*, 202, 327.

26. *RSC*, 213.

27. *RSC*, 66, 69, 105, 107, 170, 185, 202, 322; Silas Garrett affidavit, Affidavits Relating to Outrages, March 1866–August 1868, reel 34, RACST; Rachel Dills [sic] testimony, Proceedings of a Military Commission, 412T1866, reel 520, LROAG.

28. *RSC*, 66, 69, 105, 107, 183, 188, 202, 322; *Post*, 3 May 1866; Silas Garrett and S. J. Quinby affidavits, Affidavits Relating to Outrages, March 1866–August 1868, reel 34, RACST; Rachel Dills [sic] testimony, Proceedings of a Military Commission, 412T1866, reel 520, LROAG.

29. *RSC*, 161, 162, 167.

30. *RSC*, 161, 167.

31. *RSC*, 167.

32. *RSC*, 107, 161–62.

33. *RSC*, 107, 161–62, 163.

34. A. W. Allyn testimony, Proceedings of a Military Commission, 412T1866, reel 520, LROAG; *RSC*, 246, 359.

35. A. W. Allyn testimony, Proceedings of a Military Commission, 412T1866, reel 520, LROAG; *RSC*, 80, 246, 359, 360.

36. *RSC*, 246, 359, 360; A. W. Allyn testimony, Proceedings of a Military Commission, 412T1866, reel 520, LROAG.

37. *RSC*, 183, 315; Channing Richards testimony, Proceedings of a Military Commission, 412T1866, reel 520, LROAG.

38. *RSC*, 315, 318–19; Channing Richards and G. C. Worset testimonies, Proceedings of a Military Commission, 412T1866, reel 520, LROAG; *Post*, 3 May 1866.

39. *RSC*, 80, 227–28; P. M. Winters testimony, Proceedings of a Military Commission, 412T1866, reel 520, LROAG.

40. *RSC*, 314; *Appeal*, 3 May 1866.

41. *RSC*, 169, 183–85, 195, 217, 223–25.

42. *RSC*, 169, 183–84, 217, 223–25; *New York Times*, 12 May 1866.

43. *RSC*, 223, 224, 246, 359; A. W. Allyn testimony, Proceedings of a Military Commission, 412T1866, reel 520, LROAG.

44. *RSC*, 119, 122–23, 194; Channing Richards testimony, Proceedings of a Military Commission, 412T1866, reel 520, LROAG.

45. *RSC*, 119, 194, 206, 207, 223.

46. *RSC*, 194, 206, 207, 223.

47. *RSC*, 183, 185, 206, 207–208, 224, 237.

48. *RSC*, 206, 208, 224, 246, 324.

49. *RSC*, 163, 168, 176–77, 186; Rosen, *Terror in the Heart of Freedom*, 68–69, 72, 78, 80.

50. *RSC*, 80, 82, 246, 359; A. W. Allyn testimony, Proceedings of a Military Commission, 412T1866, reel 520, LROAG.

51. *RSC*, 80, 326, 339; P. M. Winters testimony, Proceedings of a Military Commission, 412T1866, reel 520, LROAG.

52. *RSC*, 246, 359; A. W. Allyn testimony, Proceedings of a Military Commission, 412T1866, reel 520, LROAG.

53. *RSC*, 314; P. M. Winters testimony, Proceedings of a Military Commission, 412T1866, reel 520, LROAG.

54. *RSC*, 80, 327; P. M. Winters testimony, Proceedings of a Military Commission, 412T1866, reel 520, LROAG.

55. P. M. Winters, A. W. Allyn, and Walter Clifford testimonies, Proceedings of a Military Commission, 412T1866, reel 520, LROAG; *RSC*, 246, 250, 252, 316, 359; *Post*, 3 May 1866.

56. *RSC*, 246, 250, 359; Walter Clifford testimony, Proceedings of a Military Commission, 412T1866, reel 520, LROAG.

57. *RSC*, 80–81, 246, 248, 359; P. M. Winters and A. W. Allyn testimonies, Proceedings of a Military Commission, 412T1866, reel 520, LROAG.

58. *RSC*, 251; Walter Clifford testimony, Proceedings of a Military Commission, 412T1866, reel 520, LROAG.

59. Walter Clifford testimony, Proceedings of a Military Commission, 412T1866, reel 520, LROAG; *RSC*, 250, 359.

60. *RSC*, 250; Walter Clifford testimony, Proceedings of a Military Commission, 412T1866, reel 520, LROAG.

61. *RSC*, 246–47, 248, 359; A. W. Allyn and Walter Clifford testimonies, Proceedings of a Military Commission, 412T1866, reel 520, LROAG.

62. *RSC*, 247, 314, 359; A. W. Allyn and P. M. Winters testimonies, Proceedings of a Military Commission, 412T1866, reel 520, LROAG.

63. *RSC*, 81; P. M. Winters testimony, Proceedings of a Military Commission, 412T1866, reel 520, LROAG.

64. *RSC*, 109, 205; *Washington Daily National Intelligencer*, 7 May 1866; *Post*, 3 May 1866.

65. *RSC*, 205; *Washington Daily National Intelligencer*, 7 May 1866. The man was possibly Reuben Alexander, a leader of Memphis's black community and in his late fifties or early sixties in 1866. See Hahn, *Land and Labor*, 275–76, and Shelby County, TN, Memphis, Ward 1, p. 17, Ward 6, p. 42, Ninth Census Returns of Inhabitants.

66. *Washington Daily National Intelligencer*, 7 May 1866; *Post*, 3 May 1866; *RSC*, 198, 205; Shelby County, TN, Memphis, Ward 2, p. 37 (B. C. Dennis), Eighth Census Returns of Free Inhabitants; *Chicago Tribune*, 3, 8 May 1866.

67. *RSC*, 108–109, 205, 370; *Washington Daily National Intelligencer*, 7 May 1866; *Post*, 3 May 1866; *New York Herald*, 5 May 1866; *Chicago Tribune*, 3, 8 May 1866.

68. *RSC*, 109, 205; *Columbus (GA) Daily Enquirer*, 8 May 1866; *Chicago Tribune*, 3 May 1866; 4 May 1866 entry, Register of Deaths, 1848–1884, reel 35, Shelby County Miscellaneous City/County Records.

69. *Avalanche*, 3 May 1866; *RSC*, 65–66, 116, 225, 313, 324; Mrs. Samuel Dills [*sic*] and A. W. Allyn testimonies, Proceedings of a Military Commission, 412T1866, reel 520, LROAG.

70. *RSC*, 66.

71. *RSC*, 66, 313, 324, 359.

72. *RSC*, 313; *Post*, 3 May 1866.

73. *RSC*, 66, 115–16, 247.

74. *RSC*, 247, 324, 359; *Little Rock (AR) Daily Gazette*, 9 May 1866; *Avalanche*, 3 May 1866; A. W. Allyn testimony, Proceedings of a Military Commission, 412T1866, reel 520, LROAG.

75. *RSC*, 66, 116, 247, 359; A. W. Allyn testimony, Proceedings of a Military Commission, 412T1866, reel 520, LROAG; *Little Rock (AR) Daily Gazette*, 9 May 1866; *Avalanche*, 3 May 1866.

76. *RSC*, 116, 247, 336.

77. *Appeal*, 3 May 1866; *Post*, 3 May 1866; *Argus*, 3 May 1866; *Washington Daily National Intelligencer*, 7 May 1866; *Memphis City Directory*, 109.

78. *Public Ledger*, 2 May 1866; *Appeal*, 2 May 1866.

79. *Columbus (GA) Daily Enquirer*, 8 May 1866; *Chicago Tribune*, 3 May 1866; *RSC*, 307, 316.

80. *RSC*, 89, 91.
81. A. W. Allyn and Walter Clifford testimonies, Proceedings of a Military Commission, 412T1866, reel 520, LROAG; *RSC*, 247, 313, 324, 359.
82. P. M. Winters testimony, Proceedings of a Military Commission, 412T1866, reel 520, LROAG; *RSC*, 81; data for Memphis, 2 May 1866, United States Naval Observatory, "Complete Sun and Moon Data."
83. Mrs. Samuel Cooper testimony, Proceedings of a Military Commission, 412T1866, reel 520, LROAG; *RSC*, 219; Mrs. Samuel Cooper affidavit, Affidavits Relating to Outrages, March 1866–August 1868, reel 34, RACST.
84. *RSC*, 219.
85. *RSC*, 219, 367; Payroll of City Day Police, 1 June 1866, reel 435, Shelby County Miscellaneous City/County Records; Mrs. Samuel Cooper testimony, Proceedings of a Military Commission, 412T1866, reel 520, LROAG; Mrs. Samuel Cooper affidavit, Affidavits Relating to Outrages, March 1866–August 1868, reel 34, RACST.
86. *RSC*, 219.
87. Ibid.; Mrs. Samuel Cooper testimony, Proceedings of a Military Commission, 412T1866, reel 520, LROAG.
88. *RSC*, 325, 328.
89. Ibid.
90. Ibid.
91. *RSC*, 193; Hannah Robinson affidavit, Affidavits Relating to Outrages, March 1866–August 1868, reel 34, RACST.
92. *RSC*, 193; Hannah Robinson affidavit, Affidavits Relating to Outrages, March 1866–August 1868, reel 34, RACST.
93. *RSC*, 226–27; Robert Church affidavit, Affidavits Relating to Outrages, March 1866–August 1868, reel 34, RACST.
94. *RSC*, 226–27; Robert Church affidavit, Affidavits Relating to Outrages, March 1866–August 1868, reel 34, RACST; *Post*, 4 May 1866.
95. P. M. Winters testimony, Proceedings of a Military Commission, 412T1866, reel 520, LROAG; *RSC*, 81.
96. *RSC*, 91; Ewing Tade testimony, Proceedings of a Military Commission, 412T1866, reel 520, LROAG.
97. *RSC*, 149, 150, 247, 251, 359; A. W. Allyn testimony, Proceedings of a Military Commission, 412T1866, reel 520, LROAG.
98. *RSC*, 149, 251, 359; A. W. Allyn testimony, Proceedings of a Military Commission, 412T1866, reel 520, LROAG.
99. *RSC*, 81, 83; P. M. Winters testimony, Proceedings of a Military Commission, 412T1866, reel 520, LROAG; *Long's Memphis Directory*, 14.
100. *RSC*, 81, 83; P. M. Winters testimony, Proceedings of a Military Commission, 412T1866, reel 520, LROAG.
101. *RSC*, 81, 83, 329–30; P. M. Winters testimony, Proceedings of a Military Commission, 412T1866, reel 520, LROAG.

102. *RSC*, 81, 83, 335–36; P. M. Winters and Ewing Tade testimonies, Proceedings of a Military Commission, 412T1866, reel 520, LROAG.

103. *RSC*, 83, 122–23; P. M. Winters and John Aldridge testimonies, Proceedings of a Military Commission, 412T1866, reel 520, LROAG.

104. *RSC*, 81; P. M. Winters testimony, Proceedings of a Military Commission, 412T1866, reel 520, LROAG.

105. *RSC*, 321, 323–24.

106. *RSC*, 323–24, 336.

107. *RSC*, 123, 324–25; John Aldridge testimony, Proceedings of a Military Commission, 412T1866, reel 520, LROAG.

108. *RSC*, 123, 324–25; John Aldridge testimony, Proceedings of a Military Commission, 412T1866, reel 520, LROAG.

109. *RSC*, 123; John Aldridge testimony, Proceedings of a Military Commission, 412T1866, reel 520, LROAG.

110. *RSC*, 123.

111. *RSC*, 247, 359; A. W. Allyn testimony, Proceedings of a Military Commission, 412T1866, reel 520, LROAG.

112. *RSC*, 247.

113. *RSC*, 102, 149, 166, 190–91, 247, 251, 330, 359; Walter Clifford testimony, Proceedings of a Military Commission, 412T1866, reel 520, LROAG.

114. Walter Clifford testimony, Proceedings of a Military Commission, 412T1866, reel 520, LROAG; *RSC*, 251.

115. *RSC*, 91, 92.

116. *RSC*, 92.

117. *RSC*, 81; P. M. Winters testimony, Proceedings of a Military Commission, 412T1866, reel 520, LROAG.

118. *RSC*, 81, 330; *Memphis City Directory*, 194; C. M. Cooley testimony, Proceedings of a Military Commission, 412T1866, reel 520, LROAG.

119. *RSC*, 309–10, 318, 330, 336; *Public Ledger*, 3 May 1866.

120. *RSC*, 247.

121. *RSC*, 79, 102–103, 103–104, 117–18, 346; Henry Alexander testimony, Proceedings of a Military Commission, 412T1866, reel 520, LROAG; *Post*, 4 May 1866; George Jones affidavit, Affidavits Relating to Outrages, March 1866–August 1868, reel 34, RACST.

122. United States Congress, *Riot at Memphis*, 2; *Post*, 4 May 1866.

123. *Post*, 4 May 1866; *Public Ledger*, 3 May 1866; Samuel Dills [sic] and Orin Waters testimonies, Proceedings of a Military Commission, 412T1866, reel 520, LROAG; Orin Waters affidavit, Affidavits Relating to Outrages, March 1866–August 1868, reel 34, RACST; United States Congress, *Reports of Assistant Commissioners of Freedmen, and Synopsis of Laws on Persons of Color in Late Slave States*, Senate Exec. Docs., 39th Cong., 2nd Sess. (1866), No. 6, Serial 1276, pp. 132–33.

124. *RSC*, 160, 162, 167–68, 332; Henry Porter testimony, Proceedings of a Military Commission, 412T1866, reel 520, LROAG.

125. *RSC*, 163, 168.
126. *RSC*, 113, 116–17, 163, 168.
127. *RSC*, 163, 168.
128. Ibid.
129. *RSC*, 171–72, 319.
130. *RSC*, 172, 319, 340.
131. Ibid.
132. Ibid.
133. Ibid.
134. *RSC*, 172, 319.
135. *RSC*, 172, 340.
136. *RSC*, 172.
137. Ibid.
138. *RSC*, 99, 100, 105, 113; Record 127, Registers of Signatures of Depositors, Memphis Branch.
139. *RSC*, 99, 116–17, 172–73.
140. *RSC*, 116, 173; Adam Lock affidavit, Affidavits Relating to Outrages, March 1866–August 1868, reel 34, RACST.
141. *RSC*, 99.
142. *RSC*, 99, 117.
143. *RSC*, 105, 117, 160, 173, 232; S. J. Quinby affidavit, Affidavits Relating to Outrages, March 1866–August 1868, reel 34, RACST.
144. *RSC*, 116, 172–73.
145. *RSC*, 99.
146. Ibid.
147. *RSC*, 99, 100; Jane Sneed testimony, Proceedings of a Military Commission, 412T1866, reel 520, LROAG; Jane Sneed affidavit, Affidavits Relating to Outrages, March 1866–August 1868, reel 34, RACST.
148. *RSC*, 99; Jane Sneed testimony, Proceedings of a Military Commission, 412T1866, reel 520, LROAG.
149. *RSC*, 99; Jane Sneed testimony, Proceedings of a Military Commission, 412T1866, reel 520, LROAG.
150. *RSC*, 99, 113, 117.
151. *RSC*, 324, 359; Walter Clifford testimony, Proceedings of a Military Commission, 412T1866, reel 520, LROAG.
152. *RSC*, 91, 92; Ewing Tade testimony, Proceedings of a Military Commission, 412T1866, reel 520, LROAG.
153. *RSC*, 105, 108, 111, 117.
154. *RSC*, 99, 105, 108, 111, 113, 117, 160; Jane Sneed testimony, Proceedings of a Military Commission, 412T1866, reel 520, LROAG; Jane Sneed affidavit, Affidavits Relating to Outrages, March 1866–August 1868, reel 34, RACST.
155. *RSC*, 172.

8. RECRIMINATIONS AND INVESTIGATIONS

1. *RSC*, 33, 276.
2. Richardson, "Memphis Race Riot," 67; *RSC*, 92, 95; *New York Independent*, 31 May 1866.
3. Richardson, "Memphis Race Riot," 67; *RSC*, 95; *New York Independent*, 31 May 1866.
4. Richardson, "Memphis Race Riot," 67; *RSC*, 95.
5. *RSC*, 51–52; *Post*, 4 May 1866; *Public Ledger*, 4 May 1866.
6. *Post*, 4 May 1866; *RSC*, 52, 264; *Public Ledger*, 4 May 1866.
7. *RSC*, 52, 56, 57, 145–46; *New York Independent*, 31 May 1866; *Post*, 4 May 1866.
8. *RSC*, 261, 275; Benjamin Runkle to O. C. Waters, 3 May 1866, vol. 134, Letters Sent by the Memphis District, Office of the Superintendent, reel 17, SRTFO; *New York Independent*, 31 May 1866.
9. *RSC*, 52, 260, 275; *New York Independent*, 31 May 1866; Benjamin Runkle to Clinton Fisk, 5 May 1866, and to W. L. Porter, 10 May 1866, vol. 134, Letters Sent by the Memphis District, Office of the Superintendent, reel 17, SRTFO; *Post*, 4 May 1866; Richardson, "Memphis Race Riot," 67–68.
10. A. W. Allyn testimony, Proceedings of a Military Commission, 412T1866, reel 520, LROAG; *RSC*, 267, 324, 359, 361.
11. Benjamin Runkle to Clinton Fisk, 23 May 1866, Reports of Outrages, Riots, and Murders, 1866–1868, reel 34, RACST.
12. *RSC*, 52, 267, 324, 359; Joseph Pidgeon testimony, Proceedings of a Military Commission, 412T1866, reel 520, LROAG; Beckey Pleasent affidavit, Affidavits Relating to Outrages, March 1866–August 1868, reel 34, RACST; *Public Ledger*, 4 May 1866; *Post*, 4 May 1866; *Washington Daily National Intelligencer*, 8 May 1866.
13. *RSC*, 95, 108–12, 181, 201, 236.
14. *RSC*, 108–12, 160, 201, 236, 249; unnamed captain to J. B. Wilson, 14 April 1866, vol. 134, Letters Sent by the Memphis District, Office of the Superintendent, reel 17, SRTFO.
15. *RSC*, 95, 181; *Washington Daily National Intelligencer*, 8 May 1866; George Stoneman to George Thomas, 5 May 1866, 287T1866, reel 519, LROAG.
16. *RSC*, 101, 153, 161–62, 171, 193, 317, 321, 348.
17. *RSC*, 78, 99, 117, 163, 343.
18. United States Congress, *Riot at Memphis*, 3; *RSC*, 53, 56, 361; *Post*, 6 May 1866; George Stoneman to George Thomas, 5 May 1866, 287T1866, reel 519, LROAG.
19. *RSC*, 53.
20. George Stoneman to George Thomas, 5 May 1866, 287T1866, reel 519, LROAG.
21. Ibid.; *RSC*, 53.

22. *RSC*, 53, 296–98; Ezra J. Warner, *Generals in Gray: Lives of the Confederate Commanders* (Baton Rouge: Louisiana State University Press, 1959), 346; Marcus Wright file, Case Files of Applications; George Stoneman to George Thomas, 19 May 1866, 287T1866, reel 519, LROAG.
23. 7 May 1866 entry, Proceedings of a Military Commission, 412T1866, reel 520, LROAG; *RSC*, 54–56.
24. Benjamin Runkle to Clinton Fisk, 31 May 1866, Narrative Reports of Operations and Conditions, February–September 1866, reel 17, RACST; "Report of an investigation . . . ," enclosed in T. W. Gilbreth to O. O. Howard, 22 May 1866, Affidavits Relating to Outrages, March 1866–August 1868, reel 34, ibid.; Benjamin Runkle to Clinton Fisk, 5 May 1866, vol. 134, Letters Sent by the Memphis District, Office of the Superintendent, reel 17, SRTFO; *RSC*, 60–61.
25. *Chicago Tribune*, 11 May 1866; *Argus*, 10 May 1866; Warner, *Generals in Blue*, 154–55; Alphonso A. Hopkins, *The Life of Clinton Bowen Fisk* (New York: Funk & Wagnalls, 1888), 1–91; J. E. Jacobs to Benjamin Runkle, 14 May 1866, Registered Letters Received, vol. 2, reel 10, RACST; R. S. Rust to Clinton Fisk, 25 June 1866, ibid., reel 11, RACST; *New York Independent*, 31 May 1866.
26. *Avalanche*, 13 May, 14 June 1866; *RSC*, 160–61, 205, 370; *Little Rock* (AR) *Daily Gazette*, 14 June 1866; George Stoneman to Elihu Washburne, 2 June 1866, Washburne Papers; *New Orleans Times*, 31 May 1866.
27. *RSC*, 137, 226; *Avalanche*, 11, 13 May 1866. A third son of the old man, iron molder Mike Pendergrast, was also arrested by the Bureau. He had not been involved in the rioting; the charge against him was "complicity" in the riot, presumably for not revealing the whereabouts of his two brothers. He posted a bond of $5,000 on 15 May and was released from confinement. See Rosen, *Terror in the Heart of Freedom*, 295n.
28. *Argus*, 4 May 1866; *RSC*, 366; *Avalanche*, 17 May 1866; George Stoneman to George Thomas, 19 May 1866, 287T1866, reel 519, LROAG.
29. *Boston Congregationalist*, 18 May 1866; *Post*, 3, 5, 6 May 1866; *Cleveland* (OH) *Daily Herald*, 11 May 1866 (quoting *Post*).
30. *Post*, 8 May 1866.
31. Ibid.
32. *RSC*, 95, 181; E. O. Tade to Samuel Hunt, 2 June 1866, H9138, and Lincoln School report for June 1866, H9150, American Missionary Association Papers; Richardson, "Memphis Race Riot," 67–69.
33. *RSC*, 236, 260–61; Benjamin Runkle to Clinton Fisk, 31 May 1866, Narrative Reports of Operations and Conditions, February–September 1866, reel 17, RACST; R. S. Rust to Clinton Fisk, 25 June 1866, Registered Letters Received, vol. 2, reel 11, ibid.; *New York Observer and Chronicle*, 9 August 1866; Benjamin Runkle to W. L. Porter, 10 May 1866, vol. 134, Letters Sent by the Memphis District, Office of the Superintendent, reel 17, SRTFO; *Chicago Tribune*, 31 May 1866.

34. *Argus*, 4 May 1866; *Washington Daily National Intelligencer*, 8 May 1866 (quoting *Bulletin*).

35. *Commercial*, 6 May 1866; *Washington Daily National Intelligencer*, 8 May 1866 (quoting *Bulletin*); *Argus*, 4 May 1866; *Avalanche*, 4, 5 May 1866.

36. *Argus*, 5 May 1866; *Appeal*, 4 May 1866; *Public Ledger*, 3 May 1866; *Macon* (GA) *Daily Telegraph*, 10 May 1866 (quoting *Avalanche*).

37. *Public Ledger*, 4, 7 May 1866; *Washington Daily National Intelligencer*, 8 May 1866 (quoting *Bulletin*); *Commercial*, 6 May 1866; *Cleveland* (OH) *Daily Herald*, 24 May 1866 (quoting *Argus*); *Post*, 8, 12 May 1866.

38. "Report of an investigation . . . ," enclosed in T. W. Gilbreth to O. O. Howard, 22 May 1866, and affidavits, passim, Affidavits Relating to Outrages, March 1866–August 1868, reel 34, RACST; *RSC*, 60–62, 336–58.

39. "Report of an investigation . . . ," enclosed in T. W. Gilbreth to O. O. Howard, 22 May 1866, Affidavits Relating to Outrages, March 1866–August 1868, reel 34, RACST; *Avalanche*, 1 July 1866.

40. Benjamin Runkle to Clinton Fisk, 23 May 1866, Reports of Outrages, Riots, and Murders, 1866–1868, reel 34, RACST.

41. Ibid.

42. 4 June 1866 entry and testimonies, passim, Proceedings of a Military Commission, 412T1866, reel 520, LROAG; *RSC*, 53, 313–36; W. H. Morgan to Elihu Washburne, 11 May 1866, Washburne Papers.

43. *RSC*, 53, 297–98; George Stoneman to George Thomas, 14 June 1866, and "Abstract of persons killed, wounded, and maltreated," Proceedings of a Military Commission, 412T1866, reel 520, LROAG; George Stoneman to George Thomas, 19 May 1866, 287T1866, reel 519, ibid.; John Y. Simon, ed., *The Papers of Ulysses S. Grant*, 24 vols. to date (Carbondale: Southern Illinois University Press, 1967–), 16:235–36n.; United States Congress, *Riot at Memphis*, 1–3.

44. George Stoneman to George Thomas, 14 June 1866, and George Thomas endorsement, 15 June 1866, Proceedings of a Military Commission, 412T1866, reel 520, LROAG; George Stoneman to George Thomas, 19 May 1866, 287T1866, reel 519, ibid.; George Stoneman to Elihu Washburne, 2 June 1866, Washburne Papers; Simon, *Papers of Ulysses S. Grant*, 16:230–31, 233–34.

45. George Stoneman to George Thomas, 19 May 1866, 287T1866, reel 519, LROAG; *RSC*, 74, 83, 137, 239–40, 264, 281–83; Hooper, "Memphis, Tennessee," 183–84. Although it refused to compensate riot victims, the city council did (in June) approve compensation for two policemen (James Finn and D. F. Slattery) wounded in the riot and also authorized reimbursement of the fire department for expenses incurred in the funeral of Henry Dunn; see Rosen, *Terror in the Heart of Freedom*, 81, 295n.

46. *RSC*, 74, 314.

47. *RSC*, 75, 77.

48. *RSC*, 160–61, 226, 239–40, 264, 281–83; George Stoneman to George Thomas, 19 May 1866, 287T1866, reel 519, LROAG; George Stoneman to Elihu Washburne, 2 June 1866, Washburne Papers; Rosen, *Terror in the Heart of Freedom*, 295n.

49. *Chicago Tribune*, 2–5 May 1866; *Cleveland* (OH) *Daily Herald*, 2, 5 May 1866; *New Orleans Weekly Times*, 5 May 1866 (quoting *Jackson [MS] Standard*); *New York Herald*, 3, 5, 7 May 1866; *New York Times*, 3, 4, 12 May 1866; *Philadelphia Inquirer*, 3 May 1866; *Milwaukee Daily Sentinel*, 3, 4 May 1866; *Bangor* (ME) *Daily Whig & Courier*, 4 May 1866; *Boston Daily Advertiser*, 7 May 1866; *Chillicothe* (OH) *Scioto Gazette*, 8 May 1866; *Columbus* (GA) *Daily Enquirer*, 8 May 1866; *Little Rock* (AR) *Daily Gazette*, 9 May 1866; *Macon* (GA) *Daily Telegraph*, 6 May 1866; *Natchez* (MS) *Daily Courier*, 8 May 1866; *New Orleans Times*, 6, 7 May 1866; *Salt Lake City Telegraph*, 12 May 1866; *San Francisco Daily Evening Bulletin*, 5 May 1866; *Savannah Daily News and Herald*, 7 May 1866; *Washington Daily National Intelligencer*, 7, 8 May 1866; *Harper's Weekly*, 26 May 1866.

50. *New Orleans Times*, 15 May 1866; *Concord* (NH) *Patriot and Gazette*, 16 May 1866 (quoting *Chicago Times*); *New York Herald*, 6 May 1866; *Milwaukee Daily Sentinel*, 10 May 1866 (quoting *Cincinnati Gazette*); *Chicago Tribune*, 5 May 1866; *The Nation*, 15 May 1866.

51. Cong. Globe, 39th Cong., 1st Sess. (1866), p. 2544.

52. Ibid., pp. 2572, 2575; *RSC*, 45; Carroll, *Twelve Americans*, 395–414; Hunt, *Israel, Elihu, and Cadwallader Washburn*, 155–96, 228–36; John Y. Simon, "From Galena to Appomattox: Grant and Washburne," *Journal of the Illinois State Historical Society* 58 (1965): 165–89.

53. *RSC*, 45.

54. *RSC*, 37, 45–49, 365–71, and 50–313, passim; *Public Ledger*, 3 May, 7 June 1866.

55. *RSC*, 289, 290, and 50–313, passim.

56. *RSC*, 2, 44, 48, 49; Cong. Globe, 39th Cong., 1st Sess. (1866), pp. 4159–60, 4266. Accounts of the riot by other historians have drawn on the witness testimonies of the three government investigations, but this book is the first to exploit them fully. The only testimonies taken by the Freedmen's Bureau and the military commission that other historians have cited are those published with the Select Committee's report and testimonies. But these do not comprise the whole corpus of the Bureau and commission testimonies. The Select Committee decided to omit in its published volume the testimonies of the Bureau and commission witnesses who also appeared before the committee. There are fifty-seven such omitted testimonies, most of them containing very useful information not brought out in the committee's questioning. These testimonies can be found only in the manuscript records of the Bureau and the commission, which I have examined. Furthermore, the compilers of the committee's published volume

inadvertently omitted nine testimonies and parts of nineteen others given by Bureau or commission witnesses who did not appear before the committee; these are likewise found only in the manuscript records.

57. *RSC*, 1–36. Among the rape victims identified in the report were twenty-six-year-old Frances Thompson and sixteen-year-old Lucy Smith, who lived together and who told the Select Committee that they were sexually assaulted by a gang of seven Irishmen, two of them policemen, who invaded their Gayoso Street home on the night of 1–2 May. This curious case deserves comment here.

In 1876 it came to public attention that Thompson was (physically) a man who since before the Civil War had been dressing and presenting himself/herself as a woman. The *Memphis Public Ledger*, which reported the story, also asserted that since emancipation Thompson had made a living by "keeping an assignation house" (i.e., running a brothel). Reminding its readers of Thompson's testimony before the Select Committee a decade earlier, the newspaper claimed that this revelation about his/her true sex—which was confirmed by four doctors who examined him/her at the request of the police department—proved that his/her testimony about the rapes was fraudulent. The paper lavished attention on this story daily for more than a week, touting it as evidence that the report of the Select Committee was nothing more than a piece of Radical propaganda based on lies.

The only historian who has heretofore investigated this issue, Hannah Rosen, argues that the doctors' report should not necessarily be taken at face value and speculates that Thompson "may have had an ambiguously sexed body." Rosen accepts as true Thompson's and Smith's accounts of being raped during the riot. She also accepts as true Thompson's statement to the Select Committee that he/she made a living as a seamstress and laundress. Rosen's arguments are bolstered by the fact that the testimonies of Thompson and Smith were quite vivid and specific and agreed closely in many details.

There are, however, other facts that call into question the statements of Thompson and Smith. The records of the Freedmen's Bureau court show that Frances Thompson and Lucy Smith appeared before the court on 30 April 1866—the day before the riot began. They had been arrested by night-squad policeman (and Irish American) G. W. Rion and charged with lewdness (a term that was applied to both prostitution and pandering). Both were found guilty and each was fined ten dollars and court costs. The court records also show that between July 1865 and January 1866, Frances Thompson was arrested and brought before the court five times on various charges. On one of these occasions, the charge—lewdness—was dismissed. On the other four occasions, Thompson was convicted—twice for disorderly conduct, once for lewdness, and once for keeping a "Disorderly House" (i.e., a house of prostitution)—and was fined. Rosen does not mention these episodes and was apparently unaware of them when writing her book.

Regarding the 30 April 1866 court appearance, the court records further note that Thompson's fine was paid, but there is no such notation for Smith. It is possible that this was merely a clerical oversight and that Smith's fine was in fact paid. But if it was not paid (the more likely scenario, for the Bureau court records seem to have been meticulously maintained), it means that Smith could not have been at home during the riot, for she would have been in police custody the whole time. Women unable to pay their Bureau court fines were remanded to the city workhouse (not the chain gang, which was reserved for male offenders), where they worked off the fines at the rate of a dollar a day. Smith's fine would have kept her in the workhouse until 12 or 13 May. (Rosen notes that the rape of Smith was reported to the Bureau "soon after the riot"—but also notes that it was reported by Thompson, not by Smith. The two appeared before the Select Committee on 1 June.)

Another fact to consider is that the three other rapes documented in testimony before the Select Committee or the other investigating bodies were all attested to by at least one neighbor of the victim as well as by the victim herself. There was no such testimony from any neighbor regarding Thompson and Smith, nor from anyone at all besides themselves.

Thus there are reasons to conclude that Thompson and Smith made up their story of being raped (perhaps to retaliate against the police or against Irishmen in general) and, having rehearsed it thoroughly, proceeded to perjure themselves quite believably before the Select Committee. At the very least, it is clear that Thompson operated a brothel and that Smith engaged in prostitution; but this of course does not prove that the two could not have been raped, if it is assumed that Smith was not in the workhouse during the riot. In the absence of absolutely conclusive evidence on this point, Rosen's argument about the rapes commands respect. Deeming both theories unproved and perhaps unprovable, I have not mentioned Thompson or Smith in the text of this book and leave it to readers to decide whether there were five rapes or three.

Thompson's and Smith's testimonies are in *RSC*, 196–97. Rosen's analysis is in Rosen, *Terror in the Heart of Freedom*, 61, 69, 70, 73, 235–41, 284n1, 285n7, 289n42, 293n79, 295n107, 353n51. On the 1876 revelation about Thompson, see, besides Rosen's book, *Public Ledger*, 11–19 July 1876, and Meriwether, *Recollections*, 178–81. On the arrests and Bureau court hearings of Thompson and Smith, See 27 July, 7 August, 1, 3 November 1865, 30 January, 30 April 1866 entries, vol. 171, Complaint Books of the Freedmen's Court in the Memphis District, reel 24, SRTFO. For evidence that a woman with an unpaid fine of ten dollars and costs would have been required to spend thirteen days in the workhouse, see 23 May 1866 entry and certificate, ibid. Policeman Rion (spelled "Ryan" in the court record) is identified in *RSC*, 369. On the exemption of women from the chain gang, see *Avalanche*, 5 May 1866. The other rape victims identified by the Select Committee were Rebecca Ann Bloom (whose rape was attested to by herself, her husband, and a neighbor), Lucy Tibbs (by herself and a neighbor), and Harriet Armour (by herself and three neighbors); see *RSC*, 13–15, 161, 163, 168, 176–77, 186, 194, 348, 351.

58. *RSC*, 33, 34.

59. *RSC*, 37–44.

60. *RSC*, 44.

61. Simon, *Papers of Ulysses S. Grant*, 16:233–34; Graf, Haskins, and Bergeron, *Papers of Andrew Johnson*, 10:688.

62. Graf, Haskins, and Bergeron, *Papers of Andrew Johnson*, 10:688–89.

63. R. Morrow to Secretary of War, 25 July 1866, Proceedings of a Military Commission, 412T1866, reel 520, LROAG.

64. *Trenton* (NJ) *Daily State Gazette*, 2 July 1866; Hopkins, *Life of Clinton Bown Fisk*, 126; Hooper, "Memphis, Tennessee," 143; United States Congress, *Reports of Assistant Commissioners of Freedmen*, 126–40; *Avalanche*, 5 September 1866; Warner, *Generals in Blue*, 481; Sefton, *United States Army and Reconstruction*, 256.

65. Simon, *Papers of Ulysses S. Grant*, 16:231–32n.; Hooper, "Memphis, Tennessee," 183–84.

66. *RSC*, 276. See also Rufus McCain to Clinton Fisk, 24 July 1866, Registered Letters Received, vol. 2, reel 10, RACST.

67. *Public Ledger*, 23 May 1866; *Post*, 23 May 1866; *Cleveland* (OH) *Daily Herald*, 24 May 1866.

68. *Public Ledger*, 23 May 1866; *Post*, 23 May 1866; *Cleveland* (OH) *Daily Herald*, 24 May 1866.

69. *Public Ledger*, 6 June 1866; *Chicago Tribune*, 31 May 1866; Hooper, "Memphis, Tennessee," 173 (quoting *Bulletin*); Walter J. Fraser Jr., "Barbour Lewis: A Carpetbagger Reconsidered," *Tennessee Historical Quarterly* 32 (1973): 154–55; Lovett, "Memphis Riots," 31.

70. Fraser, "Barbour Lewis," 154–55; LeForge, "State Colored Conventions," 241; Lovett, "Memphis Riots," 30.

71. United States Congress, *Reports of Assistant Commissioners of Freedmen*, 128; United States Congress, *Report of Commissioners of Freedmen's Bureau*, 212; *Public Ledger*, 28 May, 4, 5 June 1866; Benjamin Runkle to Clinton Fisk, 31 May 1866, Narrative Reports of Operations and Conditions, February–September 1866, reel 17, RACST.

72. Hooper, "Memphis, Tennessee," 184, 202–203, 221–23; White, *Messages of the Governors of Tennessee, 1857–1869*, 504–505; Jack D. L. Holmes, "The Effects of the Memphis Race Riot of 1866," *West Tennessee Historical Society Papers* 12 (1958): 67–69; T. E. Bliss to M. E. Strieby, 5 July 1866, H9156, American Missionary Association Papers.

73. *Avalanche*, 3 July 1866; Hooper, "Memphis, Tennessee, 222–23; *Nashville Daily Union and American*, 3 July 1866; *Argus*, 12 August 1866; *Post*, 2 July, 11 August 1866.

74. James G. Hollandsworth Jr., *An Absolute Massacre: The New Orleans Race Riot of July 30, 1866* (Baton Rouge: Louisiana State University Press, 2001), passim.

75. Graf, Haskins, and Bergeron, *Papers of Andrew Johnson*, 11:6n, 283–85. See also ibid., 11:56, and *Zion's Herald and Wesleyan Journal*, 10, 24 October 1866.

9. THE RIOT IN HISTORY AND MEMORY

1. William Archibald Dunning, *Reconstruction, Political and Economic, 1865–1877* (New York: Harper & Brothers, 1907), 80–81; Howard K. Beale, *The Critical Year: A Study of Andrew Johnson and Reconstruction* (New York: Harcourt, Brace, 1930), 343, 344; Holmes, "Effects of the Memphis Race Riot," 59, 60–64, 77–79; Michael Perman, *Reunion without Compromise: The South and Reconstruction, 1865–1868* (Cambridge: Cambridge University Press, 1973), 192; Patrick W. Riddleberger, *1866: The Critical Year Revisited* (Carbondale: Southern Illinois University Press, 1979), 177, 201; Carter, *When the War Was Over*, 249–50; Foner, *Reconstruction*, 261–63.

2. Dunning, *Reconstruction, Political and Economic*, 93; John Hope Franklin, *Reconstruction after the Civil War* (Chicago: University of Chicago Press, 1961), 62–64; Stampp, *Era of Reconstruction*, 110; Michael Les Benedict, *A Compromise of Principle: Congressional Republicans and Reconstruction, 1863–1869* (New York: Norton, 1974), 210, 214; Riddleberger, *1866*, 177; Rable, *But There Was No Peace*, 41.

3. The best general work on the subject is Foner, *Reconstruction*.

4. Holmes, "Effects of the Memphis Race Riot," 62; Riddleberger, *1866*, 201; Rable, *But There Was No Peace*, 40–41. The best general study of the reconstruction-era terrorist organizations is Allen W. Trelease, *White Terror: The Ku Klux Klan Conspiracy and Southern Reconstruction* (New York: Harper & Row, 1971). On paramilitary violence, see, among other works, Rable, *But There Was No Peace*, 144–85; Nicholas Lemann, *Redemption: The Last Battle of the Civil War* (New York: Farrar, Straus and Giroux, 2006); LeeAnna Keith, *The Colfax Massacre: The Untold Story of Black Power, White Terror, and the Death of Reconstruction* (New York: Oxford University Press, 2008); and Charles Lane, *The Day Freedom Died: The Colfax Massacre, the Supreme Court, and the Betrayal of Reconstruction* (New York: Henry Holt, 2008).

5. William Gillette, *Retreat from Reconstruction, 1869–1879* (Baton Rouge: Louisiana State University Press, 1979); Michael Perman, *The Road to Redemption: Southern Politics, 1869–1879* (Chapel Hill: University of North Carolina Press, 1984); Foner, *Reconstruction*, 512–601.

6. On Tennessee's unique reconstruction experience, see Thomas B. Alexander, *Political Reconstruction in Tennessee* (Nashville: Vanderbilt University Press, 1950); and E. Merton Coulter, *William G. Brownlow: Fighting*

Parson of the Southern Highlands (1937; repr., Knoxville: University of Tennessee Press, 1999), 311–73.

7. The other postwar Southern urban riots, particularly those at New Orleans and Norfolk, are discussed in Hollandsworth, *Absolute Massacre*; Rable, *But There Was No Peace*, 31–32, 43–58; Robert W. Coakley, *The Role of Federal Military Forces in Domestic Disorders, 1789–1878* (Washington, DC: Center of Military History, U.S. Army, 1988), 273–74; and Litwack, *Been in the Storm*, 280–81.

8. On antebellum slave insurrection panics, see David Grimsted, *American Mobbing, 1828–1861: Toward Civil War* (New York: Oxford University Press, 1998), 135–78. The Christmas insurrection scare of 1865 is discussed in chap. 2, pp. 41–42. On the New York City riot of 1863, see Iver Bernstein, *The New York City Draft Riots: Their Significance for American Society and Politics in the Age of the Civil War* (New York: Oxford University Press, 1990). (Some contemporary commentators explicitly compared the Memphis riot with the New York City riot; see, e.g., *The Nation*, 7 May 1866, and *Harper's Weekly*, 26 May 1866.) On lynching, see W. Fitzhugh Brundage, *Lynching in the New South: Georgia and Virginia, 1880–1930* (Urbana: University of Illinois Press, 1993). Another historical context is suggested by historian George Rable, who draws a parallel between the Memphis riot and the urban race riots of the latter decades of the twentieth century—Watts and its ilk—in which, although the roles of victim and perpetrator were reversed, extreme demographic, economic, and social pressures propelled blacks and whites into bloody and destructive collision; see Rable, *But There Was No Peace*, 33, 34, 39.

9. Historian Altina L. Waller argues, based on an analysis of the residence and surname of identified rioters, that most lived in South Memphis and that a large minority, perhaps even half, were non-Irish. Noting also that the blacks victimized in the riot were mostly residents of South Memphis, she interprets the riot not as an uprising of Irish Memphians but rather as a reaction by white residents of a particular section of the city to the massive influx of blacks into their neighborhood since 1862. I am not altogether persuaded by this argument. Waller's sample consists of only sixty-eight persons—of whom she could determine residence for only forty-nine—leaving a very large number of rioters unaccounted for. Moreover, surnames are not a foolproof indicator of ethnicity; many Irish immigrants in the city, including the mayor and the sheriff, had surnames that were not typically Irish. That a substantial number of rioters lived outside South Memphis is, I believe, evidenced by the fact that a good many of the mobs formed downtown (although some of these were no doubt reinforced by South Memphis residents when they marched into that area). That the great majority of the black victims of the riot resided in South Memphis can, I think, be explained by three facts: more blacks lived there than in any other section of the city; that was where the shootout that triggered the

riot took place, and was therefore the area targeted by whites who intended to put down what many of them regarded as a black insurrection; and that was where the black ex-soldiers, who were the primary targets of many rioters, were predominantly located. See Waller, "Community, Class and Race," 233–46.

10. Some historians have echoed the Republicans' insistence on the influence of the Rebel press. See, e.g., James Gilbert Ryan, "The Memphis Riots of 1866: Terror in a Black Community during Reconstruction," *Journal of Negro History* 62 (1977): 245; Rable, *But There Was No Peace*, 33–37; and Carriere, "Irresponsible Press," 2–12.

11. On Ku Klux Klan violence in west Tennessee, see Trelease, *White Terror*, chaps. 2 and 11.

12. Hollandsworth, *Absolute Massacre*, 64–68, discusses the New Orleans city government.

13. A persistent myth about the spark that touched off the riot needs to be put to rest here. Several newspapers reported at the time that the confrontation on South Street grew out of a traffic accident involving two wagon drivers (or dray or hack drivers), one black and one white, and some historians have repeated the story. It is apparently a garbled version of the run-in between two hackmen on Beale Street witnessed by Ewing and Amanda Tade. While this incident may have triggered the rioting on Beale that evening, it had nothing to do with the shootout on South, which occurred a couple of hours earlier and half a mile away. None of the reliable eyewitness accounts of the South Street fracas mention a traffic accident. Mobs had already marched down to South in response to the shootout, and had begun their bloody rampages there and on adjoining streets, by the time the Beale Street accident occurred. For contemporary press reports stating that a traffic accident set off the riot, see *Boston Daily Advertiser*, 7 May 1866; *Chicago Tribune*, 2 May 1866; *Chillicothe (OH) Scioto Gazette*, 8 May 1866; and *The Nation*, 7 May 1866. Historical studies that repeat the story include Beale, *Critical Year*, 344; Holmes, "Underlying Causes of the Memphis Race Riot," 195; Rable, *But There Was No Peace*, 37–38; and Foner, *Reconstruction*, 261–62.

14. The Select Committee report said that the evidence regarding Stevens's shooting was inconclusive, citing the fact that one doctor who examined him thought that his wound could not have been self-inflicted. But my own review of all the available evidence, including the testimony of two other doctors who examined him, persuades me that he shot himself. See *RSC*, 8, 124–25, 130–31, 133–34; R. W. Creighton testimony, Proceedings of a Military Commission, 412T1866, reel 520, LROAG; and R. W. Creighton affidavit, Affidavits Relating to Outrages, March 1866–August 1868, reel 34, RACST.

Regarding the black death toll, the investigations of the Freedmen's Bureau, the military commission, and the Select Committee arrived at different totals, but the Select Committee's deserves preference because it incorporated the findings of all three inquiries. In some cases, however, the dead blacks could not be identified by name and the circumstances of their deaths were unclear; in these instances, it is possible that a single victim seen by more than one witness was counted as multiple victims. At the same time, there may have been some victims who were not seen by any testifying witness and who therefore went uncounted (a problem acknowledged in the Select Committee's majority report). And, too, there was one black (Fayette Dickerson), and perhaps others, who died after May 3 from wounds received in the riot and who should be included in the tally of the dead. All things considered, the committee's total of forty-six blacks, while probably not exactly correct, is undoubtedly close.

15. On the triumph of the white-supremacist version of reconstruction in postreconstruction America, see Blight, *Race and Reunion*; and Bruce E. Baker, *What Reconstruction Meant: Historical Memory in the American South* (Charlottesville: University of Virginia Press, 2007). This understanding was characteristic not only of popular memory but also of historical scholarship in those years: see, for example, Dunning, *Reconstruction, Political and Economic*; Claude G. Bowers, *The Tragic Era: The Revolution after Lincoln* (New York: Literary Guild of America, 1929); and E. Merton Coulter, *The South during Reconstruction, 1865–1877* (Baton Rouge: Louisiana State University Press, 1947).

16. J. M. Keating, *History of the City of Memphis and Shelby County, Tennessee: With Illustrations and Biographical Sketches of Some of Its Prominent Citizens,* 2 vols. (Syracuse, NY: D. Mason, 1888), 1:567–69; Capers, *Biography of a River Town,* 163, 171–72, 175–78. See also Young, *Standard History of Memphis,* 138–47; Shields McIlwaine, *Memphis Down in Dixie* (New York: Dutton, 1948), 149–52; Holmes, "Underlying Causes of the Memphis Race Riot," 195–221; and White, *Messages of the Governors of Tennessee, 1857–1869,* 504.

17. Meriwether, *Recollections*.

18. Revisionist general histories of reconstruction include Franklin, *Reconstruction after the Civil War*; Stampp, *Era of Reconstruction*; and Foner, *Reconstruction*. The older interpretation of reconstruction is, unfortunately, still embraced by the large segment of the American public whose knowledge of the era derives solely from popular literature and films, especially *Gone With the Wind*. Among the revisionist studies of the Memphis riot are Ryan, "Memphis Riots of 1866"; Lovett, "Memphis Riots"; Rable, *But There Was No Peace,* chap. 3.; Hardwick, "'Your Old Father Abe Lincoln'"; and Carriere, "Irresponsible Press."

19. Modern scholarship on the Memphis riot has been influenced by certain historiographical trends of the last few decades besides reconstruction revisionism. A study that embodies the "new social history" approach, with its close attention to local communities and the experience of common

people, is Waller, "Community, Class and Race." Historians' growing interest in the role of gender in the American past is reflected in Rosen, *Terror in the Heart of Freedom*, 23–83. The concept of "whiteness," which has influenced much recent work in ethnic history, is put to use in Walker, "'This Is the White Man's Day'"; and Brian D. Page, "'An Unholy Alliance': Irish-Americans and the Political Construction of Whiteness in Memphis, Tennessee, 1866–1879," *Left History* 8 (2002): 77–96.

20. In the 1–6 May 1966 issues of two Memphis newspapers, the *Commercial Appeal* and the *Press-Scimitar*, I found not one explicit reference to the riot a century earlier. There were three very brief mentions of certain events during the riot in the *Commercial Appeal*'s daily "News of Bygone Days" column (a "today in history" feature based on past issues of the newspaper and its predecessors), but none of these made it clear that the events were part of a race riot that consumed the city for three days and claimed the lives of dozens of people. The most recent book-length history of Memphis (Wanda Rushing, *Memphis and the Paradox of Place: Globalization in the American South* [Chapel Hill: University of North Carolina Press, 2009]) does not mention the riot. On the Forrest statue, the yellow fever monument, and the Civil Rights Museum, see Rushing, *Memphis and the Paradox of Place*, 3, 38–52.

BIBLIOGRAPHY

MANUSCRIPTS

Adjutant General's Office (Tennessee) Records, 1796–1900. RG 21. Tennessee State Library and Archives, Nashville.

Allyn, Arthur W., Letters. Connecticut Historical Society, Hartford, CT.

American Missionary Association Papers, Tennessee Manuscripts. Amistad Collection. Tulane University, New Orleans.

Brownlow, Governor William G., Papers, 1865–1869. Tennessee State Library and Archives, Nashville.

Case Files of Applications from Former Confederates for Presidential Pardons ("Amnesty Papers"), 1865–1867—Tennessee Applications. M1003. National Archives and Records Administration, Washington, DC.

Compiled Military Service Records. National Archives and Records Administration, Washington, DC.

Eaton, Alice, Diary, 1865–1908. Special Collections Library. Duke University.

Eaton, John H., Jr., Papers, 1865–1881. Special Collections. University of Tennessee, Knoxville.

Eighth Census, 1860, Manuscript Returns of Free Inhabitants. National Archives and Records Administration, Washington, DC.

Eighth Census, 1860, Manuscript Returns of Slaves. National Archives and Records Administration, Washington, DC.

Eltinge-Lord Families Papers. Perkins Library. Duke University.

Letters Received by the Office of the Adjutant General (Main Series), 1861–1870. M619. National Archives and Records Administration, Washington, DC.

Ninth Census, 1870, Manuscript Returns of Inhabitants. National Archives and Records Administration, Washington, DC.

Records of the Adjutant General's Office (U.S.), 1780s–1917. RG 94. National Archives and Records Administration, Washington, DC.

Records of the Assistant Commissioner for the State of Tennessee, Bureau of Refugees, Freedmen, and Abandoned Lands, 1865–1869. RG 105, M999. National Archives and Records Administration, Washington, DC.

Records of the Superintendent of Education for the State of Tennessee, Bureau of Refugees, Freedmen, and Abandoned Lands, 1865–1870. RG 105, M1000. National Archives and Records Administration, Washington, DC.

Records of the U.S. Army Continental Commands, 1821–1920. RG 393. National Archives and Records Administration, Washington, DC.

Registers of Signatures of Depositors in Branches of the Freedman's Savings and Trust Company, 1865–1874, Memphis Branch. RG 101, M816. National Archives and Records Administration, Washington, DC.

Selected Records of the Tennessee Field Office of the Bureau of Refugees, Freedmen, and Abandoned Lands, 1865–1872. RG 105, T142. National Archives and Records Administration, Washington, DC.

Shelby County Miscellaneous City/County Records. Tennessee State Library and Archives, Nashville.

Stevens, Thaddeus, Papers. Library of Congress, Washington, DC.

Washburne, Elihu, Papers. Library of Congress, Washington, DC.

NEWSPAPERS AND JOURNALS

Bangor (ME) *Daily Whig & Courier*
Boston Congregationalist
Boston Daily Advertiser
Chicago Tribune
Chillicothe (OH) *Scioto Gazette*
Christian Advocate
Cleveland (OH) *Daily Herald*
Columbus (GA) *Daily Enquirer*
Columbus (GA) *Daily Sun*
Concord (NH) *Patriot and Gazette*
Harper's Weekly
Little Rock (AR) *Daily Gazette*
Macon (GA) *Daily Telegraph*
Macon (GA) *Weekly Telegraph*
Memphis Commercial Appeal
Memphis Daily Appeal
Memphis Daily Argus
Memphis Daily Avalanche
Memphis Daily Bulletin
Memphis Daily Commercial
Memphis Daily Post
Memphis Daily Tribune
Memphis Press-Scimitar
Memphis Public Ledger
Memphis Southern Loyalist

Milwaukee Daily Sentinel
Nashville Daily Union and American
Natchez (MS) *Daily Courier*
The Nation
New Orleans Times
New Orleans Weekly Times
New York Herald
New York Independent
New York Observer and Chronicle
New York Times
Philadelphia Inquirer
Salt Lake City Telegraph
San Francisco Daily Evening Bulletin
Savannah Daily News and Herald
Trenton (NJ) *Daily State Gazette*
Washington Daily National Intelligencer
Zion's Herald and Wesleyan Journal

PUBLISHED PRIMARY SOURCES

Berlin, Ira, et al., eds. *The Wartime Genesis of Free Labor: The Lower South.* Cambridge: Cambridge University Press, 1990.
Congressional Globe.
Digest of the Charters and Ordinances of the City of Memphis, from 1826 to 1867. Memphis: Bulletin Publishing, 1867.
Eaton, John. *Grant, Lincoln, and the Freedmen: Reminiscences of the Civil War with Special Reference to the Work for the Contrabands and Freedmen of the Mississippi Valley.* New York: Longmans, Green, 1907.
Extracts from Documents in the Office of the General Superintendent of Refugees and Freedmen, Headquarters, Memphis, Tennessee, March, 1865. Memphis: Freedmen Press, 1865.
Fraser, Walter J., Jr., and Pat C. Clark, eds. "The Letters of William Beverly Randolph Hackley: Treasury Agent in West Tennessee, 1863–1866." *West Tennessee Historical Society Papers* 25 (1971): 90–107.
Graf, LeRoy P., Ralph W. Haskins, and Paul H. Bergeron, eds. *The Papers of Andrew Johnson.* 16 vols. Knoxville: University of Tennessee Press, 1967–2000.
Hahn, Steven, Steven F. Miller, Susan E. O'Donovan, John C. Rodrigue, and Leslie S. Rowland, eds. *Land and Labor: 1865.* Chapel Hill: University of North Carolina Press, 2008.
Long's Memphis Directory . . . 1865–'66. Memphis: Blelock, 1865.
Memphis and Its Environs, 1860. Memphis: Monsarrat, Dupree, 1860.
Memphis City Directory, 1866. Memphis: Bingham, Williams, 1866.

Meriwether, Elizabeth Avery. *Recollections of 92 Years, 1824–1916*. Nashville: Tennessee Historical Commission, 1958.

Reid, Whitelaw. *After the War: A Southern Tour, May 1, 1865, to May 1, 1866*. Cincinnati: Moore, Wilstach, & Baldwin, 1866.

Report of the Select Committee on the Memphis Riots and Massacres. Washington, DC: Government Printing Office, 1866. Also published, with same pagination, as United States Congress, *Memphis Riots and Massacres*, House Rpts., 39th Cong., 1st Sess. (1866), No. 101, Serial 1274.

Richardson, Joe M., ed. "The Memphis Race Riot and Its Aftermath: Report by a Northern Missionary." *Tennessee Historical Quarterly* 24 (1965): 63–69.

Simon, John Y., ed. *The Papers of Ulysses S. Grant*. 24 vols. to date. Carbondale: Southern Illinois University Press, 1967–.

Skinner, J. E. Hilary. *After the Storm; or, Jonathan and His Neighbours in 1865–6*. 2 vols. London: Richard Bentley, 1866.

The Statistics of the Population of the United States . . . (June 1, 1870) . . . Washington, DC: Government Printing Office, 1872.

Trowbridge, J. T. *The South: A Tour of Its Battlefields and Ruined Cities, a Journey through the Desolated States, and Talks with the People*. Hartford, CT: L. Stebbins, 1866.

United States Congress. *Report of Commissioners of Freedmen's Bureau*. House Exec. Docs., 39th Cong., 1st Sess. (1866), No. 70, Serial 1256.

———. *Report of the Joint Committee on Reconstruction*. House Reports, 39th Cong., 1st Sess. (1866), No. 30, Serial 1273.

———. *Reports of Assistant Commissioners of Freedmen, and Synopsis of Laws on Persons of Color in Late Slave States*. Senate Exec. Docs., 39th Cong., 2nd Sess. (1866), No. 6, Serial 1276.

———. *Riot at Memphis*. House Exec. Docs., 39th Cong., 1st Sess. (1866), No. 122, Serial 1263.

United States Naval Observatory. "Complete Sun and Moon Data for One Day: U.S. Cities and Towns." Accessed 12 July 2009. www.usno.navy.mil/USNO /astronomical-applications/data-services/rs-one-day-US.

The War of the Rebellion: A Compilation of the Official Records of the Union and Confederate Armies. 70 vols. in 128. Washington, DC: Government Printing Office, 1880–1901.

White, Robert H., ed. *Messages of the Governors of Tennessee, 1857–1869*. Nashville: Tennessee Historical Commission, 1959.

SECONDARY SOURCES

Alexander, Thomas B. *Political Reconstruction in Tennessee*. Nashville: Vanderbilt University Press, 1950.

Ash, Stephen V. *When the Yankees Came: Conflict and Chaos in the Occupied South, 1861–1865*. Chapel Hill: University of North Carolina Press, 1995.

————. *A Year in the South: Four Lives in 1865*. New York: Palgrave Macmillan, 2002.

Baker, Bruce E. *What Reconstruction Meant: Historical Memory in the American South*. Charlottesville: University of Virginia Press, 2007.

Baker, Thomas Harrison. *The Memphis "Commercial Appeal": The History of a Southern Newspaper*. Baton Rouge: Louisiana State University Press, 1971.

Beale, Howard K. *The Critical Year: A Study of Andrew Johnson and Reconstruction*. New York: Harcourt, Brace, 1930.

Benedict, Michael Les. *A Compromise of Principle: Congressional Republicans and Reconstruction, 1863–1869*. New York: Norton, 1974.

Bergeron, Paul H. *Andrew Johnson's Civil War and Reconstruction*. Knoxville: University of Tennessee Press, 2011.

Berkeley, Kathleen C. *"Like a Plague of Locusts": From an Antebellum Town to a New South City, Memphis, Tennessee, 1850–1880*. New York: Garland, 1991.

Bernstein, Iver. *The New York City Draft Riots: Their Significance for American Society and Politics in the Age of the Civil War*. New York: Oxford University Press, 1990.

Blair, William A. *Cities of the Dead: Contesting the Memory of the Civil War in the South, 1865–1914*. Chapel Hill: University of North Carolina Press, 2004.

Blight, David W. *Race and Reunion: The Civil War in American Memory*. Cambridge, MA: Belknap Press of Harvard University, 2001.

Boatner, Mark Mayo, III. *The Civil War Dictionary*. New York: David McKay, 1959.

Bowers, Claude G. *The Tragic Era: The Revolution after Lincoln*. New York: Literary Guild of America, 1929.

Brady, Joe. "The Irish Community in Antebellum Memphis." *West Tennessee Historical Society Papers* 40 (1986): 24–44.

Brundage, W. Fitzhugh. *Lynching in the New South: Georgia and Virginia, 1880–1930*. Urbana: University of Illinois Press, 1993.

Capers, Gerald M., Jr. *Biography of a River Town: Memphis: Its Heroic Age*. Chapel Hill: University of North Carolina Press, 1939.

Carriere, Marius. "An Irresponsible Press: Memphis Newspapers and the 1866 Riot." *Tennessee Historical Quarterly* 60 (2001): 2–15.

Carroll, Howard. *Twelve Americans: Their Lives and Times*. New York: Harper & Brothers, 1883.

Carter, Dan T. *When the War Was Over: The Failure of Self-Reconstruction in the South, 1865–1867*. Baton Rouge: Louisiana State University Press, 1985.

Cimprich, John. *Fort Pillow, a Civil War Massacre, and Public Memory*. Baton Rouge: Louisiana State University Press, 2005.

————. *Slavery's End in Tennessee, 1861–1865*. University: University of Alabama Press, 1985.

Coakley, Robert W. *The Role of Federal Military Forces in Domestic Disorders, 1789–1878*. Washington, DC: Center of Military History, U.S. Army, 1988.

Connelly, Thomas L., and Barbara L. Bellows. *God and General Longstreet: The Lost Cause and the Southern Mind*. Baton Rouge: Louisiana State University Press, 1982.

Cooper, W. Raymond. "Four Fateful Years—Memphis, 1858–1861." *West Tennessee Historical Society Papers* 11 (1957): 36–75.

Coulter, E. Merton. *The South during Reconstruction, 1865–1877*. Baton Rouge: Louisiana State University Press, 1947.

———. *William G. Brownlow: Fighting Parson of the Southern Highlands*. 1937. Reprint, Knoxville: University of Tennessee Press, 1999.

Cupples, Douglas Wayne. "Memphis Confederates: The Civil War and Its Aftermath." PhD diss., University of Memphis, 1995.

Davis, Dernoral. "Hope versus Reality: The Emancipation Era Labor Struggle of Memphis Area Freedmen." In *Race, Class, and Community in Southern Labor History*, edited by Gary M. Fink and Merl E. Reed, 97–120. Tuscaloosa: University of Alabama Press, 1994.

Dunning, William Archibald. *Reconstruction, Political and Economic, 1865–1877*. New York: Harper & Brothers, 1907.

Dyer, Frederick H. *A Compendium of the War of the Rebellion*. 3 vols. New York: Thomas Yoseloff, 1959.

Foner, Eric. *Reconstruction: America's Unfinished Revolution, 1863–1877*. New York: Harper & Row, 1988.

Foster, Gaines. *Ghosts of the Confederacy: Defeat, the Lost Cause, and the Emergence of the New South, 1865–1913*. New York: Oxford University Press, 1987.

Franklin, John Hope. *Reconstruction after the Civil War*. Chicago: University of Chicago Press, 1961.

Fraser, Walter J., Jr. "Barbour Lewis: A Carpetbagger Reconsidered." *Tennessee Historical Quarterly* 32 (1973): 148–68.

Fuller, T. O. *The History of the Negro Baptists of Tennessee*. Memphis: Haskins Printing, 1936.

Gillette, William. *Retreat from Reconstruction, 1869–1879*. Baton Rouge: Louisiana State University Press, 1979.

Glatthaar, Joseph T. *Forged in Battle: The Civil War Alliance of Black Soldiers and White Officers*. New York: Free Press, 1990.

Gleeson, David T. *The Irish in the South, 1815–1877*. Chapel Hill: University of North Carolina Press, 2001.

Grimsted, David. *American Mobbing, 1828–1861: Toward Civil War*. New York: Oxford University Press, 1998.

Gutman, Herbert G. *The Black Family in Slavery and Freedom, 1750–1925*. New York: Pantheon Books, 1976.

Hahn, Steven. "'Extravagant Expectations' of Freedom: Rumour, Political Struggle, and the Christmas Insurrection Scare of 1865 in the American South." *Past and Present* 157 (1997): 122–58.

Hardwick, Kevin R. "'Your Old Father Abe Lincoln Is Dead and Damned': Black Soldiers and the Memphis Race Riot of 1866." *Journal of Social History* 27 (1993): 109–28.

Hollandsworth, James G., Jr. *An Absolute Massacre: The New Orleans Race Riot of July 30, 1866.* Baton Rouge: Louisiana State University Press, 2001.

Holmes, Jack D. L. "The Effects of the Memphis Race Riot of 1866." *West Tennessee Historical Society Papers* 12 (1958): 58–79.

———. "The Underlying Causes of the Memphis Race Riot of 1866." *Tennessee Historical Quarterly* 17 (1958): 195–221.

Hooper, Ernest W. "Memphis, Tennessee: Federal Occupation and Reconstruction, 1862–1870." PhD diss., University of North Carolina, 1957.

Hopkins, Alphonso A. *The Life of Clinton Bowen Fisk.* New York: Funk & Wagnalls, 1888.

Hunt, Gaillard. *Israel, Elihu, and Cadwallader Washburn [sic]: A Chapter in American Biography.* New York: Macmillan, 1925.

Ignatiev, Noel. *How the Irish Became White.* New York: Routledge, 1995.

Jacobson, Matthew Frye. *Whiteness of a Different Color: European Immigrants and the Alchemy of Race.* Cambridge, MA: Harvard University Press, 1998.

Janney, Caroline E. *Burying the Dead but Not the Past: Ladies' Memorial Associations and the Lost Cause.* Chapel Hill: University of North Carolina Press, 2008.

Kaplan, Michael. "New York City Tavern Violence and the Creation of a Working-Class Male Identity." *Journal of the Early Republic* 15 (1995): 591–617.

Keating, J. M. *History of the City of Memphis and Shelby County, Tennessee: With Illustrations and Biographical Sketches of Some of Its Prominent Citizens.* 2 vols. Syracuse, NY: D. Mason, 1888.

Keith, LeeAnna. *The Colfax Massacre: The Untold Story of Black Power, White Terror, and the Death of Reconstruction.* New York: Oxford University Press, 2008.

Lane, Charles. *The Day Freedom Died: The Colfax Massacre, the Supreme Court, and the Betrayal of Reconstruction.* New York: Henry Holt, 2008.

La Pointe, Patricia M. "The Disrupted Years: Memphis City Hospitals, 1860–1867." *West Tennessee Historical Society Papers* 37 (1983): 9–29.

LeForge, Judy Bussell. "State Colored Conventions of Tennessee, 1865–1866." *Tennessee Historical Quarterly* 65 (2006): 230–53.

Lemann, Nicholas. *Redemption: The Last Battle of the Civil War.* New York: Farrar, Straus and Giroux, 2006.

Litwack, Leon F. *Been in the Storm So Long: The Aftermath of Slavery.* New York: Alfred A. Knopf, 1979.

Long, John Mark. "Memphis Mayors, 1827–1866: A Collective Study." *West Tennessee Historical Society Papers* 52 (1998): 105–33.

Lovett, Bobby L. "Memphis Riots: White Reaction to Blacks in Memphis, May 1865–July 1866." *Tennessee Historical Quarterly* 38 (1979): 9–33.

Lufkin, Charles L. "The Northern Exodus from Memphis during the Secession Crisis." *West Tennessee Historical Society Papers* 42 (1988): 6–29.

Lynch-Brennan, Margaret. *The Irish Bridget: Irish Immigrant Women in Domestic Service in America, 1840–1930*. Syracuse, NY: Syracuse University Press, 2009.

McFeely, William S. *Yankee Stepfather: General O. O. Howard and the Freedmen*. New Haven, CT: Yale University Press, 1968.

McGehee, C. Stuart. "E. O. Tade, Freedmen's Education, and the Failure of Reconstruction in Tennessee." *Tennessee Historical Quarterly* 43 (1984): 376–89.

McIlwaine, Shields. *Memphis Down in Dixie*. New York: Dutton, 1948.

Page, Brian D. "'An Unholy Alliance': Irish-Americans and the Political Construction of Whiteness in Memphis, Tennessee, 1866–1879." *Left History* 8 (2002): 77–96.

Parks, Joseph H. "A Confederate Trade Center under Federal Occupation: Memphis, 1862–1865." *Journal of Southern History* 7 (1941): 289–314.

———. "Memphis under Military Rule, 1862–1865." *East Tennessee Historical Society's Publications* 14 (1942): 31–58.

Perman, Michael. *Reunion without Compromise: The South and Reconstruction, 1865–1868*. Cambridge: Cambridge University Press, 1973.

———. *The Road to Redemption: Southern Politics, 1869–1879*. Chapel Hill: University of North Carolina Press, 1984.

Phillips, Paul David. "White Reaction to the Freedmen's Bureau in Tennessee." *Tennessee Historical Quarterly* 25 (1966): 50–62.

Rable, George C. *But There Was No Peace: The Role of Violence in the Politics of Reconstruction*. Athens: University of Georgia Press, 1984.

Rauchle, Robert C. "Biographical Sketches of Prominent Germans in Memphis, Tennessee, in the Nineteenth Century." *West Tennessee Historical Society Papers* 22 (1968): 73–85.

———. "The Political Life of the Germans in Memphis, 1848–1880." *Tennessee Historical Quarterly* 27 (1968): 165–75.

Richardson, Joe M. *Christian Reconstruction: The American Missionary Association and Southern Blacks, 1861–1890*. Athens: University of Georgia Press, 1986.

Riddleberger, Patrick W. *1866: The Critical Year Revisited*. Carbondale: Southern Illinois University Press, 1979.

Roark, James L. *Masters without Slaves: Southern Planters in the Civil War and Reconstruction*. New York: Norton, 1977.

Robinson, Armstead. "Plans Dat Comed from God: Institution Building and the Emergence of Black Leadership in Reconstruction Memphis." In *Toward a New South? Studies in Post–Civil War Southern Communities*, edited by Orville V. Burton and Robert C. McMath Jr., 71–102. Westport, CT: Greenwood Press, 1982.

Roediger, David R. *The Wages of Whiteness: Race and the Making of the American Working Class*. London: Verso, 1991.

Rosen, Hannah. *Terror in the Heart of Freedom: Citizenship, Sexual Violence, and the Meaning of Race in the Postemancipation South.* Chapel Hill: University of North Carolina Press, 2009.

Rushing, Wanda. *Memphis and the Paradox of Place: Globalization in the American South.* Chapel Hill: University of North Carolina Press, 2009.

Ryan, James Gilbert. "The Memphis Riots of 1866: Terror in a Black Community during Reconstruction." *Journal of Negro History* 62 (1977): 243–57.

Samito, Christian G. *Becoming American under Fire: Irish Americans, African Americans, and the Politics of Citizenship during the Civil War.* Ithaca, NY: Cornell University Press, 2009.

Sefton, James E. *The United States Army and Reconstruction, 1865–1877.* Baton Rouge: Louisiana State University Press, 1967.

Simon, John Y. "From Galena to Appomattox: Grant and Washburne." *Journal of the Illinois State Historical Society* 58 (1965): 165–89.

Slap, Andrew L. "The Loyal Deserters: African American Soldiers and Community in Civil War Memphis." In *Weirding the War: Stories from the Civil War's Ragged Edge,* edited by Stephen Berry, 234–48. Athens: University of Georgia Press, 2011.

Smith, John David. *An Old Creed for the New South: Proslavery Ideology and Historiography, 1865–1918.* Westport, CT: Greenwood Press, 1985.

Snay, Mitchell. *Fenians, Freedmen, and Southern Whites: Race and Nationality in the Era of Reconstruction.* Baton Rouge: Louisiana State University Press, 2007.

Stampp, Kenneth M. *The Era of Reconstruction, 1865–1877.* New York: Vintage Books, 1965.

Taylor, Alrutheus Ambush. *The Negro in Tennessee, 1865–1880.* Washington, DC: Associated Publishers, 1941.

Trelease, Allen W. *White Terror: The Ku Klux Klan Conspiracy and Southern Reconstruction.* New York: Harper & Row, 1971.

Tucker, David M. *Black Pastors and Leaders: Memphis, 1819–1972.* Memphis: Memphis State University Press, 1975.

Uselton, Darrell B. "Irish Immigration and Settlement in Memphis, Tennessee, 1820s–1860s." *West Tennessee Historical Society Papers* 50 (1996): 115–29.

Walker, Barrington. "'This Is the White Man's Day': The Irish, White Racial Identity, and the Memphis Riots." *Left History* 5 (1997): 31–55.

Waller, Altina. "Community, Class and Race in the Memphis Riot of 1866." *Journal of Social History* 18 (1984): 233–46.

Warner, Ezra J. *Generals in Blue: Lives of the Union Commanders.* Baton Rouge: Louisiana State University Press, 1964.

———. *Generals in Gray: Lives of the Confederate Commanders.* Baton Rouge: Louisiana State University Press, 1959.

Wax, Rabbi James A. "The Jews of Memphis, 1860–1865." *West Tennessee Historical Society Papers* 3 (1949): 39–89.

Way, Peter. "Evil Humors and Ardent Spirits: The Rough Culture of Canal Construction Laborers." *Journal of American History* 79 (1993): 1397–1428.

Webb, Ross A. "'The Past Is Never Dead. It's Not Even Past': Benjamin P. Runkle and the Freedmen's Bureau in Kentucky, 1866–70." *Register of the Kentucky Historical Society* 84 (1986): 343–60.

Williams, Frank B. "John Eaton, Jr., Editor, Politician, and School Administrator, 1865–1870." *Tennessee Historical Quarterly* 10 (1951): 291–319.

Wooster, Ralph A. *Politicians, Planters, and Plain Folk: Courthouse and Statehouse in the Upper South, 1850–1860.* Knoxville: University of Tennessee Press, 1975.

Young, John Preston. *Standard History of Memphis, Tennessee, from a Study of the Original Sources.* Knoxville: H. W. Crew, 1912.

Zebley, Kathleen Rosa. "Rebel Salvation: The Story of Confederate Pardons." PhD diss., University of Tennessee, 1998.

ACKNOWLEDGMENTS

The debts I have accumulated over the years of working on this book are many. I wish I could repay them all, but the best I can do in most cases is simply acknowledge them. Here I gratefully tip my hat to all who have helped me along the way.

Archivists and librarians are the historian's best friends. I am indebted to legions of them for prompt, cheerful, and expert assistance. At the risk of unfairly slighting others, I will mention in particular those at the Tennessee State Library and Archives, the Connecticut Historical Society, the American Jewish Archives, and my own institution, the University of Tennessee, especially Anne Bridges.

Many fellow historians have also assisted generously. Laura-Eve Moss and Tom Coens deciphered some hard-to-read documents for me. Kathleen Zebley-Liulevicius provided information on Andrew Johnson's pardoning of Confederates. Dean Thomas gave me a copy of an 1860s map of Memphis that proved indispensable. Paul Bergeron helped me understand Andrew Johnson's response to the riot. John Cimprich, Dan Crofts, Ernie Freeberg, and Mark Wetherington read the entire manuscript of the book and offered astute comments. These men and women are not just fellow historians but also my friends; in some cases, our friendship goes back forty years or more. Other historians and friends too numerous to mention have also helped me, in ways too numerous to mention.

David Miller and Lisa Adams of the Garamond Agency have aided me at every step along the way; once again, I thank them not only for running interference in the mysterious world of book proposals and contract negotiations but also for coaching me on how to write a better book. Another person whose keen eye and good sense have made this a better book is my editor at Hill and Wang, Dan Gerstle; it has been a pleasure to work with him.

Jeanie, my wife of forty-three years, and Juanita, my mother, have always supported my work with love and encouragement, and they continue to teach me by example how to be a better person. So have other members of my family, especially Ellen, Ginger and Landon, and Margaret and Mike. My debts in this regard are overwhelming.

My grandmothers, Edna Vaughan and Elsie Bolton, have been gone for decades but live on vividly in my memory and in the memory of others who knew them. One of my great regrets is that I was too immature to really appreciate them while they lived—to appreciate their wisdom, their humor, their strength, and their selflessness. I dedicate this book to them, hoping that I might be forgiven for waiting so long to say thank you.

INDEX